SAGGISTICA 10

DISCOURSE BOUNDARY CREATION
(LOGOS NOMOS POIESIS)

DISCOURSE BOUNDARY CREATION
(LOGOS NOMOS POIESIS)

A *Festschrift* in Honor of Paolo Valesio on his 70th birthday
Held at Stony Brook University, April 23, 2010

Edited by
Peter Carravetta

BORDIGHERA PRESS

Library of Congress Control Number: 2013956388

Sponsored by
The Alfonse M. D'Amato Chair in Italian and Italian American Studies at
State University of New York at Stony Brook
Stony Brook, NY 11794 USA

© 2013 by Peter Carravetta & authors

All rights reserved. Parts of this book may be reprinted only by written permission from the respective authors, and may not be reproduced for publication in book, magazine, or electronic media of any kind, except for purposes of literary reviews by critics.

Printed in the United States.

Published by
BORDIGHERA PRESS
John D. Calandra Italian American Institute
25 West 43rd Street, 17th Floor
New York, NY 10036

SAGGISTICA 10
ISBN 978-1-59954-036-8

TABLE OF CONTENTS

FOREWORD
ix   Peter Carravetta

ESSAYS
1   Teodolinda Barolini, *Toward a Dantean Theology of Eros: From Dante's Lyrics to the* Paradiso
19   Peter Carravetta, *History, Empire, and Political Reason: Campanella and the Dawn of Modern Europe*
55   Alessandro Carrera, *The Logic of Poetic Genealogy: On Paolo Valesio's "The Dark Flame"*
76   Andrea Ciccarelli, *Abroad and Beyond: Paolo Valesio and the Empty Nest*
91   Ernesto Livorni, *Poetry, Dialogue, Silence*
116   Mario Moroni, *The Continuous Meditation / The Meditation Continues*
119   Alessandro Polcri, *L'imprendibile (note per un ritratto di Paolo Valesio)*
131   Lucia Re, *"Più che l'amore:" d'Annunzio's Bitter Passion and Mediterranean Tragedy*
148   Laura Wittman, *Undefended Communication*

TESTIMONIALS
169   Gian Maria Annovi
175   Patrizio Ceccagnoli
178   Luigi Fontanella
183   Erin Larkin
185   Michael Palma
187   Graziella Sidoli

195   Contributors
200   Conference Program
204   Index of Names

Foreword

The sponsor of this volume, the Alfonse D'Amato Chair in Italian and Italian American Studies at Stony Brook University, New York, was instituted in 2008. As the first holder of this Chair, I am committed to promoting a number of academic, cultural, and social activities across several disciplines. Among these a central concern is Critical Thinking, that is, reflection upon undertakings, publications and events that engage and stimulate historical, artistic, pedagogical and, in general, other intellectual pursuits. In order to give body to these often problematic, just as often much contested yet to some degree still elusive objectives, I have launched a *Forum in Italian American Criticism* (FIAC), which consists primarily in organizing at least one major conference a year, and sometimes half-day gatherings on more restricted topics. This collaborative project aims to create the premises for an open-ended dialogue with the most probing interdisciplinary work being done by scholars, thinkers, professionals and artists who are engaged in matters Italian, Italian American, American Italian, and, in our ever more interconnected XXI Century, more broadly Euroamerican and Global.The speakers at the first FIAC Symposium, held at Stony Brook University and at the John D. Calandra Italian American Institute on October 3-4, 2008, dealt primarily with metacritical issues and addressed the very reasons for and methods of our work in the humanities. The papers were subsequently published in a volume edited by Jerome Krase and bearing the conference title, *The Status of Interpretation in Italian American Studies* (Forum Italicum, 2011). The present volume collects the Proceedings from the second FIAC symposium. The proceedings from a third FIAC symposium, dedicated to the question of history in Italian and Italian American studies on the occasions of the 150th anniversary of the founding of the Italian state, and held at Stony Brook in March 2011, will appear in Spring 2015.

The present volume embodies the same critical spirit by focusing, rather than on a general topic, on the work done by one specific individual who has engaged in and embodied all of the perspectives listed above. I will cite a key paragraph from the Invitation to Participate in a Conference, which I sent out to about twenty scholars in early 2009:

> Dear .... I am writing to invite you to participate in a *Festschrift* in honor of Professor Paolo Valesio, on the occasion of his 70th birthday. As you well know, Valesio has been a leading Italianist in the United States for over three decades. He has made seminal contributions in linguistics, rhetoric, literary theory, poetics, religious literature, and D'Annunzio and Marinetti studies. He has moreover distinguished himself as a novelist and even more so as a poet, with a substantial production and unique voice. Valesio has been a teacher and inspiration to a great many of us, always ready to put his great learning and critical insights in so many fields at the service of his students, colleagues and the profession, and on both sides of the Atlantic. Many of us wish to honor the achievements and commitment of this internationally known intellectual, thinker and poet in our profession. Consistent with his humanity and modesty, Valesio would likely appreciate more a gathering focused on ideas and creativity than something celebrating his person. To that end, and after consulting with colleagues who know him well, the event will bear the aegis of two word-concepts under which a great many of his areas of interest can be covered: Nomos and Logos [...]

The conference title was subsequently changed (see Program, reproduced at the end of the volume) to include the word *poiesis*, since Valesio's activity in more recent years has turned with increasing intensity toward poetry.

But for these Proceedings, even the changed title, "Logos Nomos Poiesis," seemed too unwieldly, probably snob and offstandish, so I thought it opportune to give English equivalents. Needless to say, each of the three Greek words, with their broad and fluid semantic history, could have been rendered differently, and in specific contexts others would probably have been more appropriate. Yet if we bear in mind the work that our esteemed honoree has carried out during such a distinguished career, rendering *logos* with Discourse seems justified insofar as he has plumbed the depths of the word (and this in several languages) always in relation to other parts of speech, to rethoric in short, since the young linguist—at age thirty co-editor of the most important and scientifically up to date dictionary of the Italian language, the Zingarelli, 9th edition—, was already seeking to understand how meanings are carried across space and time to reach and shape other community of speakers. It is significant that one trained in structural linguistics then turns to ancient ideas about language and, in extracting the best from both worlds, creates a hybrid appropriate for our age, a contemporary theory, as the subtitle of his milestone *Novantiqua* (1980) states. Boundary for *nomos* can make one think, more much than its domain in paleojurisprudence, of the *loi du genre*, the concept of determining where one form of articulation cedes space to another and is governed by a different semiotic code. This also has been a terrain Valesio has mapped out, trod and reflected upon over the years (at one point he had introduced the notion of "semiohistory"). He has in fact written in just about all the genres, and thus has had first hand knowledge of boundaries not just as a scholar and critic, but and most impressively as author as well. Indeed the question of the limit, the frontier, the *de*finition of movement and expression has characterized his entire professional *modus operandi*. Finally, *poiesis*, which is the greater category of which *techné* is the specific real-world manifestation and concretization, has been rendered with Creation not only because it contains the general sense of creativity as, effectively, the existential and material dimension of a craft, of doing art, of ushering forth what was not there before. But also because in his research Valesio has slowly moved from the strictly philologic and linguistic to the philosophical and the theological. In fact, the question of the creation and disclosure of meaning has (pre)occupied him intensely to the point of interrogating the very *pneuma* that animates the cosmos. To frame it in Parmenidian terms, why we are (why we exist) and cannot not be, not being void, entails also asking the supreme question about Creation, thus legitimizing the adoption of this word in the broadest possible sense, a rendering apt at covering the strands and tendrils of his multifarious observations, experiments, expressions, and the relentless pursuit of gaining insights into the human condition.

Everyone I invited to the symposium considered it an honor and an intellectual duty to render homage to Valesio. Unfortunately some could not make it to the April 2010 gathering, sending in their regrets while being supportive of the initiative. Also, in the end, some of the speakers convened could not send in their papers for inclusion, having elected to publish them elsewhere; this was owed in no small part to my being late in assembling the anthology, for which I publicly apologize. Thus it is with deep appreciation that I would like to thank the authors here assembled for having waited so long before seeing their tribute finally appear in a collection dedicated to our friend and teacher. I also would like to thank them for having accepted to have my own paper included, since as organizer at the time I did not consider it opportune to take up a slot in the Program. I have written about Valesio's philosophy of language in an article that appeared in the journal *Italica* in 1995, and about his poetry in an article included in a book edited by Victoria Surliuga, *Analogia del mondo*, in 2008. The study on Campanella, though apparently not connected with Valesio's published works, is meant as a tribute to a teacher who has taught many of us how to delve into complex texts and, through rhetorical interconnections, that is, through recognition of the interplay between discourse, boundaries and the creative mind, disclose the originality and freshness of an author unduly ignored or little studied.

Finally, I would like to thank Prof. Anthony Julian Tamburri, General Editor of Bordighera Press, for having offered to publish these Proceedings, as well as to host future FIAC volumes. The first FIAC volume appeared with *Forum Italicum*, in their "Filibrary Series." After a thirty year run at Stony Brook, the journal has been acquired by Sage Publications, and the Series ended. I, and I am sure my colleagues, greatly appreciate the generous commitment of Bordighera Press to publish the present and future collections that result from Forum in Italian American Criticism conferences.

Peter Carravetta
Whitestone, NY, June 2013

TOWARD A DANTEAN THEOLOGY OF EROS
FROM DANTE'S LYRICS TO THE *PARADISO*

Teodolinda Barolini
COLUMBIA UNIVERSITY

For Paolo Valesio, *poeta-theologus*

In this paper I will discuss some of the connective threads between theology and eros in Dante's poetry, threads that revealed themselves while I was working on my commentary to Dante's youthful lyrics.[1] One of the great pleasures of working on the early Dante is to witness the spiraling process, reminiscent of the deep structure of terza rima itself in its double helix of relentless forward motion and enfolded backward glance, whereby the linguistic and poetic choices of a very young poet are revisited by the older poet later on. It is this revisiting and reimagining, this recuperation of words and ideas from the past and their transportation into new contexts and across ideological fault lines, which I will sketch here. I will offer some instances of the interwoven strands of eros and theology that forge a durable braid linking the alpha and omega of Dante's poetic praxis: on the one hand, the precocious use of theological words and concepts in early love lyrics that find their ultimate expression in the *Paradiso*; on the other, the end-of-life text where the secular, courtly, and erotic language of his youth is strangely and vibrantly alive.

Behind this paper is an agenda that I have been promot-

---

[1] Dante Alighieri, *Rime giovanili e della "Vita Nuova"*, ed. and commentary Teodolinda Barolini, with notes by Manuele Gragnolati (Milano: Rizzoli, 2009).

ing for some years now. We must move Dante studies past its reflexive dualism and focus on what the radical choice of a young mortal female as Dante's *beatrice* truly signifies. Before proceeding to my readings of specific Dantean texts, I offer a personal preamble on dualism in Dante studies.

In February 2007 I had occasion to participate in the Fordham University Press Centennial Conference, an event that involved bonafide theologians – not historians, but professors at Divinity Schools who preach and practice and write theology. One of the books being celebrated was a collection of essays entitled *Toward a Theology of Eros*, from which I have borrowed the title of this paper.[2] One of the editors, Virginia Burros, writes in her Introduction that to "reach for a theology of eros is already to question the binary opposition of divine love and human desire momentously inscribed by Anders Nygren in his magisterial tome *Agape and Eros*, initially penned in the 1930s and reissued in revised form in 1953" (xiii).[3] Burrus continues to cite from and characterize Nygren's thought:

> "There cannot actually be any doubt," he writes, "that Eros and Agape belong originally to two entirely separate spiritual worlds, between which no direct communication is possible." Observing that Platonic eros is always already a sublimation of what he names "vulgar Eros," he insists that there "is no way, not even that of sublimation, which leads over from Eros to Agape." Neither is more sublime than the other, and neither can be derived from the other; rather the two are born rivals, reflecting fundamentally different orientations. Eros is human-centered, manifesting as an acquisitive desire or longing that charts an upward path

---

[2] Virginia Burrus and Catherine Keller, eds., *Toward a Theology of Eros: Transfiguring Passion at the Limits of Discipline* (New York: Fordham University Press, 2006).
[3] Anders Nygren, *Agape and Eros*, trans. Philip S. Watson (Philadelphia: Westminster Press, 1953).

toward God as its most worthy object and transformative telos. In contrast, agape is God-centered...." (Burrus, xiv)

Nygren posits Augustine as the culprit with respect to the synthesis corrected by the Reformation: "it is Augustine's theology of *caritas*, together with Pseudo-Dionysius's Neoplatonic erotics, that Nygren credits with ultimate responsibility for medieval Christianity's thoroughgoing lapse into a synthetic, and thus counterfeit, theology of love" (xv). This sentence is fascinating to me on a variety of counts. First, as a medievalist, I consider the Christian medieval "lapse into synthetic theology" critiqued by Nygren to be anything but thoroughgoing. Rather, it is only maintained in brief high culture spurts of intensity expressed by the likes of Augustine and Dante, but hardly visible in popular culture, or indeed even in literary culture, which is instead quite unremittingly dualistic. Typically, in fact, an Occitan troubadour would recant the human desire sung in his love poetry and go into a monastery, even rising to become Bishop of Toulouse in the case of Folquet de Marselha. By the same token, when the Italian poet Guittone d'Arezzo, the greatest moral poet prior to Dante in the Italian lyric tradition, decides that he should turn to loving God, the first step is to reject what he calls "carnal voglia" ("carnal desire"). The binary *donna* versus *Dio* expressed with great clarity by the Sicilian founder of the Italian lyric tradition Giacomo da Lentini in his sonnet *Io m'aggio posto in core a Dio servire* is not anomalous within the Italian medieval corpus; rather it is Dante's synthesis of lady and God that, although not without precedents such as the poetry of Guido Guinizzelli, is anomalous in its synthetic reach. Petrarch, arguably the most imitated lyric poet who ever lived, systematically reopens the fissure that Dante seals and passed on the dichotomy between beloved and Beloved to subsequent generations.

Second, and related to the first point: given a cultural landscape in which the synthetic view of desire is hard to achieve, to the point that unified theories of desire seem in general to withstand with difficulty what seems to be an almost instinctive human reversion to moral Manichaeism, I confess surprise at the idea that a dualistic view is the more correct form of Christianity, or in general of any spiritual system.

There is no doubt that Dante himself utterly rejects the binary opposition of divine love and human desire posited by Nygren, and that he offers a sophisticated and nuanced vision of the Augustinian synthesis that Nygren critiqued. However, Dante's unified theory of desire has not fared well in the critical reception, and Dante commentaries and readings have not proved up to the task of accepting and preserving the poet's insistence on paradox. Dante criticism, with fervent exceptions,[4] has remained committed to its own versions of Nygren's binary "human desire" versus "divine love": terms like *amore corporale* versus *amore spirituale* litter the commentary tradition and are reemployed by beginning scholars. I hope that one day this way of thinking will be as outdated as a rigidly conceived body/soul dualism has already become among cultural and religious historians of the Middle Ages.[5] Dante's rejection of dualism should be recuperated as part of a deeper understanding of Christian spiritual thought.

The early sonnet *O voi che per la via d'Amor passate* illustrates both the category of biblical/courtly contamination

---

[4] See for instance Christian Moevs, *The Metaphysics of Dante's "Comedy"*, (New York: Oxford University Press, 2005), and F. Regina Psaki, "Dante's Redeemed Eroticism," *Lectura Dantis* 18–19 (1996): 12–19, "The Sexualized Body in Dante and the Medieval Context," *Annali di storia dell'esegesi* 13 (1996): 539–50, and "The Sexual Body in Dante's Celestial Paradise," in *Imagining Heaven in the Middle Ages*, ed. Jan S. Emerson and Hugh Feiss (New York: Garland, 2000), 47–61.

[5] See Caroline Bynum, *The Resurrection of the Body in Western Christianity, 200-1336* (New York: Columbia University Press, 1995).

and the category of courtly language that finds its way into the *Paradiso*. The opening verses – "O voi che per la via d'Amor passate, / attendete e guardate / s'egli è dolor quanto 'l mio grave" ("O you who walk along the path of Love / behold and see / if there be any grief as deep as mine"[6] [1–3]) – translate *Lamentations* 1:12 ("O vos omnes qui transitis per viam, attendite et videte si est dolor sicut dolor meus"), but insert the words "of Love," so that the wayfarers who in the Bible travel *per viam* are now traversing the "via d'Amor." Here Dante both theologizes *courtoisie* and "courtoisifies" the Bible. This dialectical pollination or indeed co-penetration of poetic codes – courtoisification of the Bible and theologizing of *courtoisie* – is the more noteworthy in that *O voi che per la via* is a poem that exists in a redaction that precedes the *Vita Nuova*.[7] Thus, we know with certainty that this kind of *contaminatio* interested Dante even before the theologizing that is the hallmark of the *Vita Nuova*'s prose narrative.

O voi che per la via tells of a lover who had once been happy, to the point that he became an object of envy and people were speaking of his "legiadro cor": "Dio, per qual dignitate / questi così legiadro lo core have?" ("Good lord, what worthiness / confers upon this one so glad a heart?" [11-12]). But this courtly paradise was unstable, and the following verse brings us to a present in which the poet/lover has lost his joy: "Or ho perduta tutta mia baldanza" ("Now I have lost my sense of confidence" [13]). These verses from *O voi che per la via* contain what is likely Dante's first use of key courtly terms, the adjective *leggiadro* and the noun *baldanza*; the latter indicates the lover's confidence and joy in pos-

---

[6] The translations are Richard Lansing's, prepared for the English version of *Rime giovanili e della "Vita Nuova"*, forthcoming from University of Toronto Press.

[7] I cite Dante's lyrics from the 2005 edition of Domenico De Robertis. We owe a debt of gratitude to De Robertis for having published in pre-*Vita Nuova* redaction the thirteen *Vita Nuova* poems that are thus available.

sessing his lady's love.[8] Another early poem, *Morte villana*, situated shortly after *O voi che per la via* in the *Vita Nuova*, contains what is likely Dante's first use of the noun *leggiadria*.[9]

An important lexical conduit of courtliness in Dante's thought, *leggiadria*, from the Occitan *leujairia*, is the courtly virtue to which Dante will later dedicate the moral canzone *Poscia ch'Amor*, in which he strives to preserve *cortesia* by wedding courtly values to moral values.[10] Suspended between courtly and moral values, *Poscia ch'Amor* anticipates the *Paradiso*, where courtly values resurface, transformed and rejuvenated. Thus, the *Commedia*'s only use of the word *leggiadria* – a hapax – belongs to a description of the archangel Gabriel: "*Baldezza* e *leggiadria* / quant'esser puote in angelo e in alma, / tutta è in lui" ("Boldness and cheer, as much as there can be in an angel or a soul, are all in him" [*Par.* 32.109-111]).[11] The hapax *leggiadria* is paired with *baldezza*, a variant of *baldanza* (in *Con l'altre donne mia vista gabbate* Dante uses *baldezza* in the redaction that precedes the

---

[8] Another early sonnet placed by Dante in the *Vita Nuova*, *Con l'altre donne mia vista gabbate*, contains *baldezza* in the redaction that precedes the *Vita Nuova* and *baldanza* in the redaction of the *Vita Nuova*. *Baldanza* occurs in the *rime* again in the *congedo* of *Amor, tu vedi ben*, one of the *rime petrose*.

[9] The adjective *leggiadro* appears in Dante's lyric poems four times: once in *O voi che per la via* and three times in the canzone *Poscia ch'amor*, dedicated to *leggiadria*. The noun *leggiadria* appears in Dante's lyric poems seven times: once in *Morte villana*, once in *Per una ghirlandetta*, once in *Sonar bracchetti*, three times in the canzone *Poscia ch'Amor*, and once in *Due donne in cima della mente mia*.

[10] On the canzone *Poscia ch'Amor* from this perspective, see my essay "'Sotto benda': Gender in the Lyrics of Dante and Guittone d'Arezzo" in *Dante and the Origins of Italian Literary Culture* (New York: Fordham University Press, 2006), esp. pp. 338-42.

[11] The adjective *leggiadro* appears in the *Commedia* only twice, both times in a courtly setting: "L'antico sangue e l'opere leggiadre" (*Purg.*11.61); "rime d'amore usar dolci e leggiadre" (*Purg.* 26.99).

Vita Nuova and *baldanza* in the redaction of the *Vita Nuova*),[12] so that the *Paradiso* verses bring together the two courtly words that were first in proximity in *O voi che per la via*: "Dio, per qual dignitate / questi così *legiadro* lo cor have?' / Or ho perduta tutta mia *baldanza*" (11-13). There is thus a direct lexical path from the courtly paradise of our humble *sonetto rinterzato* to the very different paradise inhabited by Gabriel. And, too, there is no avoiding the courtly – and thus, inevitably, eroticized – halo that as a result adorns the archangel Gabriel in Dante's paradise.

The categories we have considered, the theologizing of a courtly lexicon and biblical/courtly *contaminatio*, expand into the "courtoisification" not just of language but of the celestial mise-en-scène, as we find in the early canzone *Donne ch'avete*, where all of heaven clamors for the lady: "Lo cielo, che non have altro difetto / che d'aver lei, al suo segnor la chiede, / e ciascun santo ne grida merzede" ("Heaven, whose only imperfection is / the lack of her, implores its Lord to ask / for her, and all saints favor this request" [19–21]). Given that the core conceit of these verses, a defect in heaven, is, as Foster and Boyde put it, "theologically absurd,"[13] I prefer to speak of a will to "theologize" on the part of the young Dante, rather than of true theology. But the early idea stayed with him and was eventually expressed with more theological correctness in *Paradiso* 30, where Dante writes that the beauty of Beatrice is such "che solo il suo fattor tutta la goda" ("that only her Creator enjoys all of it" [*Par*. 30.21]).

---

[12] Dante seems in the *Commedia* to have resolved his uncertainty as to *baldezza* versus *baldanza* in favor of *baldezza*: in the *Commedia* we find *baldanza* only in the *Inferno*, referring to Virgilio's loss of confidence in front of the devils at the gates of Dis ("Li occhi a la terra e le ciglia avea rase / d'ogne baldanza" [*Inf*. 8.118-19]), while *baldezza* is reserved for *Paradiso*, where it indicates a supremely positive confidence (*Par*. 16.17 and 32.109).

[13] See Foster and Boyde, *Dante's Lyric Poetry*, vol. 2 (Commentary), p. 100.

The use of the celestial mise-en-scène is not in itself innovative; it was used by Guinizzelli in *Al cor gentil* and by Dante in the canzone *Lo doloroso amor*, where he details the situation of his soul when it has arrived before the divine tribunal as a means of expressing the tragic violence of his feelings. Thus, in *Lo doloroso amor* he writes that if God does not pardon the soul its sins, it will depart with the punishments it deserves ("e se del suo peccar pace no i rende, / partirassi col tormentar ch'è degna" ["and should He grant its sin no amnesty, / it will depart with torments that are just"] [35–36]), but in such a way as to not be afraid ("sì·cche non ne paventa" "but which it does not dread" [37]). How can it be that the soul of the poet will not be afraid of the punishments of hell? In a reprise of Giacomo da Lentini's Sicilian topos of the image of the lady painted in the heart of the lover, the poet explains that his soul will be so intent on imagining his lady that it will not feel any pain: "e starà tanto attenta / d'immaginar colei per cui s'è mossa, / che nulla pena averà che ella senta" ("it will be so intent / on contemplating her who made it leave / that there will be no pain that it might feel" [38–40]).

Lo doloroso amor is one of the very few of Dante's lyrics to contain the name "Beatrice",[14] and in it Dante thematizes the name and the issue of naming, albeit in a negative fashion that will be surprising to readers of the *Commedia*: "Per quella moro c'ha nome Beatrice" ("I die for her whose name is Beatrice" [*Lo doloroso amor*, 14]). *Lo doloroso amor* will reverberate in Dante's memory in the seventh canto of *Paradiso*, where we find, as in the canzone, the link between the name of Beatrice, first divided "pur per *Be* e per *ice*" (*Par.* 7.14) and

---

[14] In the lyrics that do not belong to the *Vita Nuova*, the name "Beatrice" appears only in *Lo doloroso amor*; in those belonging to the *Vita Nuova* it appears twice in the canzone *Li occhi dolenti* and once in the sonnet *Oltre la spera*, while the sonnet *Deh pellegrini* contains the noun "beatrice." The diminutive "Bice" appears only in the sonnet *Io mi senti' svegliar*, placed in the *Vita Nuova*.

then written whole in verse 16, and the hyperbole of the lover who does not feel the punishments of hell:

> Ma quella reverenza che *s'indonna*
> di tutto me, pur *per Be e per ice*,
> mi richinava come l'uom ch'assonna.
> Poco sofferse me cotal *Beatrice*
> e cominciò, raggiandomi d'un riso
> tal, che nel foco faria l'uom felice...
>
> [But that reverence that rules all of me, even just with *Be* and with *ice*, made me bow like a man falling asleep. Beatrice didn't let me suffer for long, and she began, dazzling me with a smile such that would make a man happy in the fire... (*Par.* 7.13-18)]

Here are the vestiges of *Lo doloroso amor* in *Paradiso* 7: the courtly world that is invoked in the neologism "s'indonna" (*Par.* 7.13); the reference to the *nomen* as a *signum*, the name made sign by the division into syllables, *Be* and *ice*, the name that we "see written", as in the words of *Lo doloroso amor*: "Quel dolce nome che mi fa il cor agro, / tutte fiate ch'i' lo vedrò scritto" (*Lo doloroso amor*, 15-16); and above all the description of the lady's laughter, capable of immunizing her lover from the pains of hell: "un riso / tal, che nel foco faria l'uom felice" (*Par.* 7.17-18).

The courtliness of Dante's *Paradiso* will require more investigation if we are to understand the deep social implications of the ongoing expression of feudal values on the part of a poet who grew up in an urban commune. My focus is on the ways in which the *cortesia* of *Paradiso* supports the creation of a non-boundary between eros and divine love, impulses that Dante places on a continuum. Let us now turn to the theology that we can see *in potentia* in secular and courtly verse: the category of theological ideas that we can

"Toward a Dantean Theology of Eros"

trace back to early texts where these ideas appear as poetry that is not yet overtly theological. I am referring to secular poems – not overtly theologized like *Donne ch'avete* (in bono) and *Lo doloroso amor* (in malo) – that are nonetheless witnesses to the *longue durée* of Dante's theological thought. One such is the great sonnet on friendship *Guido, i' vorrei che tu e Lapo ed io*. Perhaps not surprisingly, given that friendship is a subset of love, *Guido, i' vorrei* tackles issues that will haunt Dante throughout his life, in particular the tension between the self and the other, a variant of the metaphysical problem of the one and the many. *Guido, i' vorrei* is about the desire for non-difference, for complete reciprocity and transparency. From the names and pronouns of the first verse that indicate the ontologically individual state of the three friends – Guido, Lapo, and Dante himself are three separate subjects, even grammatically – we pass to the unitary state in the plural verb at the beginning of the second verse: "Guido, i' vorrei che tu e Lapo ed io / fossimo presi per incantamento" ("Guido, I wish that Lapo, you, and I / were carried off by some enchanter's spell" [1-2]). The *three* identities, whose individuality is signified by the pronouns "io" and "tu," will become part of *one* unity, carried off in *one* boat. Already we hear in this program a distant announcement of the many attempts in the *Paradiso* to give poetic life to the idea that the Three will become One while always remaining Three.

In the octave of *Guido, i' vorrei*, Dante imagines a state of complete and achronic harmony, in which the friends are protected from the flux of time and the multiple; the dream in fact includes immortality as well, living "*sempre* in un talento" – always in one desire. In this state of atemporality, of absolute non-difference (for time is what condemns us to difference: "Lo tempo, secondo che dice Aristotile nel quarto de la Fisica, è 'numero di movimento, secondo prima e poi'" [*Convivio* 4.2.6]), the desire for further harmony – "star *insieme*" – can only grow: this is a virtuous circularity, in which living always according to a single desire will make the desire to continue living together ever stronger. The sonnet imagines individuals that, while still remaining individuals – while still remaining Dante, Guido, and Lapo – are capable of suspending their every individual desire, and thus avoiding every "impedimento," every conflict. Dante proposes to eliminate the different wills of the three protagonists, without however nullifying the ontologically separate and irreducible beings indicated through the succession of names and pronouns. We have here, projected onto a profane and magical screen, a reality that is only verifiable in theological or supernatural terms: in daily reality, our separate identities necessarily imply divergent wills, hence conflict. Outside of a supernatural context, perfect unity is not possible without violating individual identity.

The melancholy of *Guido, i' vorrei* is inherent in the fact that this dream of avoiding difference remains a dream, even in the language of the poet that recounts it. The similarities with certain passages from *Paradiso* are instructive: in *Paradiso* these desires are related in the present or the future, while *Guido, i' vorrei* inhabits the conditional from beginning to end. In *Paradiso* these are not dreams, but imagined realities, in the same way that in *Paradiso* Piccarda's verse is not "*vorrei* che nella sua volontade *fosse* nostra pace" ("I wish that in His will *were* our peace") but "'n la sua voluntate *è* nostra pace" ("in His will *is* our peace" [*Par.* 3.85]).

Another youthful and secular poem with latent theological content is the courtly canzone *La dispietata mente che pur mira*. Particularly interesting here from our perspective is the Dantean variation of the Sicilian topos of the image of the lady painted in the heart of the lover. In the canzone, Dante compares the duty of the lady to the lover, who carries her image painted in his heart, to the duty of God to human beings, created in His image:

> E certo la sua doglia più m'incende
> quand'io mi penso ben, donna, che voi

> per man d'Amor là entro *pinta* sète:
> così e voi dovete
> vie maggiormente aver cura di lui,
> ché Que' da cui convien che 'l ben s'appari
> per l'*imagine* sua ne tien più cari.
>
> [And more intensely is its pain inflamed
> when I reflect, my lady, that it's you
> inside who's painted by the hand of Love.
> And so indeed you must
> devote to its wellbeing much greater care,
> for He from Whom we learn about the good,
> holds us more dear because we bear His image
> (*La dispietata mente*, 20–26)]

The poet declares that the suffering of his heart increases when he thinks that the lady's image is painted there. The lady should take care of the heart on which her image is impressed, just as God takes care of us human beings because he sees in us His own image. Dante has radically transformed the ancient Sicilian topos of the lady painted on the heart of her beloved, moving it in a theological direction through the analogy between the lover who bears the lady's image impressed upon his heart and the human creature who bears the divine image of his Creator impressed upon him.

At the end of the *Paradiso* the image of the lady painted in the heart of the lover becomes the human image painted in the "heart" of the Trinity, that is, our image painted in Christ. The second of the three circumferences seen by the pilgrim, the one that represents Christ, "parve *pinta*" – "pinta" is a word that originates with Giacomo da Lentini's *Meravigliosamente* – "de la nostra *effige*" ("appeared painted with our effigy" [*Par.* 33.131]). The word "effige," deriving from *effingere*, "to paint," here substitutes the word more typical in the lyric tradition, "figura" (as in Giacomo's "'nfra lo core meo / porto la tua *figura*" ["within my heart I carry your image" [*Meravigliosamente*, 8–9]), and reinforces the meaning of "pinta." As if to underline the path that leads from the old lyric topos to *Paradiso*, the only other use of "effige" in the *Commedia* refers to the "effige" of Beatrice in *Paradiso* 31: "ché süa *effige* / non discendëa a me per mezzo mista" ("her image / came down undimmed by anything between" [*Par.* 31.77-78]). The final incarnation of the lyric lady and the theology of the incarnation are linked by a meditation on image-making and on the relationship between image and reality, between the flesh and the spirit, that has its roots for Dante in Giacomo's *Meravigliosamente*.

A canzone like *Donne ch'avete* features not only the overtly theologized mise-en-scéne that we have discussed but a more latent theology. The fourth stanza of *Donne ch'avete* begins with the provocative question of a new interlocutor, Love: "Dice di lei Amor: 'Cosa mortale/ come esser pò sì adorna e sì pura?'" ("Love says of her, 'How can a mortal thing / become so perfect and so beautiful?'" [43–44]). Mortality and purity, values that are usually antithetical (mortality equals corruption), are here united. This is the stanza that according to the *Vita Nuova* prose is about "la nobilitate del suo corpo" ("the nobility of her body" *VN* XIX.18 [10.29]) and it is important to note the dignity that Dante here confers upon the body, the "cosa mortale" that is not eliminated or absorbed or sublimated but consecrated: this "cosa mortale" is – Love teaches – so wondrous and pure, "sì adorna e sì pura" (44), that "Dio ne 'ntenda di far cosa nova" ("God means to make of her a new and wondrous thing" [46]). The two facts – the lady's mortality and her miraculousness, her newness with respect to all other beings – are in this way tightly linked, even by the *dispositio* of the verses, where "cosa mortale" and "cosa nova" mirror one another:

> Dice di lei Amor: "*Cosa mortale*
> come esser pò sì adorna e sì pura?"

"Toward a Dantean Theology of Eros"

> Poi la reguarda, e fra se stesso giura
> che Dio ne 'ntenda di far *cosa nova*
>
> [Love says of her: "How can a mortal thing
> be so attractive and as well so pure?"
> He look at her and to himself he swears
> that God intends to make a thing that's new.
> (*Donne ch'avete* 43-46)]

The fourth stanza of *Donne ch'avete* presents a lady who is a miraculous being but who conserves at the same time the characteristics of a mortal woman: "Color di perle ha quasi, in forma quale / convene a donna aver, non for misura: / ella è quanto de ben pò far natura" ("Her color is like pearl, of such a hue / as well befits a lady, not too much. / She is the best that nature can create" [47–49]). She is not, like the Cavalcantian lady of *Fresca rosa novella*, "oltra natura" ("beyond nature" [31]). Instead, she is the best that nature can create: "ella è quanto de ben pò far natura" (49).

Dante does not deny the lady's mortality in the canzone that confirms her radical exceptionality. Her mortality is essential, as will be seen in the meeting with Beatrice in *Purgatorio* 31, where "cosa mortale" echoes our canzone: "e se 'l sommo piacer sì ti fallio / per la mia morte, qual *cosa mortale* / dovea poi trarre te nel suo disio?" ("and if the highest beauty thus failed you with my death, what mortal thing should later have drawn you to desire it?" [*Purg.* 31.52-54]). In the end, Dante's great discovery with regard to his lady lies precisely in her being both "cosa mortale" and "cosa nova": simultaneously inside and outside of the natural order.

The conflation of "cosa mortale" and "cosa nova" is prefigured by the conflation with which *Donne ch'avete* begins, the radical copula "intelletto d'amore," whose fusion of intellect and will anticipates *Paradiso*. We need only think – to give two stunning examples among the many possible – of the fusion of the faculties of intellect and will in the verses "Imagini, chi bene intender cupe" ("Imagine, you who desire to understand" [*Par.* 13.1]), where "intender" is the verb of the intellect and "cupe" is the verb of desire, and "Affetto al suo piacer, quel contemplante" ("Absorbed in his pleasure, that contemplative" [*Par.* 32.1]), where the first clause coincides with desire and the second with the intellect. The mystical fusion of the faculties at the end of *Paradiso* is anticipated by the preposition *di* in the *iunctura* "intelletto d'amore," an early intuition of the achieved theology behind *Paradiso* 30's magnificent verses: "luce intellettüal, piena d'amore / amor di vero ben, pien di letizia" ("intellectual light, full of love, / love of true good, full of joy" [*Par.* 40-41]).

As I noted at the outset, we have created in Dante studies a critical edifice that has never properly accommodated the eroticized language that Dante uses in paradise, language that he uses to characterize not only Beatrice but also the Transcendent Principle itself. The suggestion that there is an erotic component to Dante's love – that love is best expressed through language that is sometimes eroticized – is not an idea that easily acquires traction in our critical tradition. To illustrate what I mean, I will conclude by sharing a very witty joke from the Italian University milieu, which came to me courtesy of Paolo Valesio. The joke takes the form of a box with a pharmacological appearance; on the box is inscribed, as though the name of the medication within, the first verse of Dante's famous stilnovist sonnet *Tanto gentile e tanto onesta pare*. The sonnet of Dante's youth is literally (in the world of this literary joke) a contraceptive. Reading the sonnet is prescribed to diminish and eliminate sexual desire, thus preventing conception; the package contains dosages of the poem to be taken daily according to a strict schedule. The medication is composed of 14 hendecasyllables and one concept, "l'amor platonico" ("platonic love"): "Tanto gentile e tanto onesta pare, contiene 14 endecasillabi (11 sillabe x 14 versi) ed un concetto, l'amor platonico."

"Toward a Dantean Theology of Eros"

Under the heading "interazioni" the instructions explain that the contraceptive efficacy of *Tanto gentile* will be impaired if taken contemporaneously with other treatments, poems or prose of erotic content, of ambivalent significance, as for example the erotic *pastorella* of Guido Cavalcanti, *In un boschetto*, Boccaccio's *Ninfale fiesolano*, the Introduction to Day 4 of the *Decameron*, and Boiardo's *Amorum libri*: "Meditazioni irregolari ed una diminuzione della sicurezza contraccettiva si possono verificare allorché i contraccettivi orali siano stati assunti contemporaneamente ad altri trattamenti quali poesie e/o prose di contenuto erotico, di significato ambiguo, d'inno all'amor venereo (es. In un boschetto trova' pasturella dei laboratori G. Cavalcanti s.p.a.; Ninfale fiesolano o l'introduzione del giorno IV del Decameron della G. Boccaccio s.r.l.; gli Amorum Libri del gruppo M. & M. Boiardo s.p.a.)."

Here, in extremely concentrated and witty form, we have the fundamental cliché that infuses so much discussion of the concept of love in Dante. And we see moreover that the cliché has triumphed: it has entered the cultural imaginary as a given. Our task is to disseminate and make equally clichéd a more accurate assessment. First of all, the poem *Tanto gentile e tanto onesta pare* deserves a more nuanced reading: the lover's sigh has clear erotic connotations in the courtly lyric, and the sonnet's famous concluding command that the lover ex-press himself in a sigh – "Sospira" – is not therefore without a subtle but irreducible eroticism. Moreover, as we have discussed, Dante is a poet who has no qualms about importing physical erotics into the transcendent sphere, creating in *Paradiso* his own theology of eros. Thus he depicts divine co-penetration with magnificent neologisms, forging verbs from the pronouns *lui*, *mi*, and *tu*: "Dio vede tutto, e tuo veder s'inluia ... s'io m'intuassi, come tu t'inmii" ("God sees everything, and your sight in-hims itself ... if I were to in-you myself, as you in-me yourself" [*Par.* 8.73, 81]).

Dante does not seem able, or willing, to discuss love without reference to eros. In the examination on *caritas* administered by St. John, the apostle examiner poses a question regarding God's love whose language – "with how many teeth does this love bite you?" – echoes the erotic aggression of one of the *rime petrose*. The Italian verse, "con quanti denti questo amor ti morde" (*Par.* 26.51), closely echoes "co li denti d'Amor già mi manduca" from the youthful canzone of violent and deadly eros, *Così nel mio parlar* (32). Dante challenges us to fashion for ourselves a divinity that does not disembrace human eros, but rather makes it one with *l'ultima salute. L'eros s'inleia, la salute s'inluia*.[15]

WORKS CITED

Barolini, Teodolinda. "'Sotto benda': Gender in the Lyrics of Dante and Guittone d'Arezzo." In *Dante and the Origins of Italian Literary Culture*. New York: Fordham University Press, 2006.

Burrus, Virginia, and Catherine Keller, eds. *Toward a Theology of Eros: Transfiguring Passion at the Limits of Discipline*. New York: Fordham University Press, 2006.

Bynum, Caroline. *The Resurrection of the Body in Western Christianity, 200-1336*. New York: Columbia University Press, 1995.

Dante Alighieri. *Dante's Lyric Poetry*. Ed. Kenelm Foster and Patrick Boyde. 2 vols. Oxford: Oxford University Press, 1967.

———. *Rime*. Ed. Domenico De Robertis, with commentary. Florence: Edizioni del Galluzzo, 2005.

———. *Rime giovanili e della "Vita Nuova"*. Ed. and commentary Teodolinda Barolini, notes by Manuele Gragnolati. Milan: Rizzoli, 2009.

———. *Dante's Lyric Poetry: Poems of Youth and of the "Vita Nuova."* Ed. and commentary Teodolinda Barolini. With new verse translations by Richard Lansing. Toronto: University of Toronto Press, 2014.

Moevs, Christian. *The Metaphysics of Dante's "Comedy."* New York: Oxford University Press, 2005.

---

[15] The verb is based on *Paradiso* 22.127, "prima che tu più t'inlei" ("before you more in-her yourself," where the "her" referred to is "l'ultima salute," "the final blessedness" of *Par.* 22.124).

Nygren, Anders. *Agape and Eros*. Trans. Philip S. Watson. Philadelphia: Westminster Press, 1953.
Psaki, F. Regina. "Dante's Redeemed Eroticism." *Lectura Dantis* 18–19 (1996): 12–19.
———. "The Sexualized Body in Dante and the Medieval Context." *Annali di storia dell'esegesi* 13 (1996): 539–50.
———. "The Sexual Body in Dante's Celestial Paradise." In *Imagining Heaven in the Middle Ages*, edited by Jan S. Emerson and Hugh Feiss. New York: Garland, 2000. 47–61.

HISTORY, EMPIRE, AND POLITICAL REASON
CAMPANELLA AND THE DAWN OF MODERN EUROPE[1]

Peter Carravetta
Stony Brook University

> Cosa il mondo non ha che non si muti,
> Né che del suo mutarsi non si doglia...
>
> [There is nothing in the world that does not change,
> And of this change the world feels the pain...]
>
> T. Campanella, *Poesie filosofiche* (73.8)

> La filosofia contempla la ragione, onde viene la scienza del vero; la filologia osserva l'autorità dell' umano arbitrio, onde viene la coscienza del certo.
>
> [Philosophy contemplates reason, from which we derive abstract knowledge of what is true. Philology observes that of which human choice is the author, from which we derive awareness of what is certain]
>
> G.B. Vico, *Principi di scienza nuova*
> (1744; I,ii,x; *New Science*, § 138)

> ...una tale critica retorica ricerca in tutti i testi...i temi più brucianti che costellano la lotta (la lotta primariamente simbolica) per assicurare posizioni di potere.

---

[1] A shorter version of this paper was first read at the Renaissance Society of America annual conference, in Chicago, April 5, 2008. It was subsequently further developed and read, in conference format and titled "Eclipse of the Sun: Campanella and the Rhetoric of History," at the 34th annual convention of The Society for Utopian Studies, in Wrightsville Beach, NC, Oct 31, 2009. It is the first half of a study on Campanella's thought. A Spanish translation of the present text appeared in *Despalabro* (Madrid), 2012, Vol. VI, pp. 45-60.

From: *Discourse Boundary Creation*. Bordighera Press, 2013

> [...such rhetorical critique seeks in all texts...the most problematic topics that inform the (primarily symbolic) struggle to gain positions of power.]
>
> P. Valesio, *Ascoltare il silenzio* (1986, p. 171)

I

The publication of Tommaso's Campanella's *The Spanish Monarchy* and *The French Monarchy* in 1997 in one volume,[2] edited by the indefatigable Germana Ernst and with facing translations in French, provided the spontaneous yet necessary critical locus to consider how the thought of the Calabrian monk evolved during a forty-year period, which comprises the majority of his life's work and experiences, including of course the prison years between 1600 and 1627. Against the background of his tenacious though evolving belief in the possibility of a Universal Monarchy based on natural religion, yet under the leadership of the pope, Campanella's two treatises open a window into late XVI century world politics and the early Modern European conceptions of power and hegemony, as well as afford us the possibility to study the role church and empire were to play in the unfolding of Western history. This was a time of great strife among religious denominations as well as, more broadly, between religion and science, and counter-reformation politics versus growing secularization. Campanella has often been considered a belated humanist whose ideas were soon to be swept away by the consolidation of absolute monarchies, the Treaty of Westphal, mercantilism, and the spread of European influence outside of Europe and the Mediterranean. And yet, I believe that that is a reductive assessment owed in part to latent XIX and early XX century historio-

---

[2] Campanella, Tommaso. *Monarchie d'Espagne et Monarchie de France*, ed. by G. Ernst, transl. by N. Fabry and S. Waldbaum (Paris, puf, 1997). See also the earlier, shorter edition, *La Monarchia di Spagna*, ed. by G.Ernst (Napoli, Istituto Superiore per gli Studi Filosofici, 1989).

graphical conceptions of social evolution, progress, and periodization. My interest in looking at these texts resides *not* in terms of what they did not foresee – the Enlightenment, the French revolution and the rise of nation-states – which is typical of the linear retrojection of a teleological imperative whereby the history of ideas ought to be narrated in a nearly logical, consequential "march of progress." Rather, I would like to examine these two little studied major works in terms of what they might still tell us, heirs of the postmodern critique of precisely these later developments, about the critique of political reason, the reframing of empire and the birth pangs of proto-nation-states, the then new internationalism and globalization, the forces that may or may not be channeled in structuring a society, and the recent thinking of the possibilities of empire in the XXI century.[3]

II

First, however, we need a note about the actual texts under consideration. Up until about a decade ago it was believed, on the authority of scholars of the rank of Luigi Amabile and Luigi Firpo, that *The Spanish Monarchy* (hereafter SP) was written in 1600, immediately *after* Campanella's incarceration for the insurrection of the previous year that took place in Calabria. This view in a sense explained or partly justified the adamant philohispanic tenor of the text, considered a sort of panegyric to the greatness of Catholic Spain which might have had the unstated but hoped for result of softening the Viceroy when sentencing came up. But continued philological spade work by Germana Ernst, aided also by subtle stylistic and historical analyses, has demonstrated that, first, there were two versions of the *Monarchy*, one short-

---

[3] I should also add, to better contextualize the theoretical horizon within which I am reading Campanella, that this paper is part of a larger project on Humanism, which revolves around the construction of social space, the role and primacy of free will in human endeavors, and the rhetoric of power.

er one written between June, 1593, and September, 1595; and one larger one, which is the one printed in the puf edition in 1997, written upon his presumably definitive return to Stilo in 1598.[4] This alone, writes Ernst in the Introduction citing in support Campanella's letters, should exclude the thesis about the "instrumentality" of the treatise. (xvi) The work appeared in print during the author's lifetime in Germany in 1620 and then again 1623, but with many interpolations.

The French Monarchy (hereonafter FM) on the other hand, was written a year *after* his arrival in France in 1634. The philosopher-prophet had to flee Rome – where he had finally been cleared of all charges in 1629 – in incognito, under false name, in the autumn of 1634, because he was once again in the cross hairs of the Holy Office on account of a former student of his who had been accused of heresy and in his deposition had mentioned Campanella's name. In France, where he was already well known and was well received,[5] he could finally attend to the revision and publication of his immense production. Yet, driven as he was by prophetic vision all his life, he couldn't abstain from participating in the current affairs, in a city that saw the emergence of Richeleau as the great manipulator of an ascending French hegemony aimed primarily at creating a wedge between the two trunks of the Hapsburgs. We will return to this stage of his *engagèment* further down.

III

Subdivided into 32 chapters, SM belongs to the literature of didactic counsel to a Lord or Ruler and was written in an

---

[4] On the over thirty codices of *The Spanish Monarchy* reviewed by De Mattei, the great majority state in the proem that they were written in 1598, "in questo mio conventino di Stilo." Cf. Rodolfo De Mattei, *Studi Campanelliani*. (Firenze, Sansoni, 1934), 57-81. See also the "Note philologique" by G. Ernst (1997), 607-15

[5] Cf. Michel Pierre Lerner, *Tommaso Campanella en France au XVII siècle*. (Napoli, Bibliopolis, 1995), 9-90.

effort to advise and warn on matters of government, on how to attain or keep power, and to explain the sense of more abstract principles and values. It makes ample use of historical facts as *exempla* to convey a point, and in a way, during the century in which rhetoric yields to method as the legitimate approach to knowledge,[6] it is simultaneously very rhetorical and very methodic. That it was also written to curry favor from the powerful – in this case, the King of Spain, although Philip II died precisely in September 1598 – was the custom of the era, a practice which has deep roots in Humanism, and which with Machiavelli reaches its apex.

Campanella states right from the beginning that the causes of human principalities are three: God, prudence and opportunity, which when taken together are called destiny (fato). He then offers a paradigmatic example: The Monarchy of Christ gave its followers the prudence of the snake (positively embodied by the apostles and the pope), and the opportunity to take advantage of a situation (which consisted in knowing how to capitalize on timely events, "del tempo"). Example furnished here is what happened with the subdivisions of the Roman Empire and the tragic end of the monarchy of the Jews. And yet, moving from historical philology to philosophy, we soon read that it is the last two terms of the triad that matter most: Human affairs – *le cose umane* – whether good or bad, if known by us, are due to prudence, if not, they are called fortune, chance or fate:

---

[6] Cf. Neil Gilbert, *Renaissance Concepts of Method*. (New York, Columbia University Press, 1963); Walter J. Ong. *Ramus, Method and the Decay of Dialogue*. (Cambridge, Harvard University Press, 1958). Matters were a bit more complicated regarding the proper reading of history and its impact on jurisprudence. See for example Julian H. Franklin, *Jean Bodin and the Sixteenth-Century Revolution in the Methodology of Law and History* (New York, Columbia University Press, 1963). On the ontological and pragmatic links between method and rhetoric, see now Peter Carravetta, *The Elusive Hermes. Method, Discourse, Interpreting* (Aurora (CO), Davies Group, 2012).

> Come ritrovare una cosa a uno che l'andava cercando è senno e prudenza, e a un altro che non badava né la sapea, è caso o fortuna. (SM 4)[7]

As we move to ch. 2, on "La cagioni dell'Imperio spagnolo," (10-12) we learn that, though God is the first and last mover of all, and has rewarded the Spanish for their 800-year struggle against the Moors, it is *human agency* that makes and undoes empires, and the book will soon read as a *realist approach* to an understanding of the forces that shape human destiny. In line with a rhetorical strategy that can be perceived in other early humanists, for instance in Lorenzo Valla and Pico della Mirandola, and without having to challenge the authenticity of these authors' deepest belief in the Supreme Being, God is soon left out of the equation, becoming a regulatory principle or ideal of transcendence that can actually accommodate – again in line with Pico – believers from other religious faiths, including Muslim and Jews.[8] More broadly, though, interactions in human history are subject to the interplay mainly of *prudenza* and *occasione*.

At this juncture we must introduce a necessary external frame of reference inasmuch as, judging not only by these two loaded lexemes, but also by the stylemes and the structure of logical deductions in the remaining chapters, it becomes soon clear that, as one critic observed, Campanella

---

[7] "It is like when someone finds something he was looking for already, we call it wisdom and prudence, whereas when someone finds something that he neither knew about nor paid attention to, we call it chance or fortune." Except where indicated, all translations are my own.

[8] The second time in his life that Campanella got into serious trouble with the Holy Office, when he was in Padua, in the early 1590's, was owed to the fact that he befriended a Jewish scholar and that, according to testimony furnished to the accusers, he conversed "da ebraizzante" ("as a Jew sympathizer"), raising the suspicions of local religious authorities. We should not forget that this is the high point of the Counter-Reformation, and mere suspicion of heresy was punishable by torture or death.

may have had a copy of Machiavelli's *The Prince* and of the *Discourses* close at hand when he wrote SM.⁹ We will turn to the importance of this hypothesis in more detail further down, but we must bear it in mind as we progress.

What are the reasons behind Spanish greatness that afford them the possibility of becoming the ultimate Universal Monarchy? Placed against the tapestry of history, Campanella argues that in the past Goths, Longobards and the French won empires with lances and horses, and before them the Romans with swords, but now that the Spanish through their long struggles have acquired the support of the Church – who rewarded them by bestowing upon their leadership the title of Catholic King – and developed *astuzia*, they won their empire also thanks to superior weapons, like the *archibugio*, the early flint rifles or blunderbuss, and the printing press! Apart from this clear-headed understanding of the transforming power of technology, he closes in on the fact that opportunity played its role when the two great families of Castile and Aragon joined together, and when the Genoese, who had put their own seafaring traditions at the service of the Spanish crown, discovered a New World for them – "l'invenzione del nuovo mondo." ["the invention of the New World"].¹⁰ – But there is more, for at that particular juncture

---

⁹ Cf. Vittorio Frajese. *Profezia e machiavellismo. Il giovane Campanella*. (Roma, Carocci, 2002), 58-83, especially 67-9.

¹⁰ The expression "Invention of the New World" is particularly salient when in *our* era so many books, whose aim is to undermine the Enlightenment and XIX Century notion of foundations and the transcendent origins of nations and people, bear titles such as: Eric Hobsbawn and Terence Ranger's *The Invention of Tradition*, Mudimbe's *The Invention of Africa*, Ali Jimale Ahmed's *The Invention of Somalia*, Alain Dieckhoff's *L'invention d'une nation. Israël et la modernité politique*, Roberto Martucci's *L'invenzione dell'Italia Unita* and so on. Clearly the major influence here has been Benedict Anderson's *Imagined Communities* (1983). But steeped in the humanist tradition, coming up with "in-venire" was for Campanella a natural gesture, which can fruitfully be juxtaposed to the notion of dis-covery, employed for centuries. Besides the 1596 *Poetica*, available in Latin only after 1638, Campanella also wrote a still unpublished *Rhetori-*

in history, the French, the Germans, and the English, owing to their internicine religious strife, were "depressed," meaning in deplorable condition, so the only, though formidable, task for the Spanish crown was to knock down – "abbattere" – the Turkish empire, and the world would be theirs, emulating what Alexander had done with the Persians and Rome with Carthage.

We have to read Campanella's text carefully to appreciate how he seems to be operating at two or more levels at the same time. Although the heading for ch. 3 states that the first cause of empire resides in God, the opening sentence reads as follows:

> All nations have learned that chance (occasione) and human prudence (prudenza umana) alone are not enough to either acquire things or govern, inasmuch as we can see that in specific cases the will may be free to choose (l'arbitrio è libero nel volere), but not in matters of doing and feeling, for we can all think that tomorrow one goes to sow and another to court and some hunting and some traveling, and so on, and then there comes a thunderstorm the next morning which will upstage what prudence commanded, and no one will do what his will tells him, but will act according to what the fated occasion will allow. Whoever can subject the prudence of the will to superior causes will however somehow succeed. (SM 14)[11]

---

ca: cf. Luigi Firpo, "Introduzione" to Tommaso Campanella, *Poetica* (Roma, Reale Accademia d'Italia, 1944): 62-63.

[11] "Ogni nazione ha conosciuto che la prudenza umana sola con l'occasione non basta all'acquisto delle cose né al governo, poiché veggiamo nelle cose particolari che l'arbitrio è libero nel volere, ma non nel fare e nel patire, con ció che sia questa sera tutti pensiamo per dimane chi ad andare ad arare, chi alla corte, chi a caccia, chi in viaggio, etc., ecco che sul mattino verrà una pioggia, e guasterà tutti i consigli della prudenza, e nessuno farà secondo il suo arbitrio, ma secondo l'occasione fatale permetterà. Ma chi saprà supporre la prudenza dell'arbitrio alle cause superiori, riuscirà a suo modo." (SM 14).

Superior causes can be nature's or God's will, but there is no immanence sought here, rather, he will look for those causes that may reveal the historical unfolding of a Messianic monarchy, as he will write in the 1606 book by that title. Later, he will demonstrate that without the Christians' deity the ancient empires *had to* fall, whereas in recent history, he argues, "unfolding" of the past was more clearly designed, going from Rome to Byzantium to France and finally to Spain, in short, there seemed to be a human *telos* acting in or through history. And despite the fact that as a millenarian he prophetized shattering revelations by the year 1600, the possibility open to the crown of Spain to achieve the universal monarchy were linked to religious, moral, and ethical responsibility. There is an implied emphasis on *human agency*. In the same breath he in fact reiterates that there are different ways of seeking or understanding God, for instance, philosophers might search in nature or, like Pythagoras, seek God through numbers, while the Hebrews did it through their prophets, and the Romans through their spirits. One cannot but think of how much this is in the trajectory sketched by Pico's syncretism. He finally arrives at the notion – which had long been a major *topos* in allegorical interpretation – that one must recognize the angel – the messenger – who travels through historical time from empire to empire, from people to people, transforming the tutelage of and abeyance to the Supreme Being into a search for patterns, guiding forces, and linguistic traces.

A case can be made that in some ways Campanella is here proleptically looking at Vico's *New Science*. But he is actually more of a realist than the Neapolitan philosopher, perhaps more in line with Thomas Hobbes and, in our day, Carl Schmidt. He goes on to manifest this in ch. 4, where the achievements of ancient empires and monarchies are juxtaposed to the achievements of Spain, the Hapsburgs specifically, and where he systematically inserts concrete references concerning which other existing powers the crown should ally itself with, taking advantage of the fact – important for our understanding of the next book we will examine, – that France *has had* this opportunity in the Christian era but had squandered it. Passing sweeping historical judgment was not alien to these early historiographers. On the strength of his deductions, the Calabrian monk finally suggests that the Monarch, "the King of Kings," should seek to have the pope himself crown him Emperor, thus relocating at the same time the political center of the Holy Roman Empire from Austria-Germany to Spain, by now considered the new *caput mundi*. In a sense trusting in predestination, which as a believer he had to include in his sociopolitical analyses, Campanella makes it clear that Spain has now a golden opportunity to achieve, and consider itself, the universal Christian monarchy. Yet in the passage cited there is also present, as suggested, an awareness of the relative autonomy of *human agency*, which can be characterized as a balancing act between what one is ready to do, and what one can actually do in the face of unforeseen circumstances: a realist must also be an opportunist, and in the chess game of *Realpolitick*, that is a necessary, crucial trait.

Here we are again in Machiavellian territory, for Campanella clearly understood that religion is the glue of societies, and that no political power can be achieved without having the church as an ally. From ch. 5 onward, the argument turns in fact to political philosophy in order to explain the differences between his vision of history and that of the Florentine. The second cause of the rise of empires is *prudenza* (36) which, consistent with his Telesian roots and the philosophy of the senses, is rooted in nature: "and who is guided by nature cannot lack in prudence, as we can see with plants, ants, wasps, cranes and fishes, whereby men often learn to govern from these realms." (ib.) And here comes the explicit reference:

> It should be borne in mind however that *prudenza* is different from *astuzia*, which some call *ragion di stato*, because, first, *prudenza* accords with the first cause, which is God, and is therefore mindful of prophecies and the divine sciences in order to foretell the future. Second, *astuzia* is concerned only with taste and one's own brain, calling itself wisdom... *prudenza* is magnanimous and looks to things to find a greater truth, *astuzia* is pusillanimous and in order to appear magnanimous ends up in arrogance (superbia); without a scale of values (scala di virtù) it aspires to greatness while focusing on meaningless minutiae. *Prudenza* shows clemency and truthfulness, *astuzia* is cruel and adulatory. (SM 36)

In short, the wily seek and execute lowly tricks and fraud against the people in order to debase and debilitate them, aiming to satisfy primarily themselves, as the "empio Macchiavello" (38) holds, whereas the prudent is concerned with and respects the customs of the people. Hence he becomes stronger in conquest as befits the audacious, like Columbus, Alexander, and Caesar. The prudent ruler is definitely liberal, capable of generosity and appropriate firmness (giusta severità), even while deploying useful and loving lies (inganni amorosi).

Is Campanella's juxtaposition of *astuzia* and *prudenza* proof he was so naïve as not to have learned anything from Machiavelli? Not quite, although in order to get by the censors, after his third brush with the Holy Office – he was on trial and then jailed in Santa Maria sopra Minerva in 1597 – he had to make his anti-Machiavellism very explicit. Yet in the same chapter, when it comes to the practical aspect of doing politics, he is clearly echoing *The Prince* and in part *The Discourses*.[12] According to Campanella, once he acquires a

---

[12] Cf. the thorough analysis of this complex relationship in John M. Headley, *Tommaso Campanella and the Transformation of the World* (Princeton,

reign a King should be generous but not prodigal, in order to avoid being taken for granted by the populace; on the other hand, he should not rob and disrespect his subjects, as Caligula did. Moreoever, the King should fear "mutabilità della fortuna," the unpredictability of chance, but in other cases he should not be too confident, like Charles V, who failed as a just King because he used the same audaciousness in conquering as in maintaining his reign. Concerning the military, Campanella writes that severity must be exercised to keep the soldiers bound to duty, and a King should modulate the aftermath of military victories otherwise disobedience and mutiny may ensue, as happened to Tiberius in Germany; soldiers moreover should not be insolent and plunder, otherwise a victory turns to defeat, as happened to Corradino Svevo with respect to Charles d'Anjou. Above all, after a conquest, a ruler should take care to satisfy the people, otherwise they divide and turn to foreigners for support, as happened to the Carthagenians after the first Punic War, and to Ezzelino, to whom "Padua shut its gates," and Nero, who was declared an enemy by the "patria" of which he was the prince. (40)

Other examples abound, and at the level of *method* of historical analysis the Dominican monk is not ever so far off the field disclosed by the Florentine secretary. Yet what sets them apart emerges at a *theoretical* level, especially there where the grounding ethos, the conception of man's essence, and the finality of political power are concerned. Machiavelli's *ragion di stato*, that great discovery that introduced a brutal realism in the analysis of power acquisition and management and set political science toward what much later would be called the autonomy of the political, is in SM coun-

---

Princeton University Press, 1997), 180-96, a chapter which was previously published as an article with the title "On the Rearming of Heaven: The Machiavellism of Tommaso Campanella," in *Journal of the History of Ideas* 49 (1988), 387-404.

tered by the *ragione politica* (44). On the divergence between Campanella and Machiavelli, John Headley wrote:

> Apparently horrified by Machiavelli's total subjection of religion to the principle of utility, the Calabrian prophet, gazing northward, sees that in those kingdoms the *politici* have made religion a suit or hat that can be changed at will. Yet while rejecting this Machiavellian view of politicized religion, Campanella himself affirms religion's political utility, although on a different basis. He insists that no community can last a day without religion; in fact the social necessity of religion is axiomatic for Campanella. As the very soul of the political, religion exercises a natural magic in uniting members of a community.[13]

In Campanella's own words:

> Perché la religione o vera o falsa sempre ha vinto quando ha credito, perché lega gli animi, onde pendono i corpi e le spade e le lingue, che sono strumenti d'imperio. (MS 44)[14]

And in a truly prophetic – these days we would say proleptical – assertion, he writes that "Giammai imperio più certamente rovinó che col mutare della religione, se l'istorie ben

---

[13] John Headley, *Tommaso Campanella*, cit., p. 187.
[14] "Because whether true or false religion has always won when people believed in it, because it binds the souls, from which depend the *bodies*, the *swords* and the *languages*, which are the instruments of empire" (my emphasis). Developed further down, this trichotomy appears both in *The City of the Sun* and the *De Politica*. The book that makes his anti-Machiavellism explicit is *L'ateismo trionfato*, written between 1605 and 1607, but which he had to rewrite in Latin, with strong emendations, in 1631, because deemed too Pelagian, and too "soft" on Protestan theology. See the review of the publication of the earlier Italian edition by Edward Gosselin in *Renaissance Quarterly*, Vol. 58, No. 2 (Summer 2005): 589-590.

si leggono." (46)[15] We cannot but think, of course, of the fate of the historically recent socialist or communist states that sought to abolish religion altogether. But that's another topic.

IV

The notion of *ragione politica*, apparently not as useful to the achieving and maintaining a single state, is crucial instead to a Monarchy made up of several princedoms or, by extension, to an Empire which subsumes many kingdoms, principalities, duchies, counties, and so on. Campanella's universalist ecumenical mind-set understands political reason as the capacity to work on at least *two levels at the same time*: on the one hand, power requires endorsing belief (of the extant or dominant religion) and the language (but not necessarily the arms) required to protect one religion against another. Yet on the other it must recognize the need to resort concretely to the use of arms when it comes to conquering and annexing a different country of the same faith. Again, he provides ample documentation for his thesis. Against the separation of powers and the idea, championed foolishly ("scioccamente") (48) by Dante – and, we might add, Marsilius of Padua, Lorenzo Valla, and the whole tradition of antidecretalists, – that the Pope should just tend to the souls and the *decime*, Campanella holds that, in the real world, the prophet *must be* armed, and that the papacy is the central socio-political power which can galvanize Europe. Aware that his are no longer the days of Alexander VI or Julius II, *ragione politica* demonstrates that there is always someone ready to take up arms to support the Pope, even should the Pope not have arms of his own. In fact, he argues, some may be driven by zeal, as countess Matilda did against emperor Henry (Arrigo), others by discord or jealousy, as the Vene-

---

[15] "Properly read, history will reveal that when religions change empires fall."

tians did against emperor Fredric, and others still for both reasons, as did Pepin and Charlemagne, who united to fight for the Pope against Longbards, Saracens and others (46): fighting for the premiership of the pope is the politically advantageous position to assume.

V

From this point on, the lesson to impart to the Spanish royals is clear: "the King must declare himself dependent on the Pope," (50) while essaying to "propose marvelous things, which make the King of Spain admirable in matters of religion, prudence, valor and prophecy, because where these things occur, there the empire will lean." In addition, since these *grandi cose* must occur "under the auspices of the Italian empire, which today is German, it is clear that he must take it over, a feat possible only through the Pope, who can damn the three Protestant heretics who threaten Rome." (54) As we will see, and announcing what will be the core of the *The French Monarchy* 35 years later, it is on Italian soil that the struggle to attain a Universal Monarchy must be waged. Further on in the 1598 text he advises on the necessity to elect a Spanish Pope, preferably from the Austrian branch, and that other concerted efforts should include sending cardinals to the New World, install two or three religious sages in all administrative positions, confer to Domenicans, Francescans "and others" all high offices, and further that in time of war all captains should have a religious counselor (56, 58).

In ch. 8, having reiterated that "it is proper of prudence to take advantage of opportunity" (66), Campanella writes down a list of matters the King should attend to, almost like a memo with Do's and Don't's, and then goes on to sketch, in ch. 9, all the noble traits this glorious leader of the Christian Monarchy should display. But it is in light of the above glossed *ragione politica*, and in order to avoid "ruin," that he

"History, Empire, and Political Reason"

advises the monarch to carry this out slowly and, again, *prudently*,[16] by resorting to such public legislation as changing the names of the months, timetables, vary the habits of the populace, introduce new observances in religious practice, in short, make science and religion permeate the tenor and activities of the kingdom, so that the final effect will be, as elsewhere declared and repeated, both to Christianize *and* to Hispanize. Campanella here exhibits an astounding insight into population control, government craft, and the timely deployment of ideologhemes, which we might reasonably compare to contemporary state-sponsored programmes, agencies, schools, propaganda and techniques for social behavior modification.

This general plan has made some scholars, such as Francesco Clemente, see a direct connection between *SM* and *City of the Sun*, which is a defensible position,[17] we might add,

---

[16] Although further down, in chapter XVI, as he gets more and more specific about the actual history of Spain and the misgoverning of foreign lands, he does get carried away on Machiavellian wings, sounding like he is giving advice to a chief of staff on how to carry out an occupation: "che quando si occupa paese strano di religione e di dominio, si debba spopolare e trasmigrare le genti facendole schiave, e battezzare i figli o farne serraglio o mandarli nel Mondo nuovo, e mandare una colonna dei tuoi, e un governatore fedele e prudente. E questo si dovea fare in Tunisi da Carlo V...." However, as we saw above, his political realism shows also when he states that matters are to be handled differently when the religion is the same: "quando poi si occupa paese strano di dominio, ma non di religione, non si deve spopulare né mutar legge, ma presidiarlo e mandar i supremi officiali dei tuoi, e i bassi officiali siano del popolo del paese, e a poco a poco mutar le leggi loro nelle tue, però più strettamente o largamente secondo il clima comporta." (154)

[17] Cf. Francesco Clemente, "Fra realismo politico e vocazione utopica. La Monarchia di Spagna di Tommaso Campanella," in *Segni & Comprensione* (Univ. del Salento) Anno XXII (Nuova Serie), N. 64, gennaio-aprile 2008:103-25. Yet in chapter 30, dedicated to the "altro emisfero, cioè del Mondo novo," Campanella vacillates between harsh *political realism*, which demands that Catechism be taught in the Amerindians' language but also that, in populating these lands (apparently he was unaware that millions had already died of diseases spread by the Europeans), the Spaniards avoid killing them while enslaving non-converts, "as the Ro-

but only up to a point, since the latter was written in his darkest hour, in 1602, perhaps in fear of death following the torture. Nevertheless, if there exists a thematic link between the socio-historical analyses of *SM* and the theoretical speculations of *City of the Sun*, then we have to take a short detour and a leap ahead in time in order to see if and how it is developed further. This can be done by recalling that the triad *language, sword* and *wealth* remains fundamental in Campanella's political thought, as he reiterates in his *De Politica*, which is a volume from his larger *Realis Philosophia*, published in Frankfurt in 1623 but written much earlier, some sections around the time he composed *The City of the Sun*, and a more detailed draft, with the title *Aforismi politici*, sometime before 1611. We can assume that this is a definitive version of his political ideas insofar as he oversaw its publication in 1637 while in Paris.[18] Here we read that when it comes to power (il potere): "It appears that what is most useful is language in order to acquire, arms in order to defend, and wealth in order to maintain (conservare)." (113) Earlier in this canonical text on politics, he had written that, at the theoretical level, "The primalities (It. primalità, Lat. primalitates) entail activities which are distinct as to their essences. Power (Potenza) is what can do [or has agency], Wisdom (Sapienza) is what knows, and Love (Amore) is what loves or wants...and there is therefore difference between right,

---

mans did;" (348) and a sort of *enlightened socialist monarchy* not averse to *using* church personnel: "The third union is that of goods, wherefore I believe that the King should divide all the occupied lands among those who do not practice war and respect agrarian laws, which is to say to all Africans and Indians who have been brought there. And the King ought also make sure that no one among them, except for the priests, own anything, but that everything belong to the crown, so that from time to time he can distribute the fields and other offices, in guise that in the end they have but love for the sovereign who hands these gifts." (ib.)

[18] Cf. Tommaso Campanella, *De Politica*, ed. by Tommaso Cesaro (Napoli, Guida, 2001:9-20). The chapter titled "Language, sword, and wealth" is on pages 113-33.

"History, Empire, and Political Reason"

dominion, and benefit." (49) Further down, in ch. 8, he writes once again:

> Three are the means by which to acquire, maintain and govern kingdoms: language, sword and wealth. Language, to be sure, is the instrument of religion and prudence, that is, of the deeds (beni) of the souls. The sword is instrument of the body and its goods. Wealth is the province of fortune, which is useful to the body and only secondarily to the soul. (103)

Bearing in mind the content of *De Politica* can cast light both on the earlier *Spanish Monarchy* as well as the later *The French Monarchy*. Returning to SM, Campanella is very clear and concrete about a number of sociohistorical issues that impacted on the lives of peoples and governments. His attention to detail leaves no stone unturned. He remarks on the necessity to lower taxes in order to have the population appreciate and applaud the Monarch – "perché nessuna cosa nuoce più al Re che l'odio de popoli," (XVII, 176) –; then on the comparisons of how the Turks and the Spanish have handled the creation of empire, (XIX, 208) explicating in what ways the Spanish government has been found wanting in realizing its quest for Hispano-Christian hegemony (254); he then stresses the need to curtail the power of barons, especially in the South of Italy (118), perhaps thinking of the perverse feudalism rampant in his native Calabria! Finally, from chapter 21 to 30, the thinker moves on to a country by country analysis of their political structure and social and religious habits, the techniques required to conquer or bring them into the Monarch's sphere of influence, discusses comparatively the then existing power blocks of the Euro-Mediterranean area, closing with a chapter on the new world (ch. 31), which is explicit about how the Spanish are mismanaging it, and one on navigation (ch. 32), which makes the case for the cruciality of sea power to world dominion. A politically prophetic highlight is his having understood that Holland was the Achille's heel of the Spanish empire, as it effectively turned out to be, and that the only real competition was France, to which he dedicates one of the longest chapters. In the Appendix (364-66), perhaps by then aware that Philip II was dying or had died, he expresses the hope that such an enlightened leader may soon come again to realize his vision.

Throughout the 164 pages of the original edition, at key moments Campanella restates his grounding belief that, after the prime mover, the ultimate wealth for the Monarch resides not in gold but in people, (156, 158, 346) that the most important instrument for empire-building is language, and second is the sword – "primo instrumento d'imperio è la lingua, e il secondo la spada;" (190) and that on the basis of historical, prophetic, and astral knowledge, Spain is destined to achieve the universal Christian Monarchy.

VI

Well, it did not quite turn out that way, as he dramatically learned in the ensuing three decades trying to survive in various dungeons in Naples' forbidding castles. When we turn to *The French Monarchy* (FM), we know that 37 years have passed and the world picture is now quite different. Religious antagonism has increased with the spread of Calvinism, both the Church and the Spanish empire have become more odious reactionary powers, new power blocs such as the Bohemians, the Swedes, and the Dutch are on the rise, and less than a year after Campanella arrives in Paris France is plunged in The Thirty Year's War on the side of the Lutherans in order to weaken the Spanish Empire's mires on the Holy Roman Empire, itself caught in unmentionable strife among tens of warring factions.[19] There is no doubt that upon close analysis Campanella's writings after 1634 have lost some of their religious fervor, and that his support for the Church is really motivated more by pragmatic ends than by missionary zeal. After all, had not Church authorities – under four different popes[20] – kept him confined for a total of 31 years in various dungeons? His faith must have been both strong and lucid to see the total separation between God and man, and he can definitely be considered a participatory voice in the evolution of secularization, if only we bring into the critical horizon his other more philosophical writings: for he saw no ontological difference between the emerging scientific and rationalistic currents – think of his *Apologia per Galileo* of 1616 – and the search for truth that his own brand of naturalism allowed *even within* a transcendent, non-mythological conception of the divinity.[21]

VII

Campanella had begun to champion the cause of a unified France with a discourse, of which we have no extant text, on the taking of the castle of La Rochelle in 1628, in which he bemoaned the disagreements between the King and his mother Marie de Médicis, and which saw the latter side with the King's younger brother Gaston d'Orléans. In 1632 he wrote a dialogue, *Dialogo politico tra un Veneziano, Spagnolo e Francese circa li rumori passati di Francia*, in which,

---

[19] The war between France and Spain continues beyond the 1648 Treaty of Westphalia, until 1659, when France emerges as the *de facto* strongest power in Europe.

[20] I am excluding the 27-day reign of Leo XI in 1605. The popes who had a direct impact on Campanella's life were Clement VIII (1592-1605), Paul V (1605-1621), Gregory XV (1621-1623), and of course Urban VIII (1623-1644).

[21] See also his *Compendio di filosofia della natura*, ed. by G. Ernst and P. Ponzio (Santarcangelo di Romagna, Rusconi, 1999), composed around 1613 according to L. Amabile, and after 1619 according to L. Firpo. For details, see the "Introduzione" to this volume by Ponzio, 5-19.

Peter Carravetta

speaking through the Venetian, he upholds the politics of Cardinal Richelieu,[22] and once again makes a case for the cruciality of Italy in the geopolitical and military power-play between Spain and France. Concerning the role of Italy in European struggles, Campanella had stated similar views already in his 1607 *Discorsi ai Principi d'Italia*, except that the King who should have intervened, consistently with what we saw he believed in the text of the SM, was to be the King of Spain. This time, Campanella makes the case for France, for as we saw the scenario had radically changed. Early in 1635 he intervenes once again but in a different literary form, composing *Aforismi politici per le presenti necessità di Francia*, in which he very plainly states that the tricephalus Spanish colossus needs to be brought down, and that France ought to claim its rightful place as the leading Monarchy on the way to achieving the Universal Monarchy of God. Once again, he reiterates that Italy must be thought of as the fulcrum, or the theater, for such a shift in European and Christian domination. He explains the allegory as follows: the Spanish Monarchy has three heads, one which represents its essence, located in Germany, the second embodying its existence, situated in Spain, and finally a third which reveals its prowess (valeur) residing in Italy.[23] Elaborating on the image, he claims

---

[22] Richelieu was instrumental in quelling domestic squabbles, abolished political rights to the Protestants, besieged the Huguenots at La Rochelle, and led an army into Northern Italy to slow down Spanish advances in the region. He survived an attempt at dismissal in 1630. As the first "Prime Minister" in the modern sense of the word, he was acutely aware of the growing power of the Hapsburgs (in the person of Holy Roman Emperor Ferdinand II) during the ongoing war in central Europe (what later became known as "The Thirty Year's War"). He persuaded the Swedes to attack the emperor and secretly financed them. This was the scenario when Campanella reaches Paris.

[23] Cf. Tommaso Campanella, *Sur la mission de France*. Transl. by Florence Plouchart-Cohn (Paris, Editions Rue d'Ulm, 2005), 85. This book – to which I referred in the paragraph above – contains, in their French titles, the *Dialogue politique entre un Vénetien, un Espagnol et un Français à propos des récents troubles de France* (9-82), *Aphorismes politiques en faveur des*

that it is difficult to beat the Spanish without attacking the head bearing its acknowledged valor, that is, its Italian viceroyalty, with its baronates and garrisons throughout the peninsula, which is effectively what keeps the other two heads standing. To this end, and in order to attack its "essential" core, namely its German presence and interests, it becomes crucial to play up to the Pope: "Seul le pape, incité et soutenu par le roi de France, peut abattre la tête de l'essence de cette monarchie."[24]

In this incendiary pamphlet in which he rips Spain apart and incites the French to remember that Europe was first united under the Charles the Great, the Christian Emperor who kept Islam at bay and effectively began the process of Christianization of the continent, Campanella leverages history, national stereotypes, the balance of power in the central European states, and then recalls that the rise of the Spanish monarchy has been too rapid for it not to be in immediate danger of collapsing, inasmuch as

> elle a occupé en cent ans plus de pays que ne le firent les Romains en sept cents ans; on peut donc estimer qu'elle est désormais en déclin.[25]

In May 1635, switching rhetorical approach, he writes a *Documenta ad Gallorum nationem*[26] in the first person, becoming Carolus Magnus *lui-même*, and who as the spiritual "père de la France" returns to instruct his descendants and explain

---

nécessités présentes de la France, (83-97) *Advertissements à la nation française* (105-45), and the *Discours politique en faveur du siècle présent* (157-80). For in-depth analyses on the meaning of Campanella's francophile position, see in this volume Plouchart-Cohen's "Postface" (187-249) as well as the above cited – footnote 3 – Pierre Lerner, *Tommaso Campa-nella en France*.
[24] *Sur la mission de France*, 85.
[25] Ibid., 87.
[26] Ibid., 105-45.

to his fellow citizens why Richelieu's politics is the best course to follow in international affairs.

VIII

Thus, when we turn to *The French Monarchy*, we fairly anticipate his arguments.[27] Still convinced that the Pope must be a "sacerdote armato" (FM 378) he appeals to historical evidence to prove that the French have ruled as long as piety in politics and the "arts" of the Church were adequately respected and manifested. Then he avers once again that a Universal Monarchy can be perceived as having come close to be realized over time in what appears to be a linear conception of history and, if we stretch it a bit, as constituting what Immanuel Wallerstein would call a "world system." Campanella returns upon the earlier SM to claim that he was not wrong in his thesis whereby Spain was pre-destined to be the one Monarchy to achieve the Universal Christian Monarchy he believed in, it is just that the Spanish crown missed its opportunity to do so, sort of "messed it up," having failed for a number of reasons, among which he lists faulty political strategies and atrocious crimes committed everywhere, (390) including the New World.

It is therefore France's turn to champion his cause, and their first order of the day must be to seek a true alliance with the Pope and fight to dethrone the Hapsburgs, thus reconstituting a new social and political equilibrium in Europe. He then spends nearly fifty pages to demonstrate why the star of Spanish power is declining, making recourse, though less so than in most of his earlier writings, to astrology to shore up his argument. In the 12 articles that make up ch. 7 Campanella goes meticulously yet forcefully through all the misguided actions of the Spanish, from unwarranted

---

[27] As Plouchart-Cohn observed, op. cit., 223, Campanella's writings of this period tend to be repetitive and in some cases entire sentences reappeared in the four opuscles as well as in FM.

marriages to shameless cunning, from deploying "foreign troops" to creating a visible drop in social values, from failing to act according to the golden rule of "prudence" and "art" (422) to relying on the genius of other people – engineers from Italy and Flandres, navigators from Genoa, Italian military captains, etc – thus showing, over time, what he termed their servile mentality, propensity for trickery, and a feigned and bigoted religiosity. He writes: "li Spagnoli si servono di Dio e della fede cattolica romana, ma non servono a Dio, né alla fede," (426) ["The Spanish make use of God and of the Roman Catholic faith, but they do not serve either God or the faith."]. He repeats that Charles V had a chance to stop the Lutherans on their tracks and failed to do so, (498) that he threatened the Pope himself and in so doing exposed the Church to growing instability, fostered the growth of an increasing number of heretics, and in the process lost forty states!

Here, once again, appears the Cerberus-like personification of the Austrian empire as a three-headed monster, which failed to Hispanize the reign through carefully conferred vassallages or by not encouraging inter-ethnic marriages. In ch. 8 the philippic against Spain continues with a battery of arguments aimed at showing that the "Monarchia austriaca spagnolizzata" should finally relinquish its quest to control the Holy Roman Empire and cede the historical mission to a joint partnership between the Pope and the King of France. Not forgetful of his earlier more explicit though as we saw partly masked Machiavellism, he is confident that fear of the common enemy, the Turkish tyranny, would probably see Catholics and heretics fight side by side, a prevision which turned out to be true when France declared war on Spain. Extrapolating in terms of the development of a European identity above the political, religious and ethnic differences *within* Europe, this follows the ancient (initially Greek) pattern of a Europe versus Asia syndrome, which relies on necessary distrust of the Other in order to shape one's overarching cultural identity.[28]

Showing that his analyses are not ranting propaganda but rooted in what at the time were accepted topics in public discourse, Campanella does not desist – we might say, courageously – from pointing out that the French have to deal with their own intrinsic problems. Citing an earlier work of his, now lost, titled *Cosmographia*, he claims that the French have been and can be again the best, but also the worst, people to dominate the world. Basically, he is saying that they should "get their act together," for if they do not succeed in replacing the Spanish to achieve the Universal Monarchy, it is probably due to some endemic cultural or ethnic trait, such as were parleyed loosely but effectively even through the following century. Thus we read of how the French often are impatient, disobedient, brawling, rebellious. Yet consistent with what we already saw as his capacity to turn *prudenza* at the service of *occasione*, the Dominican monk holds that these characteristics can be turned into a positive set of national traits because, by juxtaposition, as the Spaniards are typically slovenly in their actions, so the French are impulsive and quick, and this can translate into a great asset in the domain of military policy.

In the final part of this rich and revealing text, Campanella returns to his favorite strategy of arguing from history, reminding his interlocutor that in the past it was the Pope who granted the right to Spain to make an empire, and that

---

[28] The notion that Europe is intrinsically different from the Middle and Far East, in effect a sort of paleo-Eurocentrism, originates with Herodotus when he discusses the alliance of the Greek city-states to fend off the Persians, has been held by Federico Chabod, *L'idea di Europa* (Bari, Laterza, 1957 [1944 & 1948]); Denys Hay, *Europe. The Emergence of an Idea* (Edinburgh, Edinburgh University Press, 1968 [1957]); and Henri Mendras, *L'Europe des Europeens* (Paris, folio, 1997). See also the article by Peter Carravetta, "La questione dell'identità nella formazione dell'Europa," in Franca Sinopoli, ed., *La letteratura europea vista dagli altri* (Roma, Meltemi, 2003),19-66.

he can thus take that privilege away. (532) He shows his earlier perspicuity in making explicit suggestions in policy that would ensure the King of France capillary control of his subjects by gaining control of key offices, for example, by strategically placing French officials in the hierarchy of the Holy Office Commissary, in each Congregation, in the Office of the Clerk of the Index, and in the more dispersed Vicariats. From this he turns yet again, much as Dante and Machiavelli had done earlier, to the cruciality of Italy as the theater of future geopolitical events. As in SM, here again he does a nation by nation analysis of the distribution of power in continental Europe, but in FM he goes beyond, sketching a region by region and city-state by city-state analysis of all the power blocks distributed along the peninsula, illustrating their strategic value, suggesting how to bring them into the fold of a bilateral Rome-Paris alliance, and even what the King should say to their leaders to make this alliance palatable. Rehashing his belief, now become a political principle, that it is acceptable for the Pope to wield temporal power, he strongly suggests that if the French would divide the Spanish possessions among the Italians themselves, the Italian princes would stand to gain so much that they would be ready to side with the French, (538) a strategy that would be most successful in the case of Naples. (548) This would ultimately crown France as the *de facto* superpower in Europe.

IX

What, in conclusion, can we say of Campanella's understanding of world history and his conception of empire at the dawn of Modern Europe? First of all, it must be acknowledged that Campanella the unrestrainable prophet, utopist, and missionary was also a true and proven realist when it came to political analysis, as his application, both covert and explicit, of some Machiavellian insights clearly demonstrates. But it is important to point out the profound differences as well.

Although Machiavelli is credited with being the first thinker of Italian Humanism whose sociopolitical theory is no longer based on what the world *should be*, but on what *it is* or *has actually been*; and although he is also in line with earlier Humanists, beginning with Dante, that there should be a net separation of powers between Church and Empire, with the latter regulating all mundane affairs and the former simply the spiritual world; in the end one might perceive in both *The Prince* and the *Discourses* a sort of "nostalgia for an earlier age when a basic religious fervor infused civil society with greater fear, reverence, and natural discipline,"[29] which was sadly lacking at the end of the XV century. Besides, that age was also marked by a growing individualism and an exacerbated public illegitimacy of the political process, and the Florentine never tired of excoriating representatives both secular and religious for their self-interest and wickedness. In a way, having ontologically separated religion from politics, he could now only understand religion in an ontic, instrumental way.

On the other hand, as we hinted throughout, above and beyond his own personal conception of Christianity, Campanella understood that religion, as the very word implies, is a linking, cementing force among people in any given society, and it would be anathema to suggest, as the avatars of *ragion di stato* from Machiavelli to Richelieu to Hobbes and beyond have too often believed, that it can be either abolished, removed, or played upon as if just another sociopolitical entity, such as city-states, entitlements, principalities, nations and even empires. Proleptically looking to Vico's *New Science*, Campanella understands religion as a primordial force in society, indeed as founding the community. As he observed in *Discorsi universali del governo ecclesiastico per fare una gregge e un pastor*,

---

[29] Headley, *Tommaso Campanella*, op. cit., 194-5.

"History, Empire, and Political Reason"

> And this [the political capability of the Papacy working among Christian princes and states] did not understand the very astute Machiavelli, who admires the stability of the papacy...When the Pope will be the Lord of Italy he will also be Lord of the world; but he must [first] make sure he tries every possible way to attain this end."[30]

The statement points to a deeper understanding of the social role of religion and its binding power in keeping communities together and make them act in a more or less homogeneous or socially cohesive way. The evolution of this extended belief becomes the epistemological grid of that culture. The validity or better truth of the process becomes evident less than two centuries later when the erupting nationalisms all around Europe understood that a people's dominant religion is a major and integral part of their social identification, together with language, specific customs, rituals and a set of collective habits,[31] establishing their cultural unconscious, so to speak, fueling the rhetoric of national or ethnic identities. Campanella's observations will resonate not much later with Thomas Hobbes' *Leviathan*, in the several chapters dedicated to Ecclesiastical Common-Wealths (Pt III, ch. 35, 39, 42 et infra), both on the issue of the structure and functioning of religion as an institution, and as a dynamic fluid force which binds citizens together. The allegiance and support of the people – or, later, after 1789, the citizens, – can be manipulated through the rhetorical use of various symbolisms, including clearly the religious one, and in fact must be admin-

---

[30] Cited in Headley, *cit.*, 192-3n. "Questo [...] non conobbe l'astutissimo Machiavello, che si ammira della stabilità del papato...Quando il Papa sarà signore d'Italia, sarà anche del mondo; però deve procurar ogni via di arrivar a questo."

[31] Cf. Athena Leoussi, ed. *Encyclopedia of Nationalism* (New Brunswick, NJ, Transaction Publishers, 2001); and Anthony Smith, *Theories of Nationalism* (New York, Holmes & Meier, 1983)

istered, justified and, if necessary, coerced, but cannot be dispensed with.[32]

X

Our discussion here could continue with a chapter on the ideological context within which Campanella lived, specifically by identifying and comparing him with authors he could have possibly read. We know he was an insatiable reader, but though he still managed to get books during his continuous 27 years in jail, we can't possibly speak of his personal "library," other than inferring it from his letters and citations (often incorrect because from memory).[33] Still, living under Aragonese rule, had he read Alonso de Castrillo? Were the *Comunidades* an inspiration for his failed "revolution" in Calabria in 1599, which caused him inhuman suffering for the rest of his life? How much of La Boëtie, of Bodin, of Sepúlveda, of Suárez did he know of and had assimilated?[34] A broader interpretation of the originality of

---

[32] Cf. *Leviathan*, Pt II, ch. 18: "for there is no Covenant with God, but by mediation of some body that representeth Gods Person. Indeed the "Spirituall Good" is pre-eminent even above "Temporall" ones." (cf. also Pt II, ch. 17) Earlier, in the section "Of Man," Hobbes establishes that there must be a relativistic dimension to morality, and the ultimate role of reason is not so much to find the truth but to devise ways of getting on in the world. In ch. 5 he writes: "For Reason …is nothing but Reckoning (that is, Adding and Subtracting) of the Consequences of general names agreed upon, for the making and signifying of our thoughts…" But thoughts are always connected to something else.

[33] Here of course one must rely on the indefatigable work carried out by Luigi Firpo and Germana Ernst, whose discovery, redaction and commentary on innumerable texts unknown to previous generations have created the premises for more objective approaches to his labyrinthine production. See E. Baldini. *Luigi Firpo e Campanella* (Pisa: Istituti Editoriali e Poligrafici Internazionali, 2000); and Germana Ernst. *Tommaso Campanella* (Bari: Laterza, 2002).

[34] This is particularly relevant when it comes to the growing discussion, at the time, of the religious and legal status of the Amerindians; cf. J.A. Fernández-Santamaria, *The State, War and Peace. Spanish Political Thought in the Renaissance 1516-1559* (Cambridge, Cambridge University Press,

Campanella's political thought would have to engage the entire XVI century,[35] where against the twin watersheds represented by Luther and the Council of Trent, we witness a long tortuous reflection on breaking the stronghold of the One, the Unitary order of the inherited classical and then Christian middle ages, and the appearance of a more fragmented, dis-harmonius, borderline heretical mind-set. Bruno and Galileo were tried by the Church for different reasons, yet Campanella would sing the first by seeing the multiple worlds as still coherent with the transcendent unity of creation, and the second when he defended the creative scientific imagination of the individual, and the right to make discoveries based on sensory data, something he had learned from his first ideal master, Bernardino Telesio. But this task has to be postponed to another time and place.

In closing, we must recall the hermeneutic principle whereby interpretation cannot ignore the social reality of the interpreter. At a time when in the course of the last three decades of the Twentieth-century we saw the explosion of postmodern critiques of cultures as unstable entities, artifi-

---

1977), esp. pp. 220-236. For questions pertaining to law, see the above cited Julian Franklin (footnote 21). But see also Roland Crahay, *D'Erasme à Campanella* (Bruxelles: Editions de l'Université de Bruxelles, 1985) and his observations on the "utopia" of the Hutterites.

[35] As I finished this study, I learned of the appearance of Jean-Louis Fournel, *La cité du soleil et les territoires des homes. Le savoir du monde chez Campanella* (Paris, Albin Michel, 2012), a magisterial work, which I was happy to learn lends strong support to what I have developed here. Of course Fournel's far-ranging and profound study explores other topics, among which is a reading of *The City of the Sun* as a political treatise, not as escapist literature, in-depth analyses of how the New World impacted on Campanella and thus on his perception of the "World-System," and thalassocracies in general, and the centrality of Italy in the understanding of the rise of Modern Europe *even after* the opening up of the Atlantic. A key aspect, in tune with developments in critical historiography of the past quarter of a century, is reading Campanella's thought as a "geosophy." No future study on Campanella can ignore Fournel's work. I have reviewed it for *Renaissance Quarterly*, Vol. 66, no. 2 (Summer 2013): 594-596.

cially if often cynically created, and even intrinsically detached from reality by way of the dominant technological enframing of social intercourse that make and shape our very identities, as well as the rise of conservative, media savvy, politically connected right wing groups and conservative organizations such as churches and philanthropies, political action committees, and so on,[36] the reflections of a thinker such as Campanella on a, mutatis mutantis, similar world chessboard can illuminate us not only on what was peculiar of his era, but also on what appears to have cogency and validity today as well. Adapting Immanuel Wallerstein's term, the two *Monarchies* by Campanella can be used to situate a radical passage in the cultural unconscious of the Early Modern World System, and reassess the range and complexity of how many factors – linguistic, military, sociological, and above all symbolic – must interplay to describe and explain the fluid yet heterological character of an age. Campanella claimed to be a Roman Catholic believer his entire life, but his exhortations to the King of Spain in his youth, and then to the King of France in his later maturity, complemented by accurate observations of the habits and desires of people from different parts of the known world, suggest three provisional conclusions. First, that *ragion di stato* ought to be replaced with *ragione politica*. Hence the reason why we must go back and see how many of his contemporaries had understood, before Hobbes, that governments are made by *human*, not divine, choice, and sovereignty must make the individual a participant, a meaningful agent struggling to attain what will evolve into the social contract. Second, that in view of this, language, as discourse, plays a central role not only in theorization, but in the actual pragmatics of running a state, of shaping policy, of persuad-

---

[36] For a critical history of the various schools of thought that mark the postmodern age, see my study *Del postmoderno. Critica e cultura in America all'alba del duemila.* (Milano, Bompiani, 2009).

ing people, in effect stressing dialogue, debate, and diplomacy before we turn to warfare: the word before the sword was, paraphrased, one of Campanella's maxims. Third, that when rulers or governments must turn to arms, there needs be the double recognition that force must be applied carefully and that of all possible existing institutions the Church – or any specific other denomination in the decades that followed – is a key player and must be considered as such. By saying this we recognize that, in terms of *realpolitik*, the much theorized division of powers between State and Empire which was such a key element in Dante, Marsilius of Padua, Pico della Mirandola and Machiavelli, cannot be realized in any pure or transcendent manner, and cannot be enforced on principle alone, despite the later, Enlightenment-inspired American and French constitutions. Campanella understood that the Church was an effective temporal power, but at the same time that religion is a primary binding force in any society and will have a direct impact on the cohesion (or dissolution) of any given social group. Given the all-too-often nefarious record of theocracies, the movement toward keeping civil and religious institutions separate is understandable, but it will never be an easy task, as anthropological, psychological, and above all community belief in some form of supernatural deity remains an essential component of the "city of human beings."

Thus we have a paradoxical thinker. We should consider that, his declarations notwithstanding, Campanella was not really vying for a theocracy, not, at least, of the kind we have actual witness in historical memory. Although he appeals to the Pope in both treatises as the potential leader of Empire, he does so primarily because he correctly read the great sociological, psychological and often military capacity of the Pontiff to influence and impact the results of any political action, but nowhere does he state that the subjects ought to be converts or monks or priests, or "proto-comunists." His constant problems with the Holy Office were caused by his being too "liberal," too catholic, too inclusive of people who may not have been declared members of the Catholic Church. The theocracy of *City of the Sun* should *not* be used as a term of comparison to demonstrate his theocratic leanings because its leaders and functionaries are supremely enlightened, as is the entire population, making the distinction a mere taxonomic exercise, a differentiation of roles and tasks. In fact in Tapobrana citizens live and act according to their *particular* talents or *natural* inclinations and possibilities. In the actual political, social, and theoretical analyses of Spain and France at the dawn of the Modern Era, Campanella understood that it was the *idea of a net separation of temporal and spiritual powers which was utopistic*, as the tensions and struggles created by the constitutions of modern democracies to all effects demonstrate. If anything, he advocates that the main concern for rulers, and legislators as well, ought to be to focus on *the reasons of the polis* – in today's language, the needs of the citizens – much more than the reasons of either the faith or the state. These latter components, infrastructures or superstructures though they may be, must be seen as dialectically co-dependant, otherwise the supremacy of either in the name of autonomy and self-declared legitimation turns into totalitarianism, as we saw in post-Hegelian times with some Islamic theocracies, on the one hand, and variations of Fascism *and* of Communism on the other. Finally, the fact that he argued in support of two different, and historically competing and antagonistic, states within a relatively short period of time only serves to demonstrate that there is no such a thing as a universal principle of the supremacy or autonomy of either reason or faith. Nor can they be grounded on logical or transcendent (or, later, transcendental) principles, because *the political is essentially rooted in the actual transactions of the agents of the polis*, in its broadest acceptation, and what was good for a Spaniard in 1600 was probably not good for a Frenchman in 1635, and viceversa. In other words, Campanella anchors his political philosophy on the cruciality of *discourse*, which gives voice to the three elements of his basic ontology, namely Power, Knowledge, and Feeling. In actual sociohistorical settings, what matters is the *reasoned* execution of *prudentia* in the face of *occasione*, all of which is significant or makes sense with reference to a *place*, a *circumstance*, a desire for *limited action*, and in view of a particular audience, or *public*, and within that to a specific conflict.[37] In this sense, the two treatises by Campanella show that the utopist we all know from high school was in reality a political realist, and one who had understood the fundamental truth that, though arms and deities must be accounted for and judiciously used or exploited, it is discourse, the interpersonal exchange that determines and embodies human interaction, the originary element that defines and shapes the human project.

(New York, January 2012; February 2013)

Works Cited

Baldini, Enzo. *Luigi Firpo e Campanella. Cinquant'anni di ricerche e di pubblicazioni*. Pisa e Roma: Istituti e Poligrafici Internazionali, 2000.

Campanella, Tommaso. *Sur la mission de France*. Transl. Forence Plouchart-Cohn. Paris: Editions Rue d'Ulm, 2005.

_____. *De Politica*. Ed. Tommaso Cesaro. Napoli: Guida, 2001.

_____. *Compendio di filosofia della natura*. Ed. G. Ernst and P. Ponzio. Santarcangelo di Romagna: Rusconi, 1999.

_____. *Monarchie d'Espagne et Monarchie de France*. Ed. G. Ernst, transl. N. Fabry and S. Waldbaum. Paris: puf, 1997.

_____. *La città del sole / The City of the Sun*. Transl. D.J. Donno. Berkeley, University of California Press, 1981.

_____. *La Monarchia di Spagna*. Ed. G. Ernst. Napoli: Istituto Superiore per gli Studi Filosofici, 1989.

Carravetta, Peter. *The Elusive Hermes. Method, Discourse, Interpreting*. Aurora (CO): Davies Group Publishing, 2012.

---

[37] The centrality of the pragmatic dimension to discourse is a key aspect of my longer theoretical work on method and interpretation, *The Elusive Hermes*, referred to above in footnote 6.

_____. "Review" of J-L. Fournel. *La cité du soleil et les territories des hommes*, in *Renaissance Quarterly*. Vol. 66, No. 2 (Summer 2013): 594-596.

_____. *Del postmoderno. Critica e cultura in America all'alba del duemila*. Milano: Bompiani, 2009.

_____."La questione dell'identità nella formazione dell'Europa," in F. Sinopoli, ed.*La letteratura europea vista dagli altri*. Roma: Meltemi, 2003, pp.19-66.

Chabod, Federico. *L'idea di Europa*. Bari, Laterza, 1957 [1944 & 1948].

Clemente, Francesco. "Fra realismo politico e vocazione utopica. *La Monarchia di Spagna* di Tommaso Campanella," *Segni & Comprensione* XXII, 64 (2008): 103-25.

Crahay, Roland. *D'Erasme à Campanella*. Ed. Jacques Marx. Bruxelles: Editions de l'Université de Bruxelles, 1985.

De Mattei, Rodolfo. *Studi Campanelliani*. Firenze: Sansoni, 1934.

Ernst, Germana. *Tommaso Campanella*. Bari: Edizioni Laterza, 2002.

Fernández-Santamaria, J.A., *The State, War and Peace. Spanish Political Thought in the Renaissance 1516-1559* . Cambridge: Cambridge University Press, 1977.

Firpo, Luigi. "Introduzione" to Tommaso Campanella. *Poetica*. Roma: Reale Accademia d'Italia, 1944.

Fournel, Jean-Louis. *La cité du soleil et les territories des hommes. Le savoir du monde chez Campanella*. Paris: Albin Michel, 2012.

Frajese, Vittorio. *Profezia e machiavellismo. Il giovane Campanella*. Roma: Carocci, 2002.

Franklin, H. Julian. *Jean Bodin and the Sixteenth-Century Revolution in the Methodology of Law and History*. New York: Columbia University Press, 1963.

Gilbert, Neil. *Renaissance Concepts of Method*. New York: Columbia University Press, 1963.

Gosselin, Edward A. "Review" of Tommaso Campanella. *L'ateismo trionfato overo riconoscimento filosofico della religione universale contra l'antichristianesimo macchiavellesco*. 2 vols. Ed. Germana Ernst. Pisa: Scuola Normale Superiore, 2004, in *Renaissance Quarterly*, Vol. 58, No. 2 (Summer 2005): 589-590.

Hay, Denys. *Europe. The Emergence of an Idea*. Edimburgh, Edimburgh University Press, 1968 [1957].

Headley, John M. *Tommaso Campanella and the Transformation of the World*. Princeton: Princeton University Press, 1997.

———. "On the Rearming of Heaven: The Machiavellism of Tommaso Campanella," in *Journal of the History of Ideas* 49 (1988): 387-404.

Hobbes, Thomas. *Leviathan*. New York: Cambridge University Press, 1991.

Leoussi, Athena, ed. *Encyclopedia of Nationalism*. New Brunswick (NJ): Transaction Publishers, 2001.

Lerner, Michel Pierre. *Tommaso Campanella en France au XVII siècle*. Napoli: Bibliopolis, 1995.

Machiavelli, Niccoló. *The Prince*. Transl. Daniel Donno. New York: Bantam, 1966.

Mendras, Henri. *L'Europe des Europeens*. Paris: folio, 1997.

Ong, Walter J. *Ramus, Method and the Decay of Dialogue*. Cambridge: Harvard University Press, 1958.

Smith, Anthony. *Theories of Nationalism*. New York: Holmes & Meier, 1983.

Wallerstein, Immanuel. *The Modern World System*. New York: Academic Press, 1974. Vol. 2.

THE LOGIC OF POETIC GENEALOGY
ON PAOLO VALESIO'S *The Dark Flame*

Alessandro Carrera
University of Houston

> La ragione (che in grammatica spesso
> è una cosa coll'analogia)...
> [Reason (which in grammar is often
> one with analogy)...]
>
> G. Leopardi, *Sopra due voci italiane* (1817)

I. Defending Textual Coherence

When I started reading Paolo Valesio's *Gabriele D'Annunzio: The Dark Flame* shortly after it was published, initially I did not go from cover to cover, I focused on the Pasolini chapter instead. I found it intriguing not just because of its innovative approach to Pasolini, but also on account of the elusive methodology underlining the critical discourse.[1] When I went back and read the entire volume, I was struck again by the unusual dissonance that transpired from the book and that I had just glimpsed in my first partial approach. Valesio could have easily claimed to having inoculated Italian literary criticism with a highly sophisticated brand of participatory, passionate deconstructionism (and I purposely bring together terms such "passion" and "deconstruction" that usually do not appear in the same sentence). *The Dark Flame* combined a refined linguistic-stylistic approach, fully reminiscent of Jakobson's structuralist subtleties, with the adventurous mischievousness of the critic who

---

[1] Paolo Valesio, *Gabriele D'Annunzio: The Dark Flame*. From this point on, I will refer directly this text as DF followed by page number.

deliberately avoids privileged points of entry to the text examined (here is where deconstruction resonates) and lets himself be "enchanted" by the metamorphic changes of a few key words (and here is where passion makes its comeback). In truth, I soon realized that Valesio's approach could not have been farther from deconstruction. It turned upside down the deconstructionist premise that texts are inherently incoherent, and that such incoherence is better revealed if we ignore what texts ostensibly want to say and focus on *marginalia*, dead-ends, and apparently minor inconsistencies. In Valesio's analysis of the "D'Annunzio effect" on Italian literature (including retroactive effect), it was precisely at the level of basic textual organization that one single word, one single trope was enough to disclose the text's strong temporal ties with other past and future texts, regardless (it goes without saying) of the author's intentions and other authorial intrusions that neither structuralism nor deconstructionism ever cared much for.

Valesio's approach to textuality was indeed genealogical: a clever, rhetorically classical yet modern and updated defense of continuity vs. discontinuity, consistency vs. inconsistency, and reconstruction vs. deconstruction. It implied faith in the transmission of knowledge (from one author to another, and from the critic to the reader); faith that linguistic and cultural themes can be diachronically (albeit not historically) mapped out over an extensive stretch of time, and faith that the critic's task is to listen carefully to the feeble harmonics of words as they resonate from one text to another. Not to resuscitate the elusive art of close reading (in the style of the New Critics), as if the text were a safe that the critic-thief must overhear in order to find the combination that will unlock it, but to capture the coherence of literature as a whole at its most material level, where phonetics and semantics meet.

The defensive side of Valesio's approach was an easy foil for criticism. Was it out-of-sync with the then current trends?

(The early 1990s were the peak of the deconstructionist rage.) Did it put too much faith in continuity? Was it too canonical or did it attempt to re-canonize? Maybe so, and maybe not. A great deal of bold deconstructive adventures dating back to that time has already aged quickly and not so well. And Valesio has spent a great amount of energy (in English) on Gabriele D'Annunzio and Filippo Tommaso Marinetti who in North-America have never been fully recognized as part of the Italian or European dominant canon. If criticism be raised about Valesio's approach, it must be raised at the level of a serious and engaging conflict among theories. Before writing *The Dark Flame*, Valesio subtitled "Rhetorics as a Contemporary Theory" his previous book, *Novantiqua*, and "La retorica come teoria" the Italian revised version of the same book.[2] His ambition, and not a small one for that matter, was to connect the organization of language to the revelation of truth. In its essence, rhetorics-as-theory means that rhetorics must aspire to be "theory" in the original sense of *theoría*, or pageant of truth. In other words, rhetorics could and should supersede philosophy. Now, if there is a "sworn and deadly enmity," in Plato's *Republic* grave statement, between poetry and philosophy, the enmity between philosophy and rhetorics is even deeper. For rhetorics to claim the position of theory is to claim the mantle of *philosophia*, since no other discipline than philosophy has the authority to decide what is theory and what is not (the spell of Platos's *Sophist* has never been lifted).

Here, I do not wish to venture into a detailed analysis of the philosophical or counter-philosophical side of Valesio's theory of rhetorics, or rhetorics-as-theory. It is not the Valesio I met when I began reading his articles as I found them in Italian Studies journals at the end of the 1980s and when I read *The Dark Flame*. What aroused my attention then, and

---

[2] Paolo Valesio, *Novantiqua: Rhetorics as a Contemporary Theory,* and *Ascoltare il silenzio. La retorica come teoria.*

what I want to discuss now, is Valesio's theory of literary genealogy. I will try first to outline its theoretical content, and then move on to the genealogy of Valesio's genealogy or, if repetition must be avoided, its inception.

II. ANXIETY DEFERRED

Let us assume, hypothetically, that the literary artifact is a genetic structure endowed with the equivalent of textual DNA, so much so that it contains memory of its past and anticipations of its future. The basic cells of this textual DNA are what Valesio calls "semiotic signs." The syntagm *"virgo prerafaelita"* included in D'Annunzio's line, *"gelida virgo prerafaelita"* is a "semiotic sign," meaning a sign with a semiotic history or an intertextual lineage. It is not so much part of the genealogy that leads to this specific text as a "genealogy that branches out from this text" (DF 11). Valesio defines the semiotic sign "as a complex of signifier and signified" (10). With a little help from C. S. Peirce's semiotic lexicon, Valesio's semiotic sign could also be understood as an "interpretant," or a cultural code; a sign, in other words, that a specific culture employs in order to interpret other signs. Not exactly a metalanguage; no sign, in Peirce's semiotics, can transcend its "glassy essence" (Peirce quoting Shakespeare) and rise above other signs. There is no such thing as a meta-sign. In Peirce's triadic model of knowledge (sign, object, interpretant), each sign may eventually move from the position of signifier (sign) to the position of signified (object), or from signified to interpretant (code). All permutations are possible. Due to the endless nature of the interpreting process, they are indeed unavoidable. *"Virgo prerafaelita"* is therefore a signifier that includes a signified (the feminine icon in Dante Gabriel Rossetti's paintings, which D'Annunzio had in mind) for the alerted readers who understand it according to their cultural codes (their interpretants). However, D'Annunzio's line is also an interpretant in itself, since it allows the readers to "branch out" and connect the dots between the text examined and a complex intertextual constellation.

Valesio's "semiotic sign" is an obvious tautology, given that every sign partakes of the infinite movement of *semiosis* and all signs are therefore of semiotic nature (Valesio himself is well aware of the tautological inclination of semiotics, and prefers to regard his book as an exercise in hermeneutics). Yet semiotic signs are also signs that point toward *semiosis* as an ultimate goal, on the assumption that, given the proper (and ideal) conditions, there are no irretrievable break-ups in the transmission of signs and the reciprocal play of interpretants. Chronological progression is here less important than spiritual (hermeneutic) continuity. Valesio's textual genealogy is neither another theory of intertextuality nor can it be reduced to source criticism which, as Valesio himself points out, does nothing but hammering texts in a chain that imprisons them (65). Rather, Valesio's genealogy aims at liberating the potentialities of textuality through intertextuality and subtextuality. Speaking from the "folds of text" (67), Valesio's method aims to keep its distance from philosophy and theology (his genealogy, to make the point clear, is closer to Hesiod than it is to Nietzsche). By claiming the ground where rhetorics questions ontology, Valesio is trying to secure, if not rhetorics' primacy (the struggle between philosophy and rhetorics briefly resurfaces), certainly the rhetorics' right to ask pre- or anti-ontological questions. We will note in passing that deconstruction, although decidedly anti-rhetorical and anti-genealogical in its purpose, shares with genealogy the wish to put ontology in the defendant's position.

Valesio's genealogy is also a significant response to Harold Bloom's theory of literary creativity as a clinical diagnosis of the "anxiety of influence" syndrome. In the way Valesio addresses subtextuality, or better the hidden textuality that insinuates itself in the discourse that an author develops on another author, what we have is, essentially, genealogy

"The Logic of Poetic Genealogy"

without the anxiety. There are exceptions to the rule, but even exceptions refuse to be read solely along the lines of Oedipal torment. D'Annunzio's French speech on Dante, *Dant de Flourence*, which Valesio includes in his volume in its entirety, might be read as a supreme exercise in anxiety therapy. In a way, Valesio is implicitly suggesting that often the text-as-son (D'Annunzio's speech in this case) says not so much "Father, I want to kill you" (in the brutal but effective synthesis of the Oedipus myth as we hear it in Jim Morrison's *The End*) as "Father, why don't you help me?" (in the words of Ugolino's son, *Inferno* XXXIII). The latter is a plea the text-as-father may actually respond to, not by eating its children like Ugolino did but by feeding them with much needed bread—in the form of quotes, tropes, references, textual ground on which the text-as-son will be able, hopefully, to stand.

We are not free from Oedipus, though, and in Valesio's method anxiety may have been deferred rather than disposed of. Genealogy is not an abstract exercise; it implies actual parents and real offspring. "Its logic is, in fact, that of '*x* son of *y*,' and not that of '*x* effect of *y*'. When we grasp any historical relation as a concrete personal relation, we have grasped a genealogy" (14). You may look like your father even without knowing who your father is. You may also kill him without knowing his identity, which is precisely what happened to Oedipus. Genealogy is inescapable. It affects equally the pious and the murderer, the prodigal son and the obedient one. If genealogy cares so little for the anxiety of influence it is because it deals with the physiology of the text and not with its psychology. Yet Valesio's notion of genealogy is ultimately dramatic (it is, after all, "a concrete personal relation") to the extent that it brings about an endless confrontation between the living and the dead.

But the dead must be allowed to answer. The semiotic channel between us and them must not be interrupted. I may not know who my father is, but I need to establish a dialogue with the traces of him that have remained in my DNA. For this dialogue to take place, my ancestors cannot be reduced to archaeological remnants. An archaeological structure always needs to be reanimated (62). But how? To what extent can genealogy, which is always alive, reanimate archaeology, which is always dead?[3]

Archaeology is the true enemy of the flow of textuality; on this matter, Valesio could not be more explicit. Authors can be recovered in archaeological form, as it has happened to D'Annunzio, but as long as they are retrieved as ruins they remain dead: "It is necessary to recover, beyond archaeology, the urgency of a genealogy" (114). To the extent that it implies the text-as-father being rewritten, genealogy is a dialectical force pitted against the inertia of influence or, better, against the inertia of source criticism in its most archaeological form. Valesio's genealogical enterprise is based on the hope, or dream, that literature will always be capable to secure its inheritance against time, oblivion, and the breaking-up of the semiotic chain. Of course, by rewriting the primal text together with the author, genealogical critics (or critics-as-authors) may be deluding themselves into thinking that they are actually achieving time-transcending poetry (*poiesis perennis*).[4]

III. CONTINUITY AND DISCONTINUITY

Who is at work to break up the semiotic chain? Who has sided with archaeology and has plotted against genealogy?

---

[3] Valesio's genealogies are eminently male. Without making too big a fuss about it, to the extent that they refer constantly to fathers and sons, and never to mothers and daughters, they never break with the "male *logos*" tradition that has proceeded undisturbed from Plato to Derrida (and Bloom). The reader will excuse me if, for a reappraisal of maternal *logos* in the creation of poetry, I refer to Carrera, *Lo spazio materno dell'ispirazione* and *La distanza del cielo*.

[4] This only means that literature, supposedly secure in its fortress of semiotic signs, is actually in constant need of being rescued. But this is just an aside, to be developed elsewhere.

"The Logic of Poetic Genealogy"

Since the 1960s, a long list could be drawn. The battle between continuity and discontinuity is of paramount importance for the role that Italian culture has played and still plays in the post-humanist cultural landscape, primarily in Continental Europe but with ramifications that extend to the English-speaking world as well. We need now to take a long detour if we want to understand fully the implications of Valesio's genealogical choice.

Between 1968 and 1972, a few Italian intellectuals engaged themselves in the planning of a new journal that would approach literature and the human sciences from an interdisciplinary perspective. Writers Italo Calvino and Gianni Celati, historian Carlo Ginzburg, philosopher Enzo Melandri, and professor of French literature Guido Neri, were all involved in the discussion concerning the publication of a journal whose tentative name (after several others were discarded) was "Alì Babà." The journal, however, never saw the light of day. Calvino had envisioned a sophisticated yet popular magazine that could be bought at the newsstands. Celati was inclined to a more speculative enterprise. Ginzburg, Melandri, and Neri took part in the initial stages of the project until it became clear that the point of contention concerned Calvino's and Celati's diverging visions. Discussions were cut short in 1972, after Celati obtained a visiting professorship in the United States and Calvino became absorbed into a new book project that would eventually become *Invisible Cities*.[5]

Valesio was only tangentially involved in the project, yet his name came up often in the letters that Calvino and Celati exchanged at that time. His article on the "language of madness in the Renaissance" aroused much interest in both, to the extent that it contributed to the debate on the rea-

---

[5] For the exchange of letters and others documents see *Italo Calvino, Gianni Celati, Carlo Ginzburg, Enzo Melandri, Guido Neri, "Alì Babà". Progetto di una rivista 1968-1972*.

son/madness opposition that had followed the publication of Foucault's *Histoire de la folie*. Calvino also praised Valesio's introduction to the Italian translation of Edward Sapir's *Language: An Introduction to the Study of Speech*. He described it as a *"modello d'introduzione,"* arguably because Valesio emphasized the diachronic, historical implications of Sapir's linguistics vs. the purely synchronic paradigm championed by hard-core structuralists—a paradigm Calvino was uncomfortable with. But the reason why Calvino and Celati were interested in the essay on the language of madness, and the reason why Calvino found Valesio's introduction to Sapir so praiseworthy, are the same ones that brought the planned journal to its demise; namely, the growing gap between Celati's strong embrace of the new, Foucauldian, archaeological paradigm, and Calvino's much more doubtful and cautious approach to it.

Foucaut's archaeology, however, was but one link in a complex semiotic chain that included *anatomy* (Robert Burton), *allegory* (Walter Benjamin), *analogy* (Enzo Melandri) and *conjecture* (Carlo Ginzburg), each term standing for a paradigm of knowledge opposed or alternative to traditional historical continuity and syllogistic, demonstrative cogency. Celati was initially attracted to Robert Burton's *Anatomy of Melancholy* as a thematic research from which nothing having the remotest connection with the subject matter would be excluded. By expanding the model inherited from the Renaissance encyclopedias, Burton did not separate credible information from imaginary accounts. What mattered to him was analogical completeness rather than scientific accuracy. Burton's anatomy was Celati's first step toward Foucauldian archaeology, whose first manifesto was the introduction to *L'Histoire de la folie*'s first edition—which Foucault himself soon regarded as dated and did not reprint in further editions of the book. It is now virtually impossible to think of an archaeological path to knowledge without referring to Foucault's production in the 1960s. In those years, however, the

"The Logic of Poetic Genealogy"

discontinuity paradigm had other champions, Lévi-Strauss being the most visible among them. Celati was also influenced by Deleuze and even more by the discussions he had with Enzo Melandri, who was developing his own archaeological-analogical theory of knowledge and traced archaeology back to Kant.[6]

In his brief essay, "Sull'archeologia," Celati admits his fascination for objects that have lost their language and no longer have speech.[7] Not just the archaeological objects are mute, but also all objects that no longer speak to us turn *de facto* into archaeological artifacts. In semiotic terms one could say that the archaeological objects, their connection with interpretants having been severed, are now reduced to signifiers without signified. Since their code is broken and cannot be retrieved, except that in fragments, they speak in broken voices or do not speak at all. They cannot even substitute their lost language with meaningful silence, yet they do not disappear; they stand mute and meaningless, but no less ominously present for that. One must not forget that in the years of the Calvino-Celati debate the so-called "poetics of the objects," extending from French *nouveau roman* (Robbe-Grillet, Butor) and *nouvelle vague* cinema (Truffaut) to Italian modernist poetry and cinema (Vittorio Sereni, critic Luciano Anceschi, Michelangelo Antonioni) was one of the hottest topics of the day. In many ways, the poetics of the objects was also a forerunner of Derrida's *trace*. In its game of presence and absence *trace* came to show, in a negative

---

[6] According to Celati's notes, Enzo Melandri mentioned Immanuel Kant, *Schriften zur Metaphysik*, in *Werke*, Vol. III. In *La linea e il circolo*, however, Melandri refers primarily to Kant's *Critique of Judgment* (1790).

[7] Gianni Celati, "Sull'archeologia," in *Alì Babà*, cit., 153-156. The text was a first draft, submitted to Calvino and the others (Ginzburg, Melandri, Neri). It was subsequently revised for publication in "Il Verri" (12), 1975, and in Gianni Celati's *Finzioni occidental* (Turin: Einaudi, 1986) with the title, "Il Bazar archeologico." The latter version is included in *Alì Babà*, cit., 200-222.

way, the location where objects disappeared and retrieval was no longer possible.

However, Benjamin's notion of allegory as a broken code (as opposed to the transmitted cultural code of medieval allegory) had already provided the basis for a break-up paradigm long before Foucault's archaeology and Derrida's trace came along. As Renato Solmi pointed out in his 1966 introduction to an Italian anthology of Benjamin's writings, "Allegories—as Benjamin says in his essay on Baudelaire—are always allegories of the forgotten. Their true subject matter is oblivion."[8] And the torn-down Parisian neighborhoods that in Baudelaire's perception turned instantly into allegories are paralleled today by our experience of seeing an empty lot where yesterday something stood, perhaps a fast food restaurant or a gas station that we have passed by every day for years and yet can't remember what it was and how it looked like.

Calvino, on his part, did his best to bow to the *zeitgeist* and embrace the discontinuity paradigm that Celati was championing, but his heart was not in it. In 1960 he produced a brief prose piece, "Lo sguardo dell'archeologo," meant to be the introductory piece to the journal that never materialized. It was a rather clumsy article, in which Calvino catered to Celati's inclination without having really grasped, or so it seems, the implications of the archaeological point of view. Celati, in fact, did not buy Calvino's argument and answered with a letter that, friendship aside, did not go lightly on Calvino's theoretical shortcomings.[9] It was increasingly evident that intellectual reconciliation was impossible and the new journal was virtually dead. Stubbornly, years later

---

[8] "Allegorie ... sono sempre allegorie del dimenticato: il loro vero oggetto è l'oblio." Renato Solmi, *Introduzione* in Walter Benjamin, *Angelus novus*, XIX.

[9] Italo Calvino, "Lo sguardo dell'archeologo," in *Alì Babà*, cit. 197-199. See also the letter of Gianni Celati to Italo Calvino, February 6, 1972, in *Alì Babà*, cit., 145-149.

Calvino included the piece on the archaeological gaze in *Una pietra sopra*, his 1980 collection of essays, but he never came back to the topic and never expanded on it, at least in essayistic form. Yet the thorn was still in his side, and Calvino's change of heart about archaeology is in fact the subject of one of his *Mr. Palomar* stories, as we will see in the next paragraph.[10] Calvino felt a stronger affinity with Ginzburg's conjectural paradigm, which satisfied his novelistic sensibility for those little clues that are essential to the solution of a mystery. Archaeology, allegory, and discontinuity were just not his cup of tea.[11] His true ambition, as it became more and more clear to him during the 1960s and the 1970s, was to pack the classic continuity of literature, so that it could be carried on safely to the next millennium.

IV. ANALOGIES AND PERMUTATIONS

Apart from the main conversation, and yet essential to the full understanding of what was at stake, stands Enzo Melandri and his complex theory of analogy. Melandri published his massive *oeuvre*, *La linea e il circolo* in 1968, shortly before Foucault's *Archéologie du savoir* was published in France.[12] The timeline is crucial. Melandri was a logician and not a proponent of critical history, yet his approach to anal-

---

[10] Now in Italo Calvino, *Saggi, Vol. I.*, 324-327. "Lo sguardo dell'archeologo" is not included in *The Uses of Literature: Essays*, English edition of *Una pietra sopra*.

[11] Carlo Ginzburg, "Spie. Radici di un paradigma indiziario." Paper presented at the "Humanities and Social Thought Colloquium," Bellagio Foundation, 1977. First published as "Spie. Radici di un paradigma scientifico." The expanded final version is included in *Miti emblemi spie*. Also reprinted in *Alì Babà*, cit, 223-265, together with Italo Calvino's review, "L'orecchio, il cacciatore, il pettegolo" (1980), 305-309. See also the English translation, "Clues: Roots of an Evidential Paradigm" in *Clues, Myths, and the Historical Method*.

[12] Enzo Melandri, *La linea e il circolo. Studio logico-filosofico sull'analogia* (1968), now with a new introduction by Giorgio Agamben (2004). An abridged version of the first chapter, "L'archeologia," is included in *Alì Babà*, cit., 282-301.

ogy could and should have been understood in parallel with Foucault's archaeology (not just "in the light" of Foucault's archaeology), had Foucault's terminology not seized the discourse and established its hegemony. As a result, *La linea e il circolo*—an extremely demanding book—can be appreciated, even by today's Italian readers, only by mentally substituting "archaeology" every time the text says "analogy." Nonhegemonical works often suffer being incomprehensible in their own language. (Melandri's work has enjoyed a cult status since, which is a kinder way to say hardly a status at all.)

Yet *La linea e il circolo* must also be understood in its own terms. Melandri rejected systematic approach to its subject matter (analogy) as "too French," meaning too rationalistic. In a strange and surprising way, his analysis of analogy is not that far from Burton's anatomy and various Renaissance encyclopedias. *La linea e il circolo* is, or it aspires to be, a *"piazza universale dell'analogia"*—to steal the title from XVI Century Tommaso Garzoni's *Piazza universale dei mestieri*—but here is where the comparison with the Renaissance ends. In Melandri's *piazza* no one is strolling. There are no examples, there is very little that the layman can put his finger on, and the reader is asked to follow the logical treatment of a subject matter that defies logical reasoning. To provide a logic of analogy, in other words, is an impossible task, a contradiction, and Melandri's book, in the glory of its hundreds of pages, is there to prove it. As much as metaphor is central to the understanding of historical time (the past can always be read as a metaphor of the present), analogy is anarchy in action against the dream of a fully mapped-out cultural code, it is the metonymical forest where language is drunk with possibilities and prey to the endless game of permutations without reference. To echo Mallarmé's warning, analogy is truly a demon unleashed: no matter how hard he tries, the narrator in Mallarmé *Le Démon de l'analogie* will never know the meaning of the strange words ("the penultimate one is dead") that have popped up in his mind while he was walk-

"The Logic of Poetic Genealogy"

ing by a Parisian street.[13] It is here that the connection with archaeology reappears. If history works through metaphors, then archaeology works only through analogy, guessing, retrospection—the only codes that are left when cultural continuity is broken.

Melandri's approach, however, stops short from total epistemological rupture. To a certain extent, *La linea e il circolo* is very much a product of its times. It was the year 1968, and Melandri believed that analogy could be summoned up to a political task. "Good" analogies move beyond themselves, toward Hegelian-Marxist dialectics and political action; "bad" analogies force us to go back to square one and deny that movement is possible (the movement of thought, but also political movement). Obviously, this is the dated aspect of Melandri's theory. Much less dated is his observation that dialectics is always complemented by a non-dialectical moment which remains analogical, non-mediated, and possibly akin to Schelling's absolute.[14] Analogy, in other words, is the logic of immediacy, of the pure intimation of being. Dialectics overcomes it, tries to "comprehend" it, but cannot get rid of it, and will always bear analogy's invisible mark under its skin.

It is not hard to see why Melandri's archaeological-analogical paradigm, paired with Celati's preference for archaeology over dialectical history, was a direct threat to the rhetoric of continuity that Calvino was developing at the end of the 1960s. Calvino's faith in continuity, however, was based on a subtle, self-defying paradox. In *Invisible Cities* (1972), all the cities that Marco Polo describes to Kublai Khan are positively lost. They may or may not exist or have existed, in fact they are archaeological objects whose meaning is irretrievable, except in the analogical narratives that

---

[13] Stéphane Mallarmé, *The Demon of Analogy*. See also Antonio Prete, *Il demone dell'analogia*, 152-159.
[14] Enzo Melandri, *La linea e il circolo* (2004 edition), 810.

the Venetian traveler develops to make them understandable to Kublai Khan, who never leaves his palace and has never seen them. Marco Polo's flights of imagination in describing the invisible cities he claims to have visited are neither metaphors nor allegories; Kublai Khan will not get a better understanding of his kingdom by deciphering their code. Marco Polo's descriptions are analogies whose ultimate meaning will always elude the emperor of China. But analogies of what? At the end of the book Marco Polo discloses that those cities were all permutations of the same city—Venice. Their reference, their "sense," is therefore safe, as much as Venice, the precarious city on water, can be considered safe. If the cities are signifiers, Venice is the signified—as long as Venice does not sink into the Adriatic Sea. At the surface, *Invisible Cities* is a triumph of analogies. And yet, in its essence, it is a deeply genealogical work. Marco Polo holds the secret genealogy of the analogies he is piling up, but he will reveal it only at the very last moment, solving a mystery whose existence Kublai Khan did not even suspect.

V. From Genealogy to Unrelated Kinship

Our detour has been long, but the reader will now see that it was much needed. Valesio's genealogy, as we have said before, is the concern of fathers and children. They may or may not know each other, but their relationship is inscribed in their genetic nature and therefore essentially retrievable. Analogy, on its part, is the concern of brothers and/or cousins. It may have less to do with Sophocles' Oedipus than with the strife between the Kauravas and the Pandavas in the *Mahabharata*. In fact, the analogical paradigm is akin to the non-Oedipal "society without fathers," based on brotherhood alone, that Deleuze has often envisioned.[15] Which means, in fact, a society of Abels and Cains without the embarrassing presence of Father Adam (not to say Father God). But it would be wrong to ascribe Valesio's genealogy and Calvino's rescuing of meaning to the mere side of historic continuity, leaving all the fun of discontinuity to Deleuzian brotherhood. Immediacy is not the precinct of analogy alone.

In fact, no clear-cut distinction can be made between the safety of metaphor as the preferred trope of historical interpretation and the unsafe analogical jump in the presence of a past that no longer communicates with us. The belief that metaphor was but the first step on the ladder to concept was harbored by Hans Blumenberg in his 1960 *Paradigms for a Metaphorology*. However, he revised his early position and in his 1979 *Shipwreck with Spectator* spoke of the "non-conceptuality" of metaphors, which originate not in the world of concepts but in Husserl's pre-categorial "life-world".[16] Ultimately, metaphors are like fossils; their birth is obscure and their primordial meaning is unfathomable. In the early stages of scientific research they come in handy; later on, they are like old marks on the body of thought, and their role is more therapeutic than heuristic. If analogies follow the lines of invisible wounds, metaphors are the visible scars.

But no matter how far the genealogical research stretches out, and no matter how high the analogical mind wants to jump up, textuality, analogy, and genealogy all *happen at the same time*—concurrently with our reading of the text. There is no father before the child is born, and only metaphorically (and retrospectively) we can say that the father was already there before the child came into the world. In the same fashion, genealogy begins to exist the moment it is uncovered,

---

[15] See for instance Gilles Deleuze, *Bartleby o la formule,* also (in Italian translation) in Gilles Deleuze and Giorgio Agamben, *Bartleby o la formula della creazione*, 8-42.

[16] See also Remo Bodei's introduction to *Naufragio con spettatore. Paradigma di una metafora dell'esistenza*. 9-10.

and only from that moment on it "branches out." Our early assumption (Valesio's assumption in our words), that there was a textual DNA encoded in the text, must be understood now as the metaphor that it was.

In one of the travelogue chapters in Calvino's *Mr. Palomar*, the eponymous character is visiting the ruins of Tula together with a Mexican friend who is an expert in pre-Columbian civilizations and is more than willing to teach Palomar the symbolism of the Toltec culture. At the same time, a class of Mexican schoolchildren is having a field trip at the site of the ruins. A young teacher shows the columns, statues and the reliefs to his students, gives them a few facts and then, invariably, ends up saying, "*No se sabe lo qué quiere decir*," we don't know what they mean. Palomar is fascinated by his friend's erudition, yet he is even more attracted by the severe pedagogy of the young teacher. Perhaps, he thinks, the refusal to interpret the ruins of the past is the only way to show them respect. But Palomar's friend is nonplussed. At the relief-frieze known as Wall of the Serpents, when the young teacher says again that "we don't know" why each serpent is holding a skull in its open jaws, the erudite friend cannot keep silent: "Yes, we do!" he says. "It's the continuity of life and death; the serpents are life, the skulls are death!" Palomar does not know what to think. He has no idea what "life" and "death" meant to the ancient Toltecs and, for that matter, to the schoolchildren who perhaps are their descendants. He is not even sure what those words mean to him. As much as he leans toward the schoolteacher, however, he cannot blame his friend, because he sees so much of himself in him. He knows that he cannot repress in himself the need to translate, move from one language to another, and "weave and reveawe a network of analogies" ("*tessere e ritessere una rete d'analogie*").[17] In the meantime, the teacher

---

[17] Italo Calvino, "Serpenti e teschi," in *Palomar*, included in *Romanzi e racconti Vol. II*, 956. See also "Serpents and Skulls" in *Mr. Palomar*, 95-98.

———. "Serpents and Skulls." In *Mr. Palomar*. Trans. William Weaver. San Diego: Harcourt, Brace & Jovanovich, 1985, pp. 95-98.

Carrera, Alessandro. *Lo spazio materno dell'ispirazione. Agostino Blanchot Celan Zanzotto*. Fiesole: Cadmo, 2004.

———. *La distanza del cielo. Leopardi e lo spazio dell'ispirazione*. Milan: Medusa, 2011.

Celati, Gianni. "Il Bazar archeologico." In *Finzioni occidentali*. Turin: Einaudi, 1986.

———. "Sull'archeologia." In Mario Barenghi and Marco Belpoliti, eds. 1998, pp. 153-156.

———. "Il progetto 'Alì Babà,' trent'anni dopo." In Mario Barenghi and Marco Belpoliti, eds. 1998, pp. 313-21.

D'Annunzio, Gabriele. *Dant de Flourence* (1914). Trans. André Doderet. In Paolo Valesio 1992, pp. 199-209.

Deleuze, Gilles. *Bartleby o la formule*. Paris: Flammarion, 1989.

Deleuze, Gilles and Giorgio Agamben. *Bartleby o la formula della creazione*. Trans. Stefano Verdicchio. Macerata: Quodlibet, 1993.

Foucault, Michel. *Histoire de la folie à l'age classique*. Paris: Plon, 1961.

———. *L'Archéologie du savoir*. Paris: Gallimard, 1969.

Ginzburg, Carlo. "Spie. Radici di un paradigma scientifico." *Rivista di storia contemporanea* 1 (1978): 1-14.

———. "Spie. Radici di un paradigma indiziario." In *Miti emblemi spie. Morfologia e storia*. Turin: Einaudi, 1986. 158-93. Also in Barenghi and Belpoliti eds. 1998. 223-65.

———. "Clues: Roots of an Evidential Paradigm." In *Clues, Myths, and the Historical Method*. Trans. Anne C. Tedeschi and John Tedeschi. Baltimore: The Johns Hopkins University Press, 1992, pp. 96-125.

Mallarmé, Stéphane. "The Demon of Analogy." In *Collected Poems*. Trans. Henry Weinfield. Berkeley: University of California Press, 1994, pp. 93-94.

Melandri, Enzo. *La linea e il circolo. Studio logico-filosofico sull'analogia*. Macerata: Quodlibet, 2004 [First ed., Bologna: il Mulino, 1968].

Prete, Antonio. *Il demone dell'analogia. Da Leopardi a Valéry: Studi di poetica*. Milan: Feltrinelli, 1986.

Sapir, Edward. *Il linguaggio: Introduzione alla linguistica*. Ed. and with an introduction by Paolo Valesio. Turin: Einaudi, 1968

[First published as *Language: An introduction to the Study of Speech*. New York: Harcourt, Brace & Co., 1921].

Solmi, Renato. *Introduzione*. In Walter Benjamin, *Angelus novus*. Trans. Renato Solmi. Turin: Einaudi, 1962.

Valesio, Paolo. "The Language of Madness in the Renaissance." *Yearbook of Italian Studies* I (1971): 199-234.

_____. *Novantiqua: Rhetorics as a Contemporary Theory*. Bloomington: Indiana UP, 1980.

_____. *Ascoltare il silenzio. La retorica come teoria*. Bologna: il Mulino, 1986.

_____. *Gabriele D'Annunzio: The Dark Flame*. Trans. Marilyn Migiel. New Haven: Yale University Press, 1992.

Abroad and Beyond
Paolo Valesio and the Empty Nest

Andrea Ciccarelli
Indiana University

The aim of this paper is to explore the complexity of Paolo Valesio's poetics in regards to the topic of exile, particularly in his fictional works. However, I need to state right away that Valesio is one of those intellectuals (and I use the word in a weighty fashion, as I believe that this term is too often abused simply to identify academic life and work) and authors whose poetics should be addressed without the usual division between works of fiction and scholarly works. In his case, in fact, I see a unique approach both to the reading and to the writing of literature. It would be enough to look at a few excerpts from any of his major critical essays, to conclude that Valesio entrusts his uncommon hermeneutical skills not only to a profound scholarly meditation, but to an exact, lucid style which cuts through the texts analyzed, with a prose that very often respects and responds to the creative tension raised by the original works. His approach is not presumptuous: to the contrary, Valesio's critical writing always maintains the necessary humbleness and reverence for the authors analyzed; specifically, his is in case of a lucid acknowledgement of the ritual of literature as a verbal medium that cannot be challenged by an ambitious theoretical approach, unless also supported by a more than adequate stylistic understanding of the rhetorical code. If the ultimate goal of rhetoric is to persuade the reader/ listener of the importance of one's own message, it is inevitable that, when this message is openly expressed in an artistic form, the reader/ listener not only tries to decode the general struc-

From: *Discourse Boundary Creation*. Bordighera Press, 2013

ture, but she/ he also needs to find elements of creativity that support her/ his analysis. Ultimately, in Valesio's view, the pleasure of interpretation needs to correspond to the pleasure of writing: otherwise there could be no closure in the short circuit provoked by the rhetorical act of reading.[1]

To grasp this critical method, perhaps, we could briefly exemplify from one of his articles devoted to an author, Manzoni, who is not one of Valesio's favorites, at least not for his novel.[2] The critical tension felt and declared in regards to the subject examined, in fact, helps us to identify Valesio's continuous attempt to connect stylistically with the source analyzed. Valesio's main thesis is that Manzoni's use of the rhetorical figure of the *reticentia* (which allows him not to address directly the issue of love in the novel) eventually contradicts his own attempt to write a novel with a high degree of historical credibility.[3] The omissions in the narrator's interventions as well as those in the characters' dialogues, according to Valesio, make it more and more difficult to appreciate the twists of a plot initially triggered by a love story (that of Renzo and Lucia) vexed by the lust of don Rodrigo.

---

[1] This is clearly explained in what, I believe, is his most important scholarly book, *Novantiqua: Rhetorics as a Contemporary Theory* (Bloomington: Indiana University Press, 1980), ix-xiii, where he argues the independence of rhetoric as a form of human speech and therefore proposes a view of literature as an interaction between reader and author.

[2] "Lucia, ovvero la *'Reticentia'* nei *Promessi sposi.*" *Filologia e Critica.* XIII (1988): 207-238. This article, with a few amendments, was later republished in Giovanni Manetti, ed., *Leggere i Promessi sposi* (Milan: Bompiani, 1989). As a poet, Valesio seems instead to appreciate some of the aesthetic choices made by Manzoni; see, for instance, Andrea Ciccarelli, "Fuoricasa: scrittori italiani in Nord America," *Esperienze letterarie* 1 (2004): 100-101.

[3] "Che cos'è la *reticentia*? Fondamentalmente, l'interruzione di una frase già iniziata, implicante la soppressione di qualche elemento *genericamente ricostruibile* della frase stessa; l'interruzione è accompagnata di solito da una pausa di silenzio. Una volta che la nostra attenzione sia attirata su questa figura, vediamo che essa è molto frequente, sulla bocca dei più svariati personaggi, nei *Promessi sposi…*" Valesio, "Lucia ovvero," 208.

Naturally, my purpose here is not that of evaluating or debating Valesio's critical approach to Manzoni or to any specific author, for that matter.[4] This is not the right place, as my intention, I repeat, is that of pointing out Valesio's unique approach to the study of literature as an aesthetic operation that implies a dual rhetorical function, inasmuch as the writer examined triggers a persuasive power necessary to establish a complicity with the reader. In this regard, I would like to stress that even in an article aimed at criticizing both the critical interpretations as well as the unity of Manzoni's work, Valesio finds a personal way to connect, through a series of stylistic intuitions, to the author analyzed. This is the case, for instance, when he refers to the famous passage ("la notte degl'imbrogli") that causes the chain reaction of events that will separate Renzo and Lucia for a long time:

> E mentre s'avviavano, con quella commozione che non trova parole, e che si manifesta senza di esse, il padre soggiunse, con voce alterata: - il cuor mi dice che ci rivedremo presto. Certo, il cuore, chi gli dà retta, ha sempre qualche cosa da dire su quello che sarà. Ma che sa il cuore? Appena un poco di quello che è già accaduto (*I promessi sposi*, Chapter VIII).

Valesio stresses that the narrator's intervention could easily be interpreted as an ulterior sign of Manzoni's *reticentia*: his characters, not even padre Cristoforo, cannot entrust themselves to any instinctual aspects of life without paying dear consequences. To the point that these words may sound as an "elegia se non anticristiana, per lo meno acristiana."[5] Nevertheless, despite the criticism, Valesio's

---

[4] In fact, personally, I have already expressed my different approach to the same issue, see Andrea Ciccarelli, *Manzoni: la coscienza della letteratura* (Rome: Bulzoni, 1996), 114-116 and 132, n.4.

[5] Valesio, "Lucia ovvero," 233.

careful eye also notices that, in this passage, Manzoni utilizes a series of hendecasyllables to render more precious the intensity of a key-point of the novel ("Una minuscola ma vastamente suggestiva poesia incastonata nel testo narrativo").[6] It is a crucial narrative moment, in fact, as the protagonists are crushed by the unjust events out of their control and by the thought of the upcoming, inevitable exile. The lyrical tone is a rhetorical stratagem that, while not diminishing the strength of the narrator's rational incursion ("ma che sa il cuore?"), embraces the entire situation with a soothing poetic quality that, rhetorically, compensates the helpless desperation of the moment. Along the same lines, Valesio, after having argued that Manzoni literally slows down Renzo's pace in the story, normally referring to his actions in the past tense, Valesio then astutely observes that, after the episode of the *Lazzaretto*, the narration of the events related to Renzo switches to the present tense, easing, also from a verbal standpoint, his final entry into the realm of the remaining actions. Once again, we may disagree about Valesio's critical assessment. It is clear, however, that these two stylistic intuitions cannot be fully appreciated outside of an aesthetic notion that views literature as a rhetorical means that fills the empty space between an author and each one of his/her reader.

As stated at the beginning, in this essay, however, I intend to focus on Valesio's works of fiction and, specifically on one of them. But, before addressing the text in question, I would like to bring up, briefly, what I consider the cornerstone of Valesio's aesthetic dimension: his concept of exile. It is a concept which is ferociously private although it needs to find its public outlet to make sense of itself aesthetically. I believe that one passage, in particular, offers the underlining ideas behind his entire poetics:

---

[6] "Lucia ovvero," 233.

"Abroad and Beyond"

> Exile is a slinking beast; it bides its time, without hurry, but it gets you in the end [...] When all the illusions of moderation and equilibrium [...] are gone, we find ourselves face to face with a radical choice: only one of two opposite paths can be taken, and either one is difficult to walk [...] How can an author write his poems in his native language while residing in a foreign land without addressing, *in some way*, this lacerating divarication?[7]

These words marked one of the historical passages of Italian writing in North America. They are taken, in fact, from the introduction of a seminal publication – the anthology *Italian Poets in America*, a special issue of *Gradiva*, that Valesio co-edited in 1993 with Luigi Fontanella. Together with another 1993 anthology, *Poesaggio* (co-edited with Peter Carravetta),[8] this issue of *Gradiva* represents a milestone for the emancipation of poetry written in Italian in the United States. In his introduction, Valesio makes reference to the tormented choice of writing poetry in a language other than English in America (and, clearly, what is directed to poetry can easily be applied to prose fiction as well): how would/could one reconcile the divaricating factor between living abroad, *fuoricasa*, and choosing to write in one's own native language? Valesio's definition of exile is exemplary and greatly effective: "Exile is a slinking beast," a parasite that corrodes from within, that consumes one's own energy from a concealed position; and, when it is detected, it is often too late: it has eaten up our vital nourishment. Valesio's definition is not isolated in the world of literary theory dealing with the concept of exile; other authors have made designations similar to his. A few years later, for instance, Enzo Bettiza compared the condition caused by exile to a subtle gas ("gas nervino") that slowly erodes memory:

---

[7] *Italian Poets in America*. *Gradiva* 10-11 (1992-1993): 5.
[8] *Poesaggio. Poeti italiani d'America* (Treviso: Pagus Edizioni, 1993).

> L'esilio è simile a una lebbra leggera, gassosa, che, con un logorìo diluito nel tempo, sfigura e corrompe a poco a poco [...] una necrosi indolore, che non s'avventa come una fiera carnivora sui ricordi, ma s'insinua piuttosto in essi come un gas nervino, ustionandoli e strinandoli a fuoco dolce. Il gas [...] propaga e stende insicurezza mnemonica, dubbi, sospetti, buchi neri e coltri di tenebra [...] Trasforma la memoria in memoria esiliata [...] Per l'esule [...] ricordare è guarire. Ricordare è come ritrovare.[9]

Not so differently, Milan Kundera, through the voice of the narrator of one of his *French* novels dedicated to Czech exiles in Paris, writes:

> [...] for memory to function well, it needs constant practice: if recollections are not evoked again and again [...] they go. Émigrés [...] who do not spend time with their compatriots [...] are inevitably stricken with amnesia [...] For nostalgia does not heighten memory's activity [...] it suffices into itself [...] so fully absorbed is it by its suffering and nothing else.[10]

Valesio's image of the slinking beast remains the most evocative however, as it offers a contrasting solution to the nostalgia of exile, to the oozing wound that cannot heal. He points to the heart of the conflict: if exile corrodes – silently – from within, the language of choice becomes, paradoxically, both the tool that can placate and that, at the same time, can exacerbate the cultural, existential and linguistic difficulty of living abroad and writing in a native language which is alien to its creative context. Language becomes, therefore, a meas-

---

[9] Enzo Bettiza, *Esilio* (Milano: Mondadori, 1996), 443.
[10] Milan Kundera, *Ignorance*, translated by Linda Asher (New York: Harper Collins, 2002), 33 (original French edition: Paris: Gallimard, 2000).

ure of memory, and thus an instrument which explores the intellectual and physical space produced by the divaricating notion which Valesio mentioned in his introduction to *Gradiva*. Preserving one's own mother-tongue in a place where such *maternity* is not recognized serves the cause of literature, as it increases the opportunity to understand cultural conflicts otherwise forcibly and falsely pacified by a logical choice: that of choosing, if possible, the mainstream language. In a sense, Valesio's linguistic operation is not so different than that of a dialectal poet who *needs* the dialect – his or her native-language – to express an inner reality that could not be revealed as much if translated into the standard language. The linguistic signs do not correspond to the street signs, and it is precisely this alienation which causes perennial friction; and yet, it also produces the necessary poetic entanglement of creation. The zigzagging within this knotted material is possible, in fact, because of a language which is as alien to the geo-cultural situations as the author's background.

In the following pages, partially also as an homage to the city in which Valesio has spent a great part of his life in two different stages of his career in the United States, I would like to exemplify Valesio's writing analyzing, albeit schematically, one of his tales, *S'incontrano gli amanti*,[11] published in 1993, the same felicitous year in which he co-edited both the *Gradiva* anthology and *Poesaggio*. In this novella, the divergent sense of otherness between different cultures (between languages, Italian customs and American ones, between the academic world and the business world, between social classes in New York, etc.) surrounds, fills and feeds the entire tale. The protagonist, Vìttore,[12] is an Italian Professor who

---

[11] *S'incontrano gli amanti* (Rome: Empiria, 1993).
[12] The name is Vìttore, accented on the first syllable, not the most common Vittòre, normally accented on the second syllable (naturally, this last one is still not as common as Vittorio). Vìttore derives from *Victor*, he who conquers, while Vittòre and Vittorio come from *Victorius*, that is,

now lives in England, but who has previously lived in the United States. While he is in New York at a conference, he tells a colleague about an old love story that he had when he was living in an American college town.

S'incontrano gli amanti is really a philosophical tale about the constrictions of life, and its deceiving appearances. From the detailed description of Gramercy Park and its fenced garden open only to the residents of the square, to the club, "*The Players,*" also on the square, where the protagonist stays while in New York, Valesio underlines the existential condition of a humanity which plays its roles, confined within the restrictive and suffocating space of a set of rules which, ultimately, lead to self-deception. The conflicting intrusions of the outside world in this story are twofold. On one hand there is the absolute estrangement of the protagonist. Vìttore is a total "outsider," as the place (an international but, for this reason, even less forgiving New York) and the language interfere with his own cultural and linguistic heritage. The fact that he lived in the US and that he now lives in another English speaking language make this isolation even more acute, reminding him of his professional role in life – that of teaching a foreign language and culture. But the entire novella underscores the alienation of urban humanity, which is unaware of aberrations caused by societal conventions that make no logical sense:

> Gramercy park è una delle poche piazze eleganti [...] di New York – che è tanto ricca di bei posti [...] Belli, ma non eleganti [...] Perfino lo squallore può essere bello [...] Tuttavia l'eleganza produce un suo quieto, un suo limitato piacere [...] Gramercy park; una piazzetta (sarebbe, se la scala di riferimento fosse europea, una piazza); ed anche

---

conqueror, winner. Perhaps, Valesio, even in the choice of the name, suggests that his character is not a natural winner and, therefore, the only way for him to survive in a hostile environment is to impose himself.

"Abroad and Beyond"

un giardino al centro della piazzetta. Un parco privato in effetti, tutt'intorno cinto da una palizzata nera di sbarre di ferro con tocchi di vernice argentea ai cancelli le cui chiavi sono possedute [...] dai proprietari delle palazzine che circondano la piazza [...] E così [...] il passante che compia lentamente il giro del parco guardando attraverso le sbarre [...] può vedere il parco quasi completamente deserto, ma nitido nel suo ordine e ben curato [...] e alcune pensose statue bronzee che hanno anch'esse acquistato la verde patina dei cespugli [...] e due fontanelle [...] e piccioni e passeri sull'orlo che prendono rumorosamente il bagno [...] e [...] due, massimo tre, privilegiati abitanti delle palazzine che se ne stanno seduti lì (ognuno solo, con una panchina tutta per sé) [...] uniche presenze viventi in quello che altrimenti appare come un paesaggio ottocentesco bloccato, congelato, fissato [...] per lo studio delle generazioni future [...] quasi fosse un locale annesso al Metropolitan Museum of Art.[13]

We are at the beginning of the novella, and the detailed description of the square sets the tone for the entire story. The discrepancy between what is left outside (all the rest, with its "beautiful" but *not* elegant city) and what, instead, is included in this elegant and, therefore, démodé image emphasizes the friction between the desires for inclusion of the estranged protagonist and his actual excruciating solitude. The insistence on the division between the two worlds segregated by the black iron bars, which force anybody who does not possess the key to the silver gate to walk around it, is a physical symbol of the lack of communicability between the two systems. Moreover, these physical barriers portray the will to maintain such distance. They are the symbol of a city, a culture, and a society forbidden to the protagonist. But the truth is that, even if they were not forbidden, they

---

[13] *S'incontrano*, 20.

would still be incompatible to his migratory and estranged life. And yet, the rules of the game or, better, the assigned roles are played diligently by all the actors of the story, not only by Vittore (the fact that the club where he is staying, "*The Players,*" exists in both England and the US, that is, in both of the English speaking countries where he has lived and lives, accentuates his estrangement, and his playing a role according to directions which are not his own).

The opposition between the square, as a natural part of the city, and its symbolic stance is embodied by the deserted garden, with its precise geometric design, contrasted by the lively and noisy interruption caused by the birds, that are antagonistic to the "pensose statue" which were supposed to be a permanent reminder of human superiority over nature and which, instead, have become part of the garden themselves ("hanno anch'esse acquistato la verde patina dei cespugli,") and, in this, have somehow redeemed themselves from any residue of human arrogance.

It is not so, though, for the two or three "privilegiati abitanti delle palazzine" who read the newspapers sitting, alone, on separate benches. They are part of the scenery, and they are not any more real than the rest of the century-old park. These privileged inhabitants are named for what they represent in this special place: the narrator calls them "presenze viventi," living existences, as if they were well executed figures of a 19th-century painting belonging to a museum, and not to the modern pace of a city blind to elegance and quietude (only when one of these "presenze viventi" leaves the garden is he finally designated as a "man"). These living presences sit, "ognuno solo, con una panchina tutta per sé." The privilege of elegance cannot be shared; it needs to be consumed individually. It is as though the necessary counteraction (almost a *contrapasso*) associated with this limited and confined pleasure is that of being forced into solitude, to a life even more individualistic and monadic than what life normally is. Valesio, in the description of the garden, makes

"Abroad and Beyond"

it a point to stress this isolation, using a series of past participles that highlight the suffocating space devoted to the experience of elegance: "limitato, cinto, circondato, bloccato, congelato, fissato."

The alienation presented by the elegance of the out-of-place park is emphasized when the narrator's eye reflects upon the grotesqueness of a situation which draws no apparent visible contrast of wealth between the privileged few who have access to the garden inside, and those who observe from the imperfect and inelegant world outside:

> Ecco uno di questi seduti sulla panchina si è alzato. Si avvia ad uno dei cancelli, armeggia intorno alla serratura poi lo chiude accuratamente dietro di sé infilandosi la chiave in tasca: getta un'occhiata all'orologio, si guarda intorno, attraversa la strada, sale i pochi scalini che conducono ad un elegante portoncino di legno scolpito; apre rapido, quasi furtivo, ed è già scomparso dentro la palazzina. Nel tragitto fra le due serrature quest'uomo non è distinguibile: in effetti, non è distinto [...] nulla che lo differenzi da qualunque altro povero diavolo di passaggio [...] egli è abbigliato essenzialmente come questi due addormentati accanto ad uno dei cancelli del parco [...] Ma la crudeltà della differenza è percepibile sopra tutto proprio in ciò che li rende più umani, nella loro posa disarmata [...] forse questa posa è l'unico elemento che li distingue [...] essa è [...] fuor di luogo, nella società innaturale che si stende tutt'intorno [...] li rende simili alle statue dentro il parco chiuso.[14]

The narrator here refers to two homeless persons who do not seem so differently dressed than the fortunate people who own the keys to the garden; they are like the statues described before: they belong to the natural urban décor of the

---

[14] *S'incontrano*, 30.

park. The painful delimitation of this jealously guarded privilege ("chiude accuratamente [...] infilandosi la chiave in tasca") is again emphasized: the man who holds the key to this garden of Eden is a man constricted between two locks ("Nel tragitto fra due serrature"), a man who hides himself within the garden, seeks for anonymity outside (the casual dress code that makes him similar to the homeless), and disappears again within the building where he lives. Once more, the privilege of elegance can be lived only within the secrecy of precise, defined measures–off limits to the rest of the world. In postmodern society there is no apparent distinction between the *saved* and the *damned* of life, except for a ferocious paradox. The latter can blend with the natural Eden from which they are shunned precisely because of their unprotected and unguarded behavior. The two "poveri diavoli" harmonize with nature because, like the statues, they become part of the landscape themselves. Only those who have nothing to defend have nothing to fear.

The novella is built upon these impenetrable worlds that face each other without ever blending. The love story at the center of the tale, in fact, evolves within a series of narrow existential universes: that of the self-sufficient environment represented by the college town where it originated; or that of the various microcosms carved within the Big Apple; or, finally, that which strikes the alienated protagonist directly. Exemplary, in this sense, is the large bar in a huge Manhattan Hotel, where the plot reaches its climax. It is the place where Vìttore and his lover drift apart forever, for lack *and* fear of communication, for an inevitable clash between different worlds of expression. The bar has a mirrored ceiling which should reproduce the space and the action below, but, in Vìttore's memory, ends up being a low and oppressive ceiling which reproduces the restricted and breathless life of our society:

"Abroad and Beyond"

> E – tocco finale da osteria di Babilonia – tutto il soffitto è fatto di specchi. Con effetto di esaltazione: è una moltiplicazione su vasto campo [...] E con effetto di esplosione: di tutti questi crani che, sotto la specchiera in alto, sembrano essere schiacciati sui grembi [...] comprimendo gli avventori sui tavolini, schiacciando poi la poltiglia sul pavimento, scaraventando infine tutta questa materia con un gran volo là fuori sulla strada.[15]

The intended optical goal – to expand all this compressed humanity, to make it look as though it were not oppressed by its obsessive life – obtains the opposite effect. The multiplication of images reminds us only of the differences and of the communicative barriers, which separate all these individual images that fully belong to the Babylon recreated by the modern arrogance that has pushed humanity to believe that we can have a common language. It is only outside, on the street where they are sent back, that these individualities reacquire their true nature, which is made of an undistinguishable, poorly amalgamated material ("scaraventando infine tutta questa materia con un gran volo là fuori sulla strada").

The metaphor entrusted to the description of the square where Vìttore resides for his temporary visit to New York serves to explain his inability to deal with his own anxiety, his own fear of being rejected by the society where he lives and works, his struggle with his own identity, with his own memory and his own future. Only when he is asleep, alone, can he relax and snore with the spontaneity of one who knows that he has no company:

> Vìttore si è addormentato con la lampada del comodino ancora accesa, e il corpo tutto inclinato di traverso sul letto. Ogni tanto [...] russa [...] con la particolare, tranquilla

---

[15] *S'incontrano*, 96.

noncuranza che d'istinto ha il dormiente quando sa di non avere compagnia nel suo dormire.[16]

Valesio's novella accentuates the effects caused by the tragic illusion that a true insertion in an alien reality might actually be possible. This is a grand illusion that is clearly denied to the protagonist. The final image, in fact, relegates him back to his obscurity, ironically underscored by that light, distractedly or deliberately, left on, and by his unconscious attempt to occupy a space that does not belong to him and to which, above all, he does not belong to (the image of the fetal position stretched across the empty bed – "tutto inclinato di traverso sul letto").

Ultimately, the basic interpretation of the otherness implicit in this work is that the protagonists, including the city of New York with her perennial – but humanly desperate – effervescence, are lonely. All of them (Vìttore, his occasional interlocutor, his former lover Lia, his former rival, his best friend) live in an English-speaking world, and they all make a living teaching Italian: *the foreign* language in which Valesio chose to write this story about solitude and cultural emptiness in America.

WORKS CITED

Bettiza, Enzo. *Esilio*. Milano: Mondadori, 1996.
Carravetta, Peter and Valesio, Paolo, editors. *Poesaggio. Poeti italiani d'America*. Treviso, Pagus, 1993.
_____. *Manzoni: la coscienza della letteratura*. Rome: Bulzoni, 1996
Ciccarelli, Andrea. "Fuoricasa: scrittori italiani in Nord America." *Esperienze letterarie* 1 (2004): 83-104.
Fontanella, Luigi and Valesio, Paolo, editors. *Italian Poets in America. Gradiva* 10-11 (1992-1993).
Kundera, Milan. *Ignorance*. Translated by Linda Asher. New York: Harper Collins, 2002.
Valesio, Paolo. *Novantiqua: Rhetorics as a Contemporary Theory*. Bloomington: Indiana University Press, 1980.

---

[16] *S'incontrano*, 99.

_____. "Lucia, ovvero la *reticentia* nei *Promessi sposi*." *Filologia e Critica* XIII (1988): 207-238.
_____. *S'incontrano gli amanti*. Rome: Empiria, 1993.

POETRY, DIALOGUE, SILENCE

Ernesto Livorni
University of Wisconsin – Madison

The poet thinks and speaks poetry, thinks and speaks about poetry: it is in this gesture that the poet founds the *raison d'être* of poetry writing and of the gesture of speaking *en poète*.

Valesio's writing gently shakes the walls separating the different writing enterprises that he undertook in a process that has been indeed a procession of books and articles and poems throughout several decades. The ultimate goal of this apparently scattered and enormous production of writing addresses the question of poetry, of its voice and its relation to silence. Valesio is impatient and dissatisfied with a compartmental understanding of literature, indeed, of knowledge; such uneasiness with separate entities in a discourse that must be circular is rooted in a belief in the constant exchange among poles that only erroneously are considered opposite to and different from one another. This has been a main concern in some of Valesio's theoretical writings, which then found their concrete expression in other works of literary criticism: the book on D'Annunzio stands by itself and yet breathes the theory elaborated in *Ascoltare il silenzio*. In turn, the latter is only to a certain extent the translation of *Novantiqua*.[1] More importantly, these critical and theoretical

---

[1] Paolo Valesio, *Novantiqua: Rhetorics as a Contemporary Theory* (Bloomington: Indiana University Press, 1980); Paolo Valesio, *Ascoltare il silenzio. La retorica come teoria* (Bologna: Il Mulino, 1986); Paolo Valesio, *Gabriele D'Annunzio: The Dark Flame*. Transl. Marilyn Migiel (New Haven: Yale University Press, 1992).

works feed Valesio's creative writing, his novels and his books of poems.

The span of Paolo Valesio's opus reaches from studies in linguistics to those in literary theories and criticism, from the writing of short stories and novels to reflections on the creative act of writing, from books of poems to discourse on poetry. The constant cultivation of different genres and the multifaceted unfolding of his writing ultimately aim at a circularity of discourses, in which the painstaking process of the alternating of writing and existence dares to contradict itself and to become one: "Il poeta come opera" is a phrase with which Valesio iconically frames the junction of an otherwise *coincidentia oppositorum*, of a *discordia discors*: existence is writing and writing is existence.[2] Valesio's is the opus of "the writer between two worlds," to borrow the title of one of the many important essays Valesio dedicated to this issue, where the two worlds are not to be understood only geographically (in that essay, it is true, Valesio also considers the writer engaged between different countries such as Italy and United States, and different languages such as Italian and English), but also as two existential realms between which the writer moves.[3] Issues of exile and "espatrio" are

---

[2] Paolo Valesio, "Il poeta come opera," in *Il Cobold*, n.17, 1981, pp. 1-3, and "Il poeta come opera (Duologo fra un poeta e un suo amico)," in *L'ANELLO che non tiene: Journal of Modern Italian Literature*, vol. 2, n. 2, Fall 1990, pp. 107-121.

[3] Paolo Valesio, "The Writer between Two Worlds: Italian Writing in the United States Today," in *Differentia: review of italian thought*, nos. 3-4, 1989, pp. 259-276. Versions of the article also appeared in Italian sometimes with variations in the title and in length ("Lo scrittore fra i due mondi: osservazioni sulla scrittura italiana negli Stati Uniti oggi," in Maria Grazia Vacchina, ed., *"Langues et peuples:"* Actes du Colloque, Gressoney-Saint-Jean, Chateau Savoia, 8 mai 1988 (Aoste: Assessorat Règional de l'Instruction Publique, 1989), pp. 133-152; "Lo scrittore fra i due mondi," in John Picchione, Laura Pietropaolo, eds., *Italian Literature in North America: Pedagogical Strategies* [Biblioteca di *Quaderni d'Italianistica*, n.9], (Ottawa: Canadian Society for Italian Studies, 1990), pp. 211-223; in Vita Fortunati, ed., *Bologna: La cultura italiana e le letterature straniere moderne*, 3

relevant in the context of the larger embrace of aesthetics and ethics. The threshold separating such polarities lives in a contrapuntal discourse in which "A succession or procession of concrete images" is "opposed to a series of abstract statements."[4] Theory, then, is a discourse tracing "la via dei minimi," as the title of the opening and concluding sections of the novel *Il regno doloroso* reminds us: the minutest and the least remarkable accidents of existence tacitly explicate the hidden and otherwise mysterious codes of life.[5] In this novel, though, there is a more complex staging of the reflections and meditations that pile up in the book. In fact, most annotations are jotted down while observing different characters (Aurelio, Leo, Doriana) living quotidian moments, apparently insignificant until they are filled with the thoughts of the characters themselves or the omniscient voice observing them.

---

vols. (Università di Bologna, Ravenna: Longo Editore, 1992), vol. 2, pp. 105-120. Regarding the question of the "writer between two worlds," see also Peter Carravetta, "Poesaggio," and Paolo Valesio, "I Fuochi della Tribù," in Peter Carravetta, Paolo Valesio, eds., *Poesaggio. Poeti Italiani d'America* (Quinto di Treviso: Pagus Edizioni, 1993), pp. 9-26, 255-290. Valesio's reflection on the condition of in-betwenness is pervasive in his writings: see also Paolo Valesio, "Il silenzio interlunare," in Michelangelo Zizzi, *Il Sud e la Luna. Per una geografia della semantica in Vittorio Bodini attraverso la lingua,* Con un saggio introduttivo di Paolo Valesio (Bari: Levante Editori, 1999), pp. I-XIV. Among the narrative writings, see also Paolo Valesio, *S'incontrano gli amanti. Tre storie interoceaniche* (Rome: Edizioni Empiria, 1993). On this aspect of Valesio's writings, see Rosario Scrimieri, "*Prose in Poesia* de Paolo Valesio: una escritura entre dos territorios," in Aurora Conde, Ana María Leyra, eds., *La Europa de la Escritura* (Madrid: Ediciones de la Discreta, 2004), pp. 255-281; and "La poetica dell'anima naturale nelle *Prose in Poesia* di Paolo Valesio," in *Poetiche: Rivista di Letteratura,* vol.8, n.2, 2006, pp. 174-208.
[4] P. Valesio, "Writer between Two Worlds," in *Differentia,* nos. 3-4, 1989, p.260. Regarding the intersection of ethics and aesthetics in Valesio's both critical and creative works, see Enzo Neppi, "The Ethics of Aesthetics: The Theme of the Hero and the Victim in the Work of Paolo Valesio," in *Poetics Today,* vol.16, n.2, Summer 1995, pp. 345-362.
[5] Paolo Valesio, *Il Regno Doloroso* (Milan: Spirali Edizioni, 1983).

"Poetry, Dialogue, Silence"

However, this depiction of the development of Valesio's critical thinking risks to remain trapped in the very contradiction that Valesio's theory wants to avoid and solve: the counter-position of two different phases in which the first may even be considered strictly speaking scholarly and academic, followed by a second phase in which novels and collections of poems risk to overshadow and outweigh his critical and theoretical efforts. In fact, the assumption may be that with *Novantiqua* a new phase in Valesio's thinking begins, which is opposite to and totally different than the previous phase. That previous phase had been that of *Strutture dell'allitterazione*, a study that seems to belong to the technical discourse of a specific discipline that can be broadly defined as linguistics.[6] Two observations must be considered that reconcile the temptation of looking at the two phases as disjoined: one is the constant preoccupation with the study of rhetoric in the three major theoretical works (*Strutture dell'allitterazione, Novantiqua,* and *Ascoltare il silenzio*), whereas the other is a shift from the conviction of a discourse founded in the dialectical process to one that opens to a belief in the dialogue.

This is a crucial step in Valesio's writing process and in the procession of his works; indeed, this step seems to be essential in order for the procession to start. In *Strutture dell'allitterazione* there is a constant preoccupation with the oppositional order of language, where the very interest in the linguistic structure is spawned from a number of models that go from the strictly scholarly study of Edward Sapir to the Marxian and Marxist elaboration of the concept of structure itself.[7] Yet, in that book there is also the lesson of anoth-

---

[6] Paolo Valesio, *Strutture dell'Allitterazione: grammatica, retorica e folklore verbale* (Bologna: Nicola Zanichelli, 1967).
[7] Valesio translated and edited Edward Sapir, *Language: An Introduction to the Study of Speech*, New York: Harcourt, Brace & World, Inc., 1921 (*Il linguaggio. Introduzione alla linguistica,* a cura di Paolo Valesio, Turin: Giulio Einaudi Editore, 1969); Edward Sapir, *Culture, Language and Personality,*

er linguist whose own work is perhaps more congenial to Valesio's desire to break away from the constraints of a discipline, of any discipline: Roman Jakobson.[8] In the third chapter on "L'allitterazione e le figure retoriche," Valesio inserts a telling paragraph describing the overarching project of the book:

> Come abbiamo detto (e come abbiamo visto or ora, e come vedremo ancora) le distinzioni sono necessarie, anzi indispensabili. D'altra parte, precisando queste e simili distinzioni, noi non vogliamo erigere delle barriere isolatrici fra l'allitterazione e le strutture linguistiche vicine a essa: al contrario, il tema metodologicamente fondamentale di questo libro è quello della possibilità (e necessità), come alternativa da un lato alla confusione fra l'allitterazione e i fenomeni affini, dall'altro lato alla delimitazione troppo rigida di questi fenomeni, di una visione *dialettica* dei rapporti fra l'allitterazione e i fenomeni vicini.[9]

This paragraph is significant not only because it explains the object of study in the book, but also because it is structured in a dialectical fashion, where the *dialektiké* founds it-

---

Selected Essays. Edited by David G. Mandelbaum, Berkeley – Los Angeles – London: The University of California Press, 1949 (*Cultura, Linguaggio e Personalità*, Turin: Giulio Einaudi Editore, 1972). In the "Introduzione" to *Il Linguaggio,* Valesio laments the lack of "una collaborazione fra linguistica e analisi marxista della società" (p. XXV), of which he finds no traces either in Sapir or in Bloomfield. Regarding the junction of technical and ideological discourses, one might want to consider a small, yet significant, instance like the following: about ready to quote a paragraph from an article by Dwight Bolinger, Valesio refers to "a context for which I feel a technical solidarity (it is the discourse of a linguist) and an ideological sympathy (it is a critique, in a progressive perspective, of political and social jargon in the United States today)" (*Novantiqua*, p. 62).
[8] Paolo Valesio collaborated with Roman Jakobson in writing at least one article together: "*Vocabulorum Constructio* in Dante's sonnet 'Se vedi li occhi miei,'" in *Studi Danteschi*, vol. 43, 1966, pp. 7-33.
[9] P. Valesio, *Strutture dell'Allitterazione*, pp. 45-46.

self on the rhetoric of counterpart, *antístrophos*, as Aristotle calls it in the first sentence of his treatise.[10] However, as Valesio states in a later book, this is "one possible concept of dialectic" (*Novantiqua* 66), whereas he wants to go beyond this kind of dialectic. This is the task of the elaboration presented in the third chapter of *Novantiqua* on "Rhetoric, Ideology, and Dialectic."

Before moving to that work, though, it is necessary to insist on some aspects of dialectic that are at the core of the linguistic and rhetorical discourse in *Strutture dell'Allitterazione*. The fourth chapter of this book, "L'allitterazione, le figure retoriche e la grammatica," proved to be a decisive step not only for the discourse developed in the book, but also in view of the further paths that Valesio's thought took in the subsequent critical works. After pointing out how the intersection of difference and similarity in the case of *derivatio* is predominant for the former and less evident for the latter, Valesio concludes:

> [...] In questa situazione, la funzione peculiare della *derivatio* è la seguente: Mettere in risalto (contro i rapporti di differenza) i rapporti di somiglianza fra certe strutture grammaticali, illuminando un'area solitamente oscura nella struttura della lingua [...][11]

Highlighting the relations of similarity rather than those of difference is already an invitation to a shift from dialectic to dialogue: from the dialectic of the difference to the dialogue of the similarity. Valesio himself makes such a statement, which is destined to have repercussions more on the development of his intellectual interests and theoretical approach to them than on the linguistic and rhetorical studies

---

[10] Aristotle, *The "Art" of Rhetoric*, Transl. by John Henry Freese (London – New York: W. Heinemann – G. P. Putnam's Sons, 1926). Cf. also Valesio, *Novantiqua*, p. 65.
[11] *Strutture dell'allitterazione*, p. 97.

that are his primary concern in his first critical book. In fact, moving on to discuss paronomasia, Valesio reaffirms the same principle he has seen at work in the case of the derivation:[12] "[...] Anche nel caso della paronomasia, come già abbiamo visto per la derivatio, è possibile indicare, accanto alle linee fondamentali dei suoi rapporti dialettici con la struttura grammaticale, anche una serie di punti in cui si verificano incontri specifici." In these words of verification in the work of rhetorical figures, there is already the seed of that thinking process that leads Valesio to privilege the rhetoric of conjunction and inclusiveness over one of disjunction and exclusiveness.

By looking at the dialectical process in its polarities, one risks to ignore the mediating passages, which instead reveal that the shift from one state to the next does not take place according to sharp turns, but rather according to smooth nuances. It is Valesio himself who points this out in a summarizing moment of the methodological principles of his work:

> [...] In primo luogo, ogni analisi di strutture linguistiche che sia, insieme, concreta e proiettata su un orizzonte vasto (a qualunque livello, e con qualunque tipo di metalinguaggio) è uno sforzo di individuazione dei *contrasti dialet-*

---

[12] Ibid., p. 104. Paronomasia remains an important concern in Valesio's writings: see for instance Paolo Valesio, "Il reale e l'irreale sono due in uno. Valedittorio," in Victoria Surliuga, ed., *Analogie del mondo. Scritti su Paolo Valesio* (Modena: Edizioni del Laboratorio, 2008), pp. 11-39. It is worth exploring the intersection of rhetorical figures of duplicity such as paronomasia and hendiadys, which seems to be a fundamental dynamics of Valesio's critical thinking: see on this Paolo Valesio, "La macchina 'morbida' di Marinetti," in *Annali d'Italianistica*, vol. 27, 2009; Federico Luisetti and Luca Somigli, eds., *A Century of Futurism: 1909-2009*, pp. 243-262. For a significant use of paronomasia, see at least the names of the characters Nerio and Nilio in dialogue in the book of poems by Paolo Valesio, *Le Isole del Lago*, Prefazione di Mario Lunetta (Venice: Edizioni del Leone, 1990), but also Paolo Valesio, *Il volto quasi umano. Poesie-dardi 2003-2005* (Bologna: Lombar Key, 2009).

"Poetry, Dialogue, Silence"

> *tici*, ovvero delle *forze dialettiche*, della lingua; e questo vale per le strutture retoriche così come vale per le strutture più propriamente grammaticali. In secondo luogo, i *contrasti dialettici* fra strutture linguistiche diverse non debbono essere considerate (appunto perché dialettici) come divisioni nette e assolute, tali da implicare esclusioni reciproche; bensì (come abbiamo già detto più volte) come rappresentanti poli opposti, ma collegati da una vasta gamma di situazioni intermedie.[13]

This chapter is fundamental in Valesio's exploration of the dialectical nature of several aspects of linguistics and rhetorics ("il contrasto dialettico fra metafora e metonimia;" "la retorica non è un bel manto gettato sulla grammatica, ma una parte integrante della struttura generale della lingua, che si trova in un rapporto intimo e dialettico con la parte propriamente grammaticale;" "la dialettica fra livello fonologico [...] e livello morfologico nella struttura specifica dell'allitterazione.").[14] More importantly, in the last two sections of the chapter Valesio focuses on two quite different dialectical tensions. Although he still wants to discuss "la dinamicità delle figure retoriche da un punto di vista storico," [15] and the "problema della genesi, intesa sia come ontogenesi sia come filogenesi, dell'allitterazione,"[16] in doing so, he inserts two important issues that remain crucial for the remainder of Valesio's critical thinking. The reference is to another form of "rapporto dialettico: da un lato, la tendenza a privilegiare la dimensione ermeneutica della lingua (la lingua come chiara e diretta spiegazione della realtà), [...]. Dall'altro lato, la tendenza a privilegiare la dimensione estetica della lingua, che si attua nella creazione di strutture do-

---

[13] Ibid., p. 114.
[14] Ibid., pp. 126, 130, 146.
[15] Ibid., p. 184.
[16] Ibid., p 185.

tate di regolarità complesse, di figure; [...]." This tension between hermeneutics and aesthetics takes another complex turn in the last section of the chapter, when Valesio grants attention to "il ruolo dell'allitterazione sullo sfondo di due modi divergenti di costruire rituali religiosi: la religione concepita soprattutto come sistema di rapporti *chiari*, sanciti con precisione giuridica, fra l'uomo e la divinità, e al lato opposto la religione concepita soprattutto come magia, cioè concepita all'insegna della «non chiarezza» dal punto di vista del senso commune."[17] The tension between these two modes of religion is to be found not only in the theoretical reflection of *Novantiqua* and especially *Ascoltare il Silenzio*, but also, and perhaps more importantly, in the novels, short stories and collections of poems that Valesio wrote over a forty-year time span.

However, the journey toward the elaboration of those ideas is a slow process that is manifested in the conclusion of this first critical book. In fact, the next-to-the-last paragraph of *Strutture dell'Allitterazione*, in which the summarizing discourse on "l'ontogenesi dell'allitterazione" moves from a

---

[17] Ibid., p. 187. For further aspects of dialectics in *Strutture dell'Allitterazione*, see chapter 6, pp. 221, 225-226; chapter 7, pp. 255-257; chapter 10, pp. 352-353; and the "Appendice," pp. 375, 406. For his interest in the intersection between linguistics and religion, but also psychology, it may be useful to consider the two volumes by Sapir that Valesio translated and, in particular, some articles in those volumes: Edward Sapir, "The Meaning of Religion," originally in *The American Mercury*, vol. 15, September 1928, pp. 72-79; "Religions and Religious Phenomena," in Baker Brownell, ed., *Religious Life* (New York: D. Van Nostrand Company, 1929), pp. 11-33; "Cultural Anthropology and Psychiatry," in *Journal of Abnormal and Social Psychology*, vol. 27, 1933, pp. 29-42; and "Psychiatric and Cultural Pitfalls in the Business of Getting a Living," in *Mental Health*, n. 9, 1939, pp. 37-44), later collected in *Culture, Language and Personality*, pp. 120-139, 140-163, 172-193. In the meantime, in the introduction to the Italian translation of Sapir's study *Language*, Valesio recalls Sapir's interest in the expansion of his own anthropological curiosity in the direction of psychology, in particular, his engagement with Freud's and Jung's psychoanalysis (cf. in the Italian text, *Il Linguaggio*, p. XVI).

"Poetry, Dialogue, Silence"

strictly linguistic level focusing on "l'articolazione labiale" in Italian and English to a psycholinguistic one ("il fenomeno psicolinguistico della ripetizione allitterante e il fenomeno essenzialmente psicologico della ripetizione balbuziente"), concludes with a prudent, but also telling, hypothesis:

> [...] Questo porta in primo piano l'ipotesi di tipo psicoanalitico che l'allitterazione e la balbuzie siano generate dal medesimo complesso di impulsi, nell'ambito dell'erotismo orale. Crediamo di non esagerare dicendo che questo *cauto inizio di conferma* di questa ipotesi apre un nuovo periodo di studi sulle relazioni fra la dimensione retorica, "esplicita", e la dimensione psicologica, "nascosta", della struttura della lingua.[18]

If this precaution is necessary before making statements within the discipline in question, statements that actually move out of that discipline itself, then it is a prudent attitude that Valesio officially abandons only ten years later, when he writes his first novel, *L'Ospedale di Manhattan*, and his first book of poems, *Prose in poesia*.[19] These books mark the abandonment of prudence as a gesture that characterizes the scholarly works, *de facto* ending Valesio's apparently primary interest in linguistics. Furthermore, the publication of his first novel and collection of poems declares his militant engagement in all forms and genres of writing.

It is telling that the novel is preceded by a "Pre-fazione" by the author, that is, a critical intervention in which a few issues emerge that accompany Valesio's writing from this novel on for the next four decades. Among these concerns, there are a few that would relate to a reflection on the struc-

---

[18] Ibid., p. 407.
[19] Paolo Valesio, *L'Ospedale di Manhattan* (Rome: Editori Riuniti, 1978); Paolo Valesio, *Prose in Poesia* (Milan: Guanda, 1979). On Valesio's narrative, see Luigi Fontanella, "Per Paolo Valesio prosatore. Appunti di lettura," in *Analogie del Mondo*, pp. 70-81.

tural aspect of the "romanzo come discorso, cosí di cognizione come di espressione,"[20] to use Valesio's own words. But there are also others that are more concerned with the novel as an expression of "an ethics of solitude," to use a phrase from the critical essay "The Writer between Two Worlds." The narrating voice in the novel *L'Ospedale di Manhattan* oscillates in a reflection on isolation and solitude – "Un limite è che esso è stato concepito dentro un fondo isolamento" … "Nella solitudine, almeno, non si sente il chiacchierío. Certo, nella solitudine s'annidano anche la noia e la nausea, fino al terrore (è questa una situazione delineata senza indulgenza, all'apertura del romanzo.)"[21] – which are two of the most pervasive motives of Valesio's writings. The discourse of the novel, in turn, as it wants to move beyond the consideration of merely formal or structural concerns, articulates the interchange between cosmopolitanism and cosmopolitics, which is explicitly elaborated as a living between two worlds: "[...] Ma una precisazione: il cosmopolitismo non dev'essere confuso con un'alternanza puramente meccanica di due residenze, come modo di organizzare gli affari o il piacere. Cosmopolita è solo colui che è sinceramente diviso – e dilacerato – tra i due luoghi, che di volta in volta aderisce all'uno o all'altro con tutta la sua passione e la sua nostalgia di radici."[22] This interchange, in turn, requires living on the margins of micropolitics: "[...] pare che la politica del cosmopolitismo non possa essere altro che una micropolitica."[23] More importantly, that preface ends with a project for a materialist form of thought: "un pensiero materialista è fecondo soprattutto in quanto veda (traccia d'una riflessione di Heidegger) l'esistente, in suoi vari aspetti e livelli, come materiale di e-laborazione, tale che un lavorío costante lo

---

[20] *L'Ospedale di Manhattan*, p. 16.
[21] Ibid., pp. 13-14.
[22] Ibid., p. 10.
[23] Ibid., p. 9.

forma e de-forma."[24] To this follow considerations on religious discourse as object of a discourse: "Dopo il marxismo – pensava il romanziere (cosí restando nel solco della piú vulgata tradizione) – il discorso religioso è possibile soltanto come discorso-oggetto (storia delle religioni, *et similia*)." And as subject of a discourse: "Oggi, quando il discorso religioso come discorso-soggetto (discorso che spiega) sembra avere una forza rinnovata, equiparare il marxismo con il laicismo integrale significherebbe condannare questa teoria a una posizione marginale, rispetto al dibattito piú vivo."[25] To Valesio, the project then is one in which a materialist criticism assumes the task of recovering the soul and joining it with a social discourse: "l'anima si fa sentire con la forza del suo lavoro materiale. Coniugare anima e società – ecco il compito della critica materialista ... [I]l *lavoro politico* di Gesú – questo il tema di una critica materialistica."[26]

Therefore, in the novel *L'ospedale di Manhattan*, Valesio is elaborating a novel as discourse, but he is also repositioning his rhetorical interest in dialectic in terms of dialogue: "La politica del quotidiano (al livello suo minimo, senza alcuna apologia) fonde e fonda dialetticamente il pubblico con il privato."[27] The aspects that the form of the dialogue take in this context are several and perhaps the most common is that of the objection that interrupts what would otherwise be a monologue and presents the viewpoint that another entity would pose: "Opporrete: che in questo modo tutti, uomini e donne, sono eguagliati, tutti ridotti allo stesso livello; tutti,

---

[24] Ibid., p. 17.
[25] Ibid.
[26] Ibid., pp. 18, 20.
[27] Ibid., p. 33. See also p. 79. Regarding this novel and "Quotidianity," see the section with this title in the chapter "Tropics of Ordinary Experience," in Paul Colilli, *The Idea of a Living Spirit: Poetic Logic as a Contemporary Theory* (Toronto: University of Toronto Press, 1997), pp. 79-92; see also by Paul Colilli, "Le allegorie di tutti i giorni," in *La Redenzione delle Cose. Saggio sul Pensiero Poetante di Paolo Valesio* (Pesaro: Metauro Edizioni, 2006), pp. 49-79.

insomma, animali piú o meno sofferenti, in attesa del colpo di grazia."[28] This sentence is in contrast with the following questions that the narrating voice asks in vain. The objection is sometimes formulated as a question that then the narrating voice answers.[29] Then, the question is integral to the discourse so that the monologue becomes a dialogue, even when it is staged as different postures of the same voice.

However, one of the most striking moments of dialogue takes place in the first pages of the novel, in an episode recalling a moment at dawn in the house of childhood:

> Cosí: è stato amoroso il gesto di mia madre durante il piú recente tra i miei brevi ritorni (quando ho dormito, dopo quanti anni? nella casa dei genitori). Mi era accaduto (ed è raro per me) di dare un colpo o due di tosse, nel crepuscolo del mattino; e dalla loro stanza in fondo al corridoio (mio padre dormiva profondo) la madre ha subito fatto udire un suo breve colpo di tosse secca. Da anni non ci parlavamo cosí seriamente; e (ripartito da quella casa, per l'esilio abituale e fino ad un certo punto volontario) trascorreranno certo molti anni lunghi, prima che noi due possiamo di nuovo parlare a questo livello fondamentale.[30]

There are several aspects that attract attention in this paragraph and that are wrapped in the parentheses: the question without answer about the time that went by since the last time the speaking voice slept in the house of his parents; his father's deep sleep, which may assume symbolic connotations, especially vis-à-vis the mother's attentive wakefulness; the reference to an exile that is rendered bitterer by the fact that it is not as voluntary as it seems, that it is such only

---

[28] Ibid., p. 34.
[29] Ibid., p. 34, but also pp. 38, 50, 65, 85, 105, 165, 167. Perhaps it is not by chance that this questioning strategy tends to disappear in the second part of the novel.
[30] Ibid., pp. 33-34.

to a certain extent. Therefore, the parentheses are constantly opening a dialogue with the remainder of the paragraph, with the main motif of the paragraph: the cough as a dialogic device. It is the most profound dialogue because it lives on voices that, rather than uttering verbally meaningful sounds, well-rounded words, a coherent discourse, set their level of communication on the noise of a dry cough in the silence of the morning hour in the familiar house. It is a dialogue in which monologues are parenthetically inserted, in which questions significantly open new scenarios rather than look for set answers. These fragments of possible monologues are open wounds next to the unspoken detail of communication. This is already an apparition of "la via dei minimi" that frames the experiences of *Il Regno Doloroso*.[31]

To be sure, in the preface to the first novel silence is mentioned as a solution against the chatter of the different cultural sides:[32]

> Tra quei due discorsi striduli, ugualmente chiassosi ed oppressivi, s'apre una breccia; la mossa allora piú prontamente disponibile, la piú diffusa in effetto, è riempire questa trincea con un cumulo di silenzio. È il silenzio che segna la morte civile di tanti intellettuali sradicati; è il cosmopolitismo come malattia e condanna, come privilegio ambiguo vissuto con un misto di cinismo e di vergogna.[33]

It is a defensive notion of silence against the oppression of inauthentic discourses to which the uprooted expatriates

---

[31] "La via dei minimi" is the title of the opening and concluding chapters of Valesio's second novel, *Il regno doloroso*, which came out in 1983.

[32] Chatter is an important philosophical aspect explored by Martin Heidegger, *Being and Time*, Transl. Joan Stambaugh (Albany: State University of New York Press, 2010), par. 35. Regarding "idle talk" in Valesio's work, see P. Colilli, "The Folds of Everyday Being," in *The Idea of a Living Spirit*, pp. 93-123.

[33] *L'Ospedale di Manhattan*, p. 12. And see "il chiacchierío," p. 14.

are condemned. To this mortal blow they oppose silence. These first reflections on silence relate to an almost nihilistic conception of silence itself: once again, dialectic plays a crucial role not only in the theoretical elaborations of *Novantiqua*, but in the novels Valesio writes at the same time. A striking instance is found in *Il Regno Doloroso*, an instance that deserves more careful attention than what is allowed here:[34]

> Quando, in una sala congressuale appena cominciata una conferenza, un'estranea viene a sedersi accanto a un estraneo: prolungare, attraverso tutta quella conferenza ed oltre, il silenzio significa già creare un legame; anche se poi basta superare la soglia d'un momento in piú, per passare – dal legame addirittura passionale che stava per saldarsi – al reciproco negletto totale. Secondo, infatti, un ritmo preciso:
> Primo – silenzio potenzialmente ostile.
> Secondo – silenzio pieno di semi d'emozioni, scintille o facelline di sentimenti. E a questo punto, biforcazione:
> Terzo, può essere – una battuta che infrange il silenzio, intreccia (ma per tempo breve) una conversazione; crea una relazione, ma il prezzo pagato è quello di subito banalizzarla. Oppure:
> Terzo, è – continuazione ostinata nel silenzio; dunque, ogni rapporto possibile finisce – con una punta d'ostilità – nel nulla.[35]

---

[34] Interestingly enough, the fourth and last chapter in *Novantiqua* is titled "The Structure of the Rheme" (pp. 145-358), whereas the fourth (but not last anymore) chapter of *Ascoltare il Silenzio* is titled "I percorsi della ipsilon" (pp. 205-293). That is, the title itself of chapters, the latter of which may be considered the translation into Italian of the former, reveals a shift from the rhetorical strategy that is very common in *L'Ospedale di Manhattan*, of which the rheme becomes the symptomatic linguistic device, to the reflection "Alle frontiere della linguistica" (*Ascoltare il Silenzio*, p.211) on the Greek letter upsilon. The quotation from *Il Regno Doloroso* alludes to the "biforcazione" in this letter.

[35] *Il Regno Doloroso* (Milano: Spirali, 1983), pp. 111-112.

To be sure, it is silence that pulses according to a precise rhythm, rather than the lecture that plays in the background. That rhythm seems to follow the scansion of dialectic (thesis, antithesis, synthesis), but all of a sudden the third phase breaks into two options, it opens itself to a binary solution in which the order of the discourse becomes crucial: the potential hostility of the first movement becomes the temperate and continuous obstinacy of a relationship in silence. Even considering the touch of irony that concludes the logic of the passage, silence ends up being identified with "nulla." In this respect, the fifth chapter of *Ascoltare il silenzio*, that was added to the chapters that structure the discourse in *Novantiqua*, is crucial in order to measure Valesio's movement toward silence. This procession is possible thanks to an understanding of writing that, rather than keeping theory and praxis separate, joins them as though they were one act in two movements.[36] The shift from dialectic to dialogue takes place in the realm of silence. To be sure, it is a shift that finds resistance at first.[37] Perhaps the most poignant instance of such a shift is the fifth chapter of *Ascoltare il silenzio*, titled "La retorica, il silenzio e l'ascolto:" this chapter is an addition to the chapters of *Novantiqua*. It is telling that the fifth chapter added to the Italian version five years later, repeats the gesture announced in the title of the third chapter in both books: "Rhetoric, Ideology, and Dialectic," in *Novantiqua*,[38] which is basically the same, "Retorica, ideologia e dialettica," in *Ascoltare il Silenzio*.[39] This is a triad that is at the root of the narrative discourse in *L'Ospedale di Manhattan*, but the

---

[36] Paolo Valesio, "Il laboratorio di scrittura: dalla 'teoria e prassi' alla teoria/prassi," in Tullio De Mauro, Pietro Pedace, Annio G. Stasi, eds., *Teoria e pratica della scrittura creativa* (Rome: Editore Coop *Controluce*, 1996), pp. 151-156.
[37] Cf. *Novantiqua.*, p. 107.
[38] Ibid., pp 61-144.
[39] *Ascoltare il silenzio*, pp. 109-204.

chapter offers a replacement with a different triad: "La retorica, il silenzio e l'ascolto." [40] The trilogy in question in the title is the protagonist of "il *secondo* movimento della retorica-come-filosofia,"[41] in which rhetoric re-evaluates silence not so much as a limit to verbal expression, but as a source for a more profound use of language. The gesture of the statue of the so-called "Arringatore" in the Archeological Museum in Florence is evoked through a dialogue from Albert Camus' play *Caligula* (Act IV, scene 12): dialectic as dialogue leads to a reflection on silence in the possible interpretations of the gesture of the statue. By the same token, ideology (especially Marxism) and dialectic are supplanted by silence and listening, that is, two different ways in which the Greek letter upsilon, representing the essence of rhetorics, branches off.[42] The very passage from *Il Regno Doloroso* modulates the three stages on the interpretation of silence, that is, of listening to silence, in a dialectical process that, rather than culminating in the synthesis, refracts itself in the continuity of silence at the risk of nothingness.[43]

---

[40] Ibid., pp. 295-448.

[41] Ibid., p. 296.

[42] Regarding this aspect, see Paolo Valesio, "A Remark on Silence and Listening," in *Rivista di Estetica*, vol.XXVI, nn.19-20 (1985), pp. 17-44. A different version is in *Oral Tradition*, vol.2, n.1 (1987), pp. 286-300. Considering the counterpart of silence, reticence, see also Paolo Valesio, "Lucia, ovvero: La 'reticentia' nei *Promessi Sposi*," in *Filologia e Critica*, vol.13, n.2, 1988, pp. 207-238; and in Giovanni Manetti, ed., *Leggere "I Promessi Sposi"* (Milan: Bompiani, 1989), pp. 145-174. On this aspect of Valesio's poetics, see Franco Masciandaro, "La poetica dell'ascolto di Paolo Valesio: Appunti su *Piazza delle Preghiere Massacrate*," in *Il Lettore di Provincia*, n.122 (2005), pp. 43-58.

[43] Regarding silence and the role it plays in Valesio's theory and in this novel, see P. Colilli, "The Mind of Silence," in *The Idea of a Living Spirit*, pp. 49-72 (Colilli develops also a comparison between Valesio's and Giorgio Agamben's insights on silence). Regarding the importance of Carl Gustav Jung for Valesio's "rhetoric as theory," see also P. Colilli, "The Living Spirit of the Semiosphere," in *The Idea of a Living Spirit*, pp. 173-183.

Commenting in passing on the poem "Silenzio" by Vittorio Bodini, Valesio writes:[44] "Scrivere una poesia che tematizzi il silenzio è una sfida assai difficile, perché il silenzio è l'ossigeno della poesia, il suo indispensabile elemento costitutivo." "Una delle più costanti preoccupazioni nella ricerca silenziaria è quella di articolare il silenzio [...]." However, Valesio himself has accepted that challenge and in his own writings he not only critically listens to silence, but he also wants to articulate silence, as he does especially in his narrative and poetic writings.

Listening to silence is a search that from the pages of the theory elaborated in *Ascoltare il Silenzio* pours into the writing of poetry. It is not by chance that all but one of the books of poems by Valesio follow after the publication of that theoretical book, starting with *La Rosa Verde* and continuing with collections having the telling title alluding to dialogue (*Dialogo del Falco e dell'Avvoltoio*) or collections in which the dialogue is implicitly staged by the protagonists of the poems (*Le isole del lago, Avventure dell'Uomo e del Figlio*).[45] Sometimes the dialogue unfolds between two collections, especially those published in the same year, as though they were two sides of the same argument.[46] The form of the dialogue is also employed in a critical and literary essay such as *Dialogo coi Volanti*.[47] The dialogue becomes a duologue, not so much as "a reasonably well-constructed duologue for two experi-

---

[44] Valesio, "Il silenzio interlunare," in M. Zizzi, *Il Sud e la Luna*, pp. XII, XIII.

[45] Paolo Valesio, *La Rosa Verde* (Padua: Editoriale Clessidra, 1987); Paolo Valesio, *Dialogo del Falco e dell'Avvoltoio* (Milan: Editrice Nuovi Autori, 1987); Paolo Valesio, *Avventure dell'Uomo e del Figlio* (Marina di Minturno: Caramanica Editore, 1996).

[46] Besides the two collections of poems published in 1987, *La Rosa Verde* and *Dialogo del Falco e dell'Avvoltoio*, one needs to consider *Le Isole del Lago* and *La Campagna dell'Ottantasette* (Milan: Vanni Scheiwiller, 1990).

[47] Paolo Valesio, *Dialogo coi Volanti* (Naples: Edizioni Cronopio, 1997). Regarding this book, see Laura Wittman, "A proposito di un dialogo post-francescano," in *YIP: Yale Italian Poetry*, vol.VII, 2003, pp. 257-267.

enced performers," as Noel Coward would say, but rather as a complete dramatic performance that is limited to two reasoning partners.[48] Furthermore, duologue offers an etymological aspect that dialogue cannot offer and that allows Valesio to justify a further shift from dialectic to dialogue and then to duologue. Whereas the term 'dialogue' is etymologically founded on the contrast between two antagonists (the prefix /dia/ is crucial in this respect) and linked to terms such as 'dialect' and 'dialectic,' the term 'duologue' is more descriptive, as the first element of the compound word sets a contrast with 'monologue.' Therefore, the dialectical contrast implied in the dialogue is attenuated in the duologue. One of the first moments in which Valesio tacitly elaborates this understanding of the duologue is "Il poeta come opera (Duologo fra un poeta e un suo amico)."[49] Thus, the duologue overcomes once and for all the implicit dialectic of the dialogue: whereas Socrates' dialogues are supposed to prove a

---

[48] Noel Coward employed the phrase to refer to his play *Private Lives* and to his dramatic style in general.
[49] Paolo Valesio, "Il poeta come opera (Duologo fra un poeta e un suo amico)," in *L'ANELLO che non tiene: Journal of Modern Italian Literature*, op. cit., pp. 107-121. At the end of this piece, the two characters debate "una differenza tra solitudine e isolamento" (p.120), which recalls pages in *L'Ospedale di Manhattan*, with the striking difference that in the novel there is a monologue that is desperately trying to establish a dialogue or, better yet, a duologue with a partner. It is important to insist on the roles of the two characters, as they support each other in the elaboration of a thought that does not belong to either one of them and that is ultimately the expression of a thinking process or, rather, procession that takes place through them. In this respect, Leopardi's model of the *Operette Morali* must have been present to Valesio's writing of duologues, as the several poems in *Il volto quasi umano* ("Principium individuationis," "Amore-e-Morte," "Luna d'inverno:" pp. 98, 172, 228) dedicated to "il conte" seem to confirm. In particular, the first poem mentioned, which is not technically dedicated to Leopardi, is, however, a good example of duologue, as the poem itself is connected to the epigraph from the *Zibaldone* (958) as a form of reply or, better yet, collaboration, as the very double gesture of concession and contradiction in the first line of that poem ("Può aver ragione il conte; e d'altra parte") remarks.

truth that he already owned and embodied at the beginning of each dialogue, Valesio's understanding of the duologue is a further deepening of a logical path undertaken by Leopardi in his dialogues in the *Operette Morali*, in which neither agent in the dialogue possesses the truth at the beginning and not necessarily at the end either.

The book of poems *Il Volto quasi Umano* is a summa, so to speak, of an intense lustrum of Valesio's poetry writing that he himself jots in the image of the ""Dardi": "con allusione, come ho già avuto occasione di indicare, a un termine tecnico del linguaggio devozionale, giaculatoria, vale a dire: preghiera breve lanciata verso/contro il cielo come un dardo."[50] Some of these poems inevitably recall situations encountered in previous collections, but some of them even intersect concepts discussed in the critical writings. In this respect, "La Y"[51] is an emblematic poem, as the first and last lines are a lapidary summary of Valesio's journey since the writing of *Novantiqua*: "Si affaccia in questi giorni a tanti bivii: / è come un semicerchio di alberi a ipsilon / [...] è sorta l'illusione della scelta." The Greek letter upsilon now only proposes the illusion of the choice, whereas the reflection

---

[50] P. Valesio, "Nota d'autore," in *Il Volto quasi Umano*, p.15. Although the dates indicated in the book suggest otherwise, Valesio himself in that note specifies the chronology of the books on which the "dardi" piled up. Interestingly enough, Valesio digs into the etymology of the terms 'dardo' and, more importantly, '*iaculum*,' remarking that "la coincidenza etimologica fra due termini così eterogenei potrebbe prestarsi a discussione sui complicati modi di coesistenza fra il sacro e il profano: [...]" (p.15). Valesio's writing practice is a living example of such a coexistence: see for instance Paolo Valesio, *Sonetos Profanos y Sacros* [Traducción colectiva del Taller de Traducción Literaria de la Universidad de La Laguna, Taller de Traducción Literaria], (La Laguna, Tenerife: Ediciones Canarias, 1996) (these sonnets form a section in P. Valesio, *Avventure dell'Uomo e del Figlio* and in Paolo Valesio, *Every Afternoon Can Make the World Stand Still: Thirty Sonnets 1987-2000*, Transl. Michael Palma (Stony Brook, NY: Gradiva Publications, 2002).
[51] Cf. *Il volto quasi umano*, p. 144.

aims at silence: "un silenzio diverso dal suo abituale."[52] However, the need for the duologue remains constant and it takes shape in the form of several poems: "Duologo della dolenza," "*Duologus de fide*," "Il duologo occulto," "Duologo della cristologia quotidiana," "Duologo delle piccole croci."[53] Unidentified voices speak about the mystery of Christ, his Passion, the faith in him, the need to live that faith in our daily lives.

This motif, which is overtly evident in Valesio's poetry at least since *Le Isole del Lago*, is the unfolding of an intuition that resides at least in one important moment in *Novantiqua* that is worth considering. In the first pages of the second chapter, as Valesio lays out the plan for the discussion of "the Aristotelian Dilemma," he writes: "The ontology of rhetoric as developed here is not an ontology of ultimate essences: in fact, the horizons of this region are those of skepticism and dialectic (two attitudes that seem alien, not to say contrary, to the basic slant of phenomenology)."[54] In the Italian version of the book, *Ascoltare il Silenzio*, this phrase is tellingly adjusted: "L'ontologia della retorica qui sviluppata non è un'ontologia di essenze ultime in senso fenomenologico. I poli della regione che vien qui portata alla presenza sono quelli dello scetticismo da un lato, e della spiritualità in stretto colloquio con il religioso (si veda sopra tutto il capitolo quinto) dall'altro."[55] Dialectic is now translated into the dialogue between spirituality and the religious realm.

It is at this translation that Valesio's writings aim, at the dialogue and exchange between different facets, rather than phases, of the spirit, in which the logical process has become a procession. In turn, this procession lines up voices that did not talk to, but with, one another, as they mold a character

---

[52] Ibid., p. 37.
[53] Ibid., pp. 31, 47, 71, 178, 229.
[54] *Novantiqua*, p. 20.
[55] *Ascoltare il silenzio*, p. 42.

and, if not a statue (let alone that of the orator), at least a face: a *quasi* human face. In so doing, Valesio's poetry embraces the main risk with which the misunderstanding of silence, a hallmark of reticence, threatens the rhythm of the duologue, which lives on the alternation of diction as the art of speech and listening as the fulfillment of silence.[56] The parabola of Valesio's writing takes that risk, of which the poem "Interlocuzione zero" is the embodiment: "'Ti voglio bene': frase che lo aiuta / contro l'affanno del voler morire / ma poi non sa a chi lo sta dicendo."

WORKS CITED

Aristotle, *The "Art" of Rhetoric*. English transl. John Henry Freese [Loeb Classical Library], London – New York: W. Heinemann – G. P. Putnam's Sons, 1926.

Paul Colilli, *The Idea of a Living Spirit: Poetic Logic as a Contemporary Theory*, Toronto – Buffalo – London: University of Toronto Press, 1997.

_____. *La Redenzione delle Cose. Saggio sul Pensiero Poetante di Paolo Valesio*, Pesaro: Metauro Edizioni, 2006.

Luigi Fontanella, "Per Paolo Valesio prosatore. Appunti di lettura," in V. Surliuga, ed. *Analogie del Mondo. Scritti su Paolo Valesio*, Modena: Edizioni del Laboratorio, 2008, pp.70-81.

Martin Heidegger, *Being and Time*, Transl. by Joan Stambaugh, Rev. by Dennis J. Schmidt, Albany: State University of New York Press, 2010.

Roman Jakobson, Paolo Valesio, "Vocabulorum constructio in Dante's sonnet "Se vedi li occhi miei,"" in *Studi Danteschi*, vol.43, 1966, pp.7-33.

Franco Masciandaro, "La poetica dell'ascolto di Paolo Valesio: Appunti su *Piazza delle Preghiere Massacrate*," in *Il Lettore di Provincia*, n.122 (2005), pp.43-58

Enzo Neppi, "The Ethics of Aesthetics: The Theme of the Hero and the Victim in the Work of Paolo Valesio," in *Poetics Today*, vol. 16, n. 2, Summer 1995, pp.345-362

---

[56] Cf. "La piena luce è silenzio," in "*Cogitamentum de lumine*," in *Il Volto quasi Umano*, p.88.

Edward Sapir, "Cultural Anthropology and Psychiatry," in *Journal of Abnormal and Social Psychology*, vol.27, 1933, pp.29-42.

_____. *Culture, Language and Personality*. Ed by David G. Mandelbaum, Berkeley – Los Angeles – London: The University of California Press, 1949 [It. Transl. *Cultura, Linguaggio e Personalità*, Turin: Giulio Einaudi Editore, 1972].

_____. *Language: An Introduction to the Study of Speech*, New York: Harcourt, Brace & World, Inc., 1921 [It. transl. *Il linguaggio. Introduzione alla linguistica*, a cura di Paolo Valesio, Turin: Giulio Einaudi Editore, 1969].

_____. The Meaning of Religion," in *The American Mercury*, vol.15, September 1928, pp.72-79.

_____. Psychiatric and Cultural Pitfalls in the Business of Getting a Living," in *Mental Health*, n. 9, 1939, pp.37-44.

Rosario Scrimieri, "*Prose in Poesia* de Paolo Valesio: una escritura entre dos territorios," in Aurora Conde, Ana María Leyra, eds., *La Europa de la Escritura*, Madrid: Ediciones de la Discreta, 2004, pp.255-281 [It. "La poetica dell'anima naturale nelle *Prose in Poesia* di Paolo Valesio," in *Poetiche: Rivista di Letteratura*, vol. 8, n. 2, 2006, pp.174-208.

Paolo Valesio, *Ascoltare il silenzio. La retorica come teoria*, Bologna: Il Mulino, 1986.

_____. *Avventure dell'Uomo e del Figlio. Poesie*, Marina di Minturno: Caramanica Editore, 1996.

_____. *La Campagna dell'Ottantasette, Poesie e prose-in-poesia*, Prefazione di Guido Guglielmi, Milan: [All'Insegna del Pesce d'Oro] Vanni Scheiwiller, 1990.

_____. *Il Cuore del Girasole (Poesie-Dardi 2001-2002),* Preface by Alberto Bertoni, Genoa - Milan: Marietti, 2006.

_____. *Dardi*, Faenza: I Quaderni del Circolo degli Artisti, 2000.

_____. *Dialogo del Falco e dell'Avvoltoio*, Milan: Editrice Nuovi Autori, 1987.

_____. *Dialogo coi Volanti*, Naples: Edizioni Cronopio, 1997.

_____. *Every Afternoon Can Make the World Stand Still: Thirty Sonnets 1987-2000*.Transl. by Michael Palma, Intr. by John Hollander, Stony Brook, NY: Gradiva Publications, 2002.

_____. Paolo Valesio, *Gabriele D'Annunzio: The Dark Flame*, Translation by Marilyn Migiel, New Haven – London: Yale University Press, 1992.

_____. *Le Isole del Lago*, Pref. Mario Lunetta, Venice: Edizioni del Leone, 1990.

_____. "Il laboratorio di scrittura: dalla 'teoria e prassi' alla 'teoria/prassi'," in Tullio De Mauro, Pietro Pedace, Annio G. Stasi, eds., *Teoria e pratica della scrittura creativa*, Rome: Editore Coop *Controluce*, 1996, pp.151-156

_____. "Lucia, ovvero: La 'reticentia' nei *Promessi Sposi*," in *Filologia e Critica*, vol.13, n.2, 1988, pp.207-238 [then in Giovanni Manetti, ed., *Leggere "I Promessi Sposi"*, Milan: Bompiani, 1989, pp.145-174

_____. "La macchina "morbida" di Marinetti," in *Annali d'Italianistica*, vol.27, 2009: *A Century of Futurism: 1909-2009*, Ed. by Federico Luisetti and Luca Somigli, pp.243-262.

_____. *Novantiqua: Rhetorics as a Contemporary Theory*, Bloomington: Indiana University Press, 1980.

_____. *L'Ospedale di Manhattan*, Rome: Editori Riuniti, 1978.

_____. "Il poeta come opera," in *Il Cobold*, n.17, 1981, pp.1-3.

_____. *Prose in Poesia*, Milan: Guanda, 1979.

_____. "Il reale e l'irreale sono due in uno. Valedittorio," in Victoria Surliuga, ed. *Analogie del mondo. Scritti su Paolo Valesio*, Modena: Edizioni del Laboratorio, 2008, pp.11-39.

_____. *Il Regno Doloroso*, Milan: Spirali Edizioni, 1983.

_____. "A Remark on Silence and Listening," in *Rivista di Estetica*, vol.XXVI, nn.19-20 (1985), pp.17-44; in *Oral Tradition*, vol.2, n.1 (1987), pp.286-300.

_____. Paolo Valesio, *La Rosa Verde*, Padua: Editoriale Clessidra, 1987.

_____. Paolo Valesio, "Lo scrittore fra i due mondi: osservazioni sulla scrittura italiana negli Stati Uniti oggi," in Maria Grazia Vacchina, ed.,*"Langues et peuples:"* [*Actes du Colloque*, Gressoney-Saint-Jean, Chateau Savoia, 8 mai 1988], Aoste: Assessorat Règional de l'Instruction Publique, 1989, pp.133-152.

_____. "Lo scrittore fra i due mondi," in John Picchione, Laura Pietropaolo. Eds., *Italian Literature in North America: Pedagogical Strategies*, Biblioteca di *Quaderni d'Italianistica*, n.9, Ottawa: Canadian Society for Italian Studies, 1990, pp.211-223 [Reprint in Vita Fortunati (aucra di), *Bologna: La cultura italiana e le letterature straniere moderne*, Università di Bologna, Ravenna: Longo Editore, 1992, 3 vols., vol.2, pp.105-120].

_____. "Il silenzio interlunare," in Michelangelo Zizzi, *Il Sud e la Luna. Per una geografia della semantica in Vittorio Bodini attraverso la lingua*, Bari: Levante Editori, 1999, pp.I-XIV

_____. *S'Incontrano gli Amanti. Tre Storie Interoceaniche*, Rome: Edizioni Empiria, 1993.

_____. *Sonetos Profanos y Sacros* [Traducción colectiva del Taller de Traducción Literaria de la Universidad de La Laguna, Taller de Traducción Literaria], La Laguna, Tenerife: Ediciones Canarias, 1996.

_____. Paolo Valesio, *Strutture dell'Allitterazione: grammatica, retorica e folklore verbale*, Bologna: Nicola Zanichelli, 1967.

_____. with Pier Giovanni Bubani, *Volano in Cento*, Faenza: I Quaderni del Circolo degli Artisti, 2002.

_____. *Il Volto quasi Umano. Poesie-dardi, 2003-2005*, Bologna: Lombar Key, 2009.

_____. "The Writer between Two Worlds: Italian Writing in the United States Today," in *Differentia: Review of Italian Thought*, nos.3-4, 1989, pp.259-276.

Laura Wittman, "A proposito di un dialogo post-francescano," in *YIP: Yale Italian Poetry*, Vol.VII, 2003, pp.257-267

THE CONTINUOUS MEDITATION
THE MEDITATION CONTINUES

Mario Moroni
State University of New York - Binghamton

If we break these walls, I mean the walls of the self, the ego, the ego-mania that generates egolatry, or "egolatrato" (ego-barking), that is, the barking of dogs in the woods, like dogs that bark at nothing, toward nothing. If we knock this ego down, or sweep it under the rug, well hidden, leaving the ego at the door, leaving it behind to make room for silence, devoting ourselves to listening: This is Paolo Valesio's invitation. It is here that Giacomo Leopardi sits on the terrace and points out the pleasantness of listening to a voice or a sound in the distance, fading away little by little. This generates a feeling of vastness. It is here that we can hear the birds singing. But then we are shut inside the cage again, us, not the birds.

Here we are prisoners of the rain, in the glass full of salt water, with our destiny written on frosted glasses, themselves prisoners, prisoners of the light.

Here, prisoners of the rain, which seems harmless yet beats down on the still rivers. Now Giacomo Leopardi sits on the riverbank, voiceless, because delight is the only scope of the birds' voices, delight in themselves, not for vainglory or showing off, not like human voices, no, just for themselves, no other scope, just the ascertainment of beauty, an affirmation of it: the song is the form's content, it's the content's form.

Let me make a proposal: I want to include kites among the birds, yes kites, a human artifact. Yes, but at least it's a way in which we try to transcend, to fly over ourselves, by

From: *Discourse Boundary Creation*. Bordighera Press, 2013

means of extension. For is a kite a prosthetic object, like a prosthesis? I mean, it is a manmade object used to keep us in touch with altitude. We are linked to the kite by a thin cord. We send it up high, as if to search, to explore how one can see from above, over ourselves.

Because, my friends, we are still here, prisoners of the rain, while the sovereigns of the air witness the song of those dying. Not even the evening comes down to tame the artifice of time, of the passing of months and calendars, in order to solve riddles, which are coming closer and closer, eternally.

Why is beauty painful? Why is the cry of the seagulls painful? Sometimes it sounds like a tormented shout, even though there is no sacrificial victim, only free flight of seagulls, of kites. Why are we tormented, sometimes? Now we are still prisoners of the rain, we can put our dreams in a phial, in a vast area of space, corroded by clocks, if the cage does not open, then, still prisoners of the rain, in large marshes.

What are we left with? What is there left to do at the hour of evensong, which lasts from five to six o'clock in the afternoon? T.S. Eliot called it the velvet hour. At this hour, Paolo Valesio invites us to be charitable, an anonymous private charity, like this: to offer crumbs to the birds, like this, with a humbly constant act of attention. Thus Giacomo Leopardi, as materialist and atheist, did not know what those birds were saying, even though they were alone like him, solitary. Thus he saw an aesthetic dimension, which was in fact his own, while Valesio leaves the birds to their flights, and ultimately there is not even a full song (a grandiose and romantic word), but just twittering, rather.

Can we then escape the seagulls' tormented cry, from the torment itself, theirs and ours? Can we then devote ourselves to simple acts of humble generosity?

Because if we really break these walls, the walls of the self, the ego, the egomania that generates egolatry, or egobarks, barks of dogs at midnight, in the woods, as in Leo-

"The Continuous Meditation"

pardi's rural landscape, they bark at infinity, against infinity, they invite to nothingness. Giacomo Leopardi is still sitting now on this side of the hedge, he is missing, lost, shipwrecked. Here we are today, maybe on a shore, relatively safe, and we look up. Was Leopardi familiar with kites? We do not know, perhaps he had one that flew in the dark.

Here we still look like prisoners of the rain, almost bewildered by the night we spent outdoors, but alive enough to look up, humble enough to offer crumbs to the birds.

L'IMPRENDIBILE
(NOTE PER UN RITRATTO DI PAOLO VALESIO)

Alessandro Polcri
Fordham University

> *Je te donne à lire le livre qui est dans le livre*
> *et le mot qui est dans le mot.*
>
> E. Jabès, *Le livre des questions*

Già a un primo sguardo, nella biografia di Paolo Valesio è subito evidente l'estrema inquietudine culturale ed esistenziale che la caratterizza. Basta anche solo rapidamente seguire gli eventi principali della sua avventura intellettuale per rimanere colpiti dai numerosi cambiamenti degli interessi di ricerca corroborati da non meno continue oscillazioni tra l'America e l'Europa. In questo incessante movimento interiore e geografico da vero e moderno *clericus vagans* restano, dunque, fissi solo tre punti: New Haven, New York e Bologna, i tre vertici di un triangolo all'interno del quale coesistono costellazioni variegate di viaggi (insegnamento, conferenze, convegni, lezioni) e, soprattutto, di scritture: poesia, prosa poetica, romanzo, racconto, traduzione, saggio critico di vario tipo e argomento (dagli originari studi di glottologia, linguistica, strutturalismo e retorica, fino alle fondamentali ricerche sul tema del silenzio, e poi su d'Annunzio, su Marinetti e il Futurismo, a tacer degli studi su Dante, Boccaccio, sul *fool* rinascimentale, su Ariosto, Rabelais, Folengo, Manzoni, Pasolini e su molto altro come, per esempio, una innumerevole quantità di saggi, introduzioni e ritratti critici di autori contemporanei e, poi, quell'*unicum* critico-narrativo che è *Dialogo coi volanti*, senza dubbio una delle sue opere più belle, intense e 'trasversali' quanto a genere di appartenenza). Evidentemente sono più vite in una, tutte fortemente tenute insieme in una mirabile concordia, coesistenza e sovrapposizione di discipline come poesia, critica, filosofia, teologia, filologia sentite come tessere unite di un discorso che mai privilegia solo una di esse ma che tutte considera come equivalenti strumenti di indagine (per questo, per esempio, secondo Paolo – e credo abbia ragione – i libri di poesia e i romanzi dovrebbero stare assieme ai libri di saggistica nel *curriculum* di uno studioso e non relegati in fondo, in un una coda quasi da nascondere). Siamo in presenza di una ricerca coerente nella sua libertà, animata da un pensiero molto 'agitato', o meglio, sempre mosso da un'instancabile *ruminatio* profondamente avversa a formule critiche alla moda e date una volta per sempre. Ne deriva una decisa imprendibilità nel senso che l'opus di Paolo Valesio non è riconducibile sotto una sola etichetta o formula (e questa è una delle sue ragioni di forza e anche di ricchezza di esiti), ma è animata da una energia trasversale che produce nei suoi scritti una coesistenza di opposti o, meglio, un "crocevia" come ha acutamente notato Alberto Bertoni nella prefazione al volume di poesie *La mezzanotte di Spoleto* (uscito nel 2013, ma contenente testi inediti di fine anni '90):

> [...] l'altro crocevia tutto ancora da indagare che si è nel tempo incarnato dentro la poesia di Valesio è quello del nesso (vincolante, benché dissimulato con sapienza) tra il sé che coincide con uno dei massimi specialisti internazionali di strutturalismo linguistico, capace di collaborare a suo tempo con Roman Jakobson; e il poeta che esprime con andatura sciolta e pronuncia naturale una polifonia profonda, tutta incentrata su un gioco vertiginoso di anacronismi, di neologismi, ("crocefissionale," "cristiananti") o di specialismi dell'antica prosa toscana punteggiati e talora interrotti da molte sapienti aperture a una dimensione sperimentale capace di ascendere direttamente a quella fonte

futurista e marinettiana (anch'essa, va da sé, intrinsecamente plurilingue), che è oggi il centrale e prediletto oggetto di studio del Valesio critico [...].

Ma quel "crocevia" non è "incarnato" solo nella poesia, esso è proprio una delle principali caratteristiche di tutta la variegata officina scrittoria di Valesio e del suo "nesso" con i molti avatar intellettuali e autobiografici dissimulati e copiosamente dispiegati nelle pagine saggistiche e prosastiche di vario genere.

Imprendibile, dunque, ma anche imprevedibile. Del resto, a conferma di tutto questo, va ricordato che due sintagmi chiave del pensiero valesiano solo "il passo di fianco" e "oltre l'oltre." Nel *Dialogo del falco e dell'avvoltoio* (libro del 1987) si trova una magnifica prosa intitolata "La pelle del mignolo." Si tratta di una potente dichiarazione di poetica e, allo stesso tempo, di una confessione sul potere del linguaggio della poesia che ritengo esemplare. In essa, infatti, Valesio cita un passo del celebre *Brief* scritto da Hofmannsthal in cui lo scrittore Lord Chandos dichiara di abbandonare la sua attività perché è vittima di una crisi profonda che gli impedisce di pensare e di usare il linguaggio coerentemente. È un passaggio in particolare ad attirare l'attenzione di Valesio. Dice Lord Chandos:

> come una volta avevo visto in una lente di ingrandimento una zona della pelle del mio mignolo [...], e mi era parsa una pianura con solchi e buche, così ora mi accadeva con gli uomini e le loro azioni. Non riuscivo più a coglierli con lo sguardo semplificatore dell'abitudine. Ogni cosa mi si frazionava, e ogni parte ancora in altre parti, e nulla più si lasciava imbrigliare in un concetto.

In questa incertezza linguistica sul mondo e i suoi dettagli risiede una potenzialità che Valesio coglie in modo originale elaborando ne "La pelle del mignolo" un programma di ri-

"L'imprendibile"

cerca a cui mi pare egli sia rimasto fedele in ogni forma di scrittura praticata. Quello che per Lord Chandos era diventato un limite, Valesio lo sente come una possibilità di scoperta di qualcosa di inaspettato contenuto proprio in quel non riuscire più a guardare le cose con "lo sguardo semplificatore dell'abitudine." Se, infatti, il dettaglio (che è, poi, dettaglio di vita) come dice Valesio "abbacina la vista," allora "il passo di fianco s'impone," per non bruciarsi e, appunto, per non continuare a cadere nell'incertezza, nell'inespressività e nell'afasia dovuta allo sguardo condizionato da abitudine. Occorre dunque coltivare "la speranza di una parola completamente Altra."

Qui risiede la potenzialità di un'oltranza ricercata in tutte le scritture praticate da Paolo (e lui stesso ne parla nella bella intervista a cura di Theodore Cachey ora in *Analogie del mondo. Scritti su Paolo Valesio*, del 2008) sia a livello di ricerca poetica che comporta una profonda riflessione sul sacro – "io penso che la poesia dica le cose indicibli" (ivi, p. 122) –, sia a livello di critica genealogica finalizzata a un discorso ontologico che fa respirare il testo ("a me interessa la saggistica perché mi pare il modo migliore di eliminare il divorzio metalinguaggio-linguaggio," ivi p. 126), al di là di limitanti logiche esegetiche solo descrittive centrate sulla meccanica delle fonti (una critica 'parafrastica' direbbe Valesio). Si tratta di un tipo di ricerca che è avversa alle barriere storiche e ideologiche (ancora troppo condizionanti le scritture critiche più condivise nel mondo accademico) e che, per esempio, si batte per riconoscere il sacro come categoria ermeneutica necessaria e come argomento di poesia da recuperare senza timore ("[..] la persona che oggi scrive versi in una prospettiva spirituale viene spesso a trovarsi artificialmente isolata in una sorta di ghetto più o meno dorato. Evidentemente rifiuto questo isolamento e mi batto per un dialogo totale fra le esperienze più diverse," intervista a cura di Davide Rondoni, in *Analogie del mondo. Scritti su Paolo Valesio*, p. 136). Non sorprende, allora, che una delle massime che Paolo sente più sua (e che, forse, potrebbe diventare il suo motto) sia lo shakespeariano "beyond beyond" (*Cymbeline*, atto 3, scena 2; tra l'altro Shakespeare è un poeta conosciuto quasi a memoria e molto presente nella sua poesia – un aspetto ancora tutto da studiare –).

"Oltre l'oltre" è un sintagma forte che, appunto, segna una oltranza di vita e di pensiero non solo a livello di teoria e pratica della scrittura, ma anche al livello di una debordante esuberanza di pensiero quotidiano che tocca vari modi e àmbiti durante la sua giornata e gli incontri che gli accadono. Per esempio, non c'è conversazione (e con lui ne ho di giornaliere da anni) che non venga arricchita e portata in verticale da una citazione miracolosamente adatta alla situazione di vita che stiamo discutendo: che si tratti di un libro, di *Italian Poetry Review*, di un volume per la collana "Ungarettiana," di una conferenza, di una poesia e così via. Ogni volta, con una precisione implacabile, Paolo pronuncia la frase giusta citata a memoria e, ovviamente, in lingua originale da una delle sue innumerevoli letture che possono essere il suo amato Kierkegaard, una poesia, una saggio, un passo di filosofia, ma anche un articolo di giornale o un romanzo giallo (genere di cui è un cultore).

Il fatto è che Paolo vive fisiologicamente dentro le parole senza quasi avvertire alcuna differenza tra la vita e la letteratura. L'una si intreccia con l'altra e l'una si alimenta dell'altra. Le due si bilanciano a vicenda e si citano. Paolo cita dalla vita e cita dalla letteratura, ma tutto poi alla fine confluisce nella letteratura: non a caso "Lettera dalla vita" è un mirabile titolo di una delle sue cinque prose (*Pentalogie*) in corso d'opera dove vita vissuta e vita narrata si mescolano identificandosi senza mai coincidere completamente. Sono cinque imprese diaristiche che nascono dall'interscambio di vita e letteratura (diari per modo di dire, dato che contengono pezzi di saggi, romanzi, racconti, poesie e riflessioni filosofico-teologiche). Paolo, del resto, per sua stessa ammissione, è attratto più dall'accenno che dalla compiutezza, e anche a

"L'imprendibile"

livello saggistico preferisce scrivere saggi invece che libri compiuti). Una energia di sconfinamento che trasgredisce le regole retoriche di incasellamento dei generi e che è aperta a inglobare nella poesia ogni forma che viene dalla vita e dunque anche l'esperienza religiosa (si diceva sopra del sacro e del suo necessario ritorno ad esistere nella poesia come uno dei mondi con cui per un poeta contemporaneo dovrebbe essere normale dialogare). Ma qui occorre una precisazione: la sua poesia, troppo spesso definita religiosa a causa della nota conversione avvenuta dopo una giovinezza trascorsa lontano dalla fede, non lo è in senso stretto. Paolo non è un mistico esclusivo (semmai si può dire che ci sono componenti di misticismo nella sua opera), né è autore monotematico di preghiere o riflessioni oranti (come, per esempio, era padre Turoldo).

Coerentemente con quanto detto fino ad ora riguardo alla sua capacità di attraversamento di generi e scritture, anche nella sua poesia, una forte oltranza coesiste con delle realtà più o meno mondane. Non è un caso che nei suoi versi Paolo controlli molto l'energia mistica – o, meglio, "poemistica," per usare un termine da lui adottato di recente nell'editoriale per *IPR* 2010. Nelle sue poesie passano inesorabilmente e appassionatamente le vicende, le cadute e le scoperte della quotidianità in cui Dio è più un interlocutore camuffato in modeste metonimie terrestri – cose, oggetti, chiese, incontri con persone, osservazioni minute della vita e delle cose colte dallo sguardo – piuttosto che il protagonista di grandi dialoghi teologici tra l'io poetico e il tu superiore "la poesia mistica non è un genere, ma una presenza elusiva che scorre attraverso vari generi."[1] Per questo, ma posso sbagliarmi – e la

---

[1] Paolo Valesio, *Amor mi mosse (la strana bellezza del fraintendimento)*, in *Voci della poesia mistica contemporanea*, a cura di Davide Rondoni, Bologna, Lombar Key, 2010, p. 29. Dico "io poetico," perché è Valesio stesso a ben marcare la differenza: "la poesia che io scrivo non è il diario autobiografico di una conversione: è la costruzione di una voce, la costruzione di un parlante che è altro da me, che non può essere semplicisticamente identi-

cosa andrebbe verificata meglio –, non mi sorprende che nelle sue poesie non siano molto frequenti le parole Croce e Dio (per lo meno, non tanto quanto ci si aspetterebbe da un poeta che la critica definisce religioso tout court). Se la sua è, dunque, una poesia che interroga un mistero, tuttavia mantiene vivo un tono terrestre con venature ben fisiche ("l'esperienza poetica è immanente"). Il "tu" di Valesio è sempre un compagno di viaggio cercato, un interlocutore costantemente chiamato, ma sempre a sèguito di una esperienza individuale in cui vita e religiosità, inverate nella poesia, tracciano un profilo complesso e tortuoso dell'esistenza. Una "lotta nell'esistenza (piuttosto che lotta per l'esistenza)," come ebbe a dire una volta, che comporta anche aperture costanti verso il mondo materiale, a tratti anche verso il comico (avvertito come un ribaltamento che è parte della vita, oltre ad essere un mezzo di distacco) e dove le certezze sono poche e le domande molte: per questo motivo secondo Valesio il poeta agisce come un *fool*: sia lo stolto paolino (1 *Corinzi*), sia il *fool* elisabettiano che insinua dubbi nella mente dei personaggi.

Si tratta, pertanto, di una poesia che non si nasconde di fronte allo choc del vivere e riconosce una impreparazione dell'io poetico di fronte ad esso. Una poesia dell'incapacità di comprendere (stoltezza) e del dubbio come necessari esercizi che portano alla preghiera, ma senza la serenità della contemplazione (le poesie-preghiera sono molto rare nella loro purezza orante, semmai se ci sono, sono soverchiate, 'massacrate' dalla vita, come recita il titolo di uno dei suoi libri più belli, *Piazza delle preghiere massacrate* del 1999). Nell'io poetico che Paolo mette in scena c'è dunque ben poca letizia francescana (e questo malgrado il suo amore per Francesco, provato anche dal suo già menzionato *Dialogo coi*

---

ficato con il mio io esistenziale; e le cose che questa voce dice non possono essere viste meccanicamente come la conseguenza diretta di una conversione" (ivi, p. 136).

volanti) e c'è, invece, molto di Giobbe, il torchiato da Dio. Questo impianto agonistico e non sereno con la fede (siamo, lo ripeto, di fronte a un pensiero della trascendenza, ma reificato nella narrazione di una vita spirituale frammentaria ed erratica) comporta che nella poesia di Paolo ci sia, a dire il vero, una certa crudeltà (altra parola centrale della sua poetica che comporta il provare a guardare alla propria condizione umana con umiltà e senza infingimenti) o, meglio, con termine barocco a lui caro, una certa *disperanza*.[2] Si tratta di un forte disorientamento dovuto al riconoscimento che il margine di comprensione degli eventi è minimo e che perciò il lato oscuro delle cose incombe (si leggano, tra i molti esempi possibili, *Bestie divine*, oppure *L'infedeltà al dettato* del 2006, *Il volto quasi umano* del 2009). E infatti Giobbe è colui che 'disperantemente' patisce, non capisce e anche fraintende.

Tocco, così, il tema del fraintendimento, l'ultima delle parole chiave della sua poetica su cui si è concentrata la recentissima riflessione di Paolo sulla poesia.[3] Lo scandalo da cui nasce la poesia è il riconoscimento della "fondamentale

---

[2] "il compito difficilissimo del poeta contemporaneo è quello di descrivere questa speranza in tutta la sua difficoltà e in tutta la sua costante possibilità di cadere nella disperanza. Io non sento la poesia del *viator*, la poesia spirituale, la poesia della speranza. Se io non sento l'ombra continua, il timore, il brivido, la vibrazione, come volete voi, della disperanza, rischio di leggere una poesia non autentica, e temo che la poesia che leggo possa non essere autentica.[…] la disperanza provoca grande poesia; [..] la speranza in poesia può diventare un po' troppo oleografica, può diventare un po' troppo edificante, può diventare un po' troppo predicatoria e allora […] il poeta deve farci sentire sempre la possibilità della disperanza, il *valde aliud* come dice la tradizione cristiana, l'estremamente altro, il totalmente altro, che può essere anche l'altro della disperazione. […] se il poeta non ci fa sentire il rischio, lui, lei, la sua poesia, rischia la inautenticità. La speranza è dialetticamente connessa al suo opposto" (trascrizione online della conferenza "La tensione dell'arte: il poeta contemporaneo è ancora viator?" tenuta al Meeting di Rimini il 22 agosto 2004).

[3] Si veda l'editoriale di *IPR* 2009 e poi una sua versione allargata per il già citato volume *Voci della poesia mistica contemporanea*.

impossibilità di veramente intendersi fra esseri umani," è, cioè, la presa di coscienza che non si può avere una formula cristallizzata di niente: né della poesia stessa, né della letteratura, né della vita, né degli uomini, né del senso del nostro esserci. Ma si badi, Paolo non è affatto un nichilista, in lui c'è tutta la passione interrogante di colui che ha in corso un dialogo con l'Altro (lo si diceva all'inizio), solo che la poesia è ora inserita (mi pare per la prima volta nella storia della riflessione poetologica di Valesio) in un distinto processo curativo:

> ...con il suo sposalizio del fraintendimento, essa [la poesia] alza la posta e la sfida, non si fa spaventare dalla Iperfaticità; e così provvede in certo senso una cura della più o meno lieve, ma costante, alienazione da fraintendimento (una sorta di rodimento del parlante ed erosione della parola).

Siamo appena sulla soglia di un elegante edificio speculativo ancora in costruzione e la riflessione a venire che Valesio dovrà sviluppare è quella che spieghi come, grazie alla poesia, si parta dal fraintendimento e si arrivi a un *fra-intendimento* (un intendimento fra parlanti). Come si vede, si tratta di un pensiero ancora in pieno fermento, ma coerente attorno a delle idee che hanno radici lontane nella sua scrittura. Non solo nella scrittura, però. Questo gusto per la ricerca ininterrotta, un "pensiero itinerante" come Paolo giustamente lo chiama, si ritrova anche nel suo insegnamento che invece che presentare un messaggio ex cathedra ("frontale," come si dice oggi con aggettivo militareggiante), ricerca nel dialogo la strada da praticare assieme agli studenti. La lezione è cioè *lectio* all'antica, ossia lettura ravvicinata del testo e suo ascolto. "Paulus non docet" mi dice e quando lo afferma mi viene in mente Marsilio Ficino che in una lettera al tedesco Martino Uranio, descrivendo la sua scuola, definiva quelli che secondo lui davvero erano i suoi allievi: "non auditores, nec omnino discipuli sed consuetudine familiares,

"L'imprendibile"

confabulatores." Stessa dimensione dialogica si riverbera nella gestione e direzione di *IPR* che Paolo non concepisce come una rivista contenitore, ma che vuole fortemente resti una rivista di ricerca (e io sono d'accordissimo). Dunque, anche *IPR*, che ho l'onore di condirigere con lui, porta il marchio di quell'inquietudine che tanto caratterizza il suo cammino di pensatore e di scrittore.

Vorrei chiudere queste rapide e affastellate note con le parole che Jean Leclercq ha dedicato alla *compunctio*. Trovo che esse non solo corrispondano in qualche modo alla poetica delle poesie-dardi che Paolo ha elaborato in alcune delle sue raccolte recenti (almeno da *Dardi. Volano in cento* del 2000 a *Il cuore del girasole* del 2006), ma ritengo che in realtà spieghino molto della trepidazione che anima la sua ricerca. Aggiungete la parola Poesia alla parola Dio (o, se preferite, sostituite la parola Dio con Poesia) e vi potrete identificare, mi pare, la scaturigine della scrittura di Paolo Valesio, così come potrete riconoscervi una efficace descrizione di quello che per lui dovrebbe essere l'effetto curativo della letteratura nell'animo umano, ovviamente al di là di ogni fraitendimento terreno:

> Il primo risultato di questa esperienza della miseria umana, per il cristiano che la sa interpretare, è l'umiltà cioè il distacco dal mondo, da noi stessi e dal nostro peccato, la coscienza del bisogno che abbiamo di Dio. Questa è la compunzione nel suo duplice aspetto: compunzione di timore e compunzione di desiderio. Originariamente la parola *compunctio* è, nell'uso profano, un termine medico: esso designa le punture di un dolore acuto, di un male fisico. Ma è stato particolarmente usato nel vocabolario cristiano con un senso che, senza perdere contatto con quello originario, è tuttavia più ricco e molto elevato. La compunzione diventa un dolore dell'anima, un dolore che ha, contemporaneamente, due principi: da una parte la realtà del peccato e della nostra tendenza al peccato – *compunctio poeniten-*

tiae, timoris, formidinis – dall'altra il nostro desiderio di Dio e il nostro possesso, già attuale, di Dio. S. Gregorio, più di altri, ha messo l'accento su quest'ultimo aspetto: possesso oscuro, la cui coscienza è fuggevole, e da cui, per conseguenza, nasce il rimpianto di vederla scomparire e il desiderio di ritrovarla. La "compunzione del cuore," "dell'anima" – *compunctio cordis, animi* – tende perciò sempre a diventare una "compunzione d'amore," di "dilezione" e di "contemplazione" – *compunctio amoris, dilectionis, contemplationis*. La compunzione è un'azione di Dio in noi, un atto col quale Dio ci risveglia, uno choc, una scossa, una "puntura," una specie di scottatura. Dio ci scuote quasi con un pungolo: "ci punge" con insistenza (cum-pungere), come per trafiggerci. L'amore del mondo ci addormenta; ma come per un fragore di tuono, l'anima è richiamata all'attenzione a Dio.[4]

WORKS CITED

Ficino, Marsilio. *Opera I-II*. Torino: Bottega d'Erasmo, 1959 [Basel, 1563].

Hofmannsthal von, Hugo. *The Lord Chandos Letter and Other Writings*. Transl. by Joel Rotenberg. New York: New York Reviews of Books, 2005.

Leclercq, Jean. *Cultura umanistica e desiderio di Dio*. Firenze: Sansoni, 1988.

Rondoni, Davide and Valesio Paolo. "La tensione dell'arte: il poeta contemporaneo è ancora viator?" Online conference held at Rimini, August 22, 2004. Downloadable from http://www.meetingrimini.org/ default.asp?id =673&item=2097.

Surliuga, Victoria, ed., *Analogie del mondo. Scritti su Paolo Valesio*. Modena: Edizioni del laboratorio, 2008.

Valesio, Paolo. *Ascoltare il silenzio. La retorica come teoria*. Bologna: Il Mulino, 1986.

_____. *Dialogo del falco e dell'avvoltoio*. Milano: Nuovi Autori, 1987.

---

[4] Cf. J. Leclercq, *Cultura umanistica e desiderio di Dio* (Firenze, Sansoni, 1988), pp. 35-36.

"L'imprendibile"

_____. *Dialogo coi volanti*. Napoli: Cronopio, 1997.
_____. *Piazza delle preghiere massacrate*, Modena: Edizioni del Laboratorio, 1999.
_____. *Dardi. Volano in cento (Poesie 1999-2001)*, Faenza: I Quaderni del Circolo degli Artisti, 2000.
_____. *Il cuore del girasole*, Milano: Marietti, 2006.
_____. *Il volto quasi umano*. Bologna: Lombar Key, 2009.
_____. "Amor mi mosse (la strana bellezza del fraintendimento)." in *Voci della poesia mistica contemporanea*, edited by Davide Rondoni, Bologna: Lombar Key, 2010.
_____. *La mezzanotte di Spoleto*. Rimini: Raffaelli, 2013.

PIÙ CHE L'AMORE
D'ANNUNZIO'S BITTER PASSION AND MEDITERRANEAN TRAGEDY

Lucia Re
University of California / Los Angeles

> Odimi tu, latin sangue gentile!
> Odimi; ché di te sotto il velame
> io dico, e del miracolo repente
> onde un spirito fai di tanto ossame.
> Quale improvviso nella notte ardente
> di Cesarèa l'Embrìaco la tazza
> di salute rinvenne alla sua gente
> e, quella pósta su la galeazza
> come il palladio fu su la trireme,
> ricelebrò la gloria della razza,
> tal forse un genio indìgete del seme
> d'Enea ritorna a noi col divin segno
> dallo splendore delle sabbie estreme.
> Tra le palme invisibili arde il pegno
> del novo patto. Innanzi ch'Ei si sveli
> giura fede al Signor del novo regno,
> Italia, per gli aperti tuoi vangeli,
> e per la grande imagine che invoco,
> e per la gesta che t'allarga i cieli!
>
> G. d'Annunzio, *La canzone del sangue* (1911)

In *The Dark Flame*, Paolo Valesio shows how in Gabriele d'Annunzio's 1906 tragedy *Più che l'amore*, "the savage darkness of the existential antihero [shares] a family tree with Dostoevsky and Gide."[1] From the folds of the text other

---

[1] Paolo Valesio, *Gabriele d'Annunzio: The Dark Flame*, English translation by Marilyn Migiel (New Haven and London: Yale University Press, 1992), p. 67.

From: *Discourse Boundary Creation*. Bordighera Press, 2013

relations and chosen kinships may emerge, for example with Joseph Conrad's *Heart of Darkness* and Arthur Rimbaud's *Une Saison en enfer*. Rather than explore the play's intertextual and transnational genealogy, however, what I would like to trace in the following pages is the emergence and significance of the words *razza* [race] and *sangue* [blood] in this text, and the way in which *Più che l'amore* symbolically articulates the profound relationship and interconnectedness of race, blood and homosociality within a new sacralized discourse about the Italian nation at the beginning of the 20th century.

In the complex history of d'Annunzio's use of the word race (*razza* but also the strong variant *stirpe*) the campaign speech of August 1897 to the rural people and small landowners of the poet's native Abruzzi (one of the most underdeveloped regions of Italy, economically and culturally part of the South), usually known as "Discorso delle siepe," which helped elect him to the parliament, represents a turning point. [2] Various versions of this speech, later entitled "Lode dell'illaudato," were delivered by d'Annunzio all over Abruzzi in late July and August 1897, and the speech given in Pescara on August 22 appeared in *La Tribuna* on August 23, and was widely commented in national newspapers, gaining the praise of Giovanni Pascoli, among others. D'Annunzio, who ran as a candidate for the right against a candidate of the radical party, had been a resident of Francavilla in Abruzzo for three years; he was already an international celebrity, and his victory is attributable mostly to this factor. D'Annunzio at this juncture, however, was not yet

---

[2] Gabriele d'Annunzio, *Prose di Ricerca* (Milano: Mondadori, 1947) vol. 1, pp. 463-76. For a pioneering reading of the theme of race in this speech, see Jared M. Becker, *Nationalism and Culture. Gabriele d'Annunzio and Italy after the Risorgimento* (New York: Peter Lang, 1994), 47-49. See also Mario Moroni, "1897, scrivere i confini: la retorica della siepe in D'Annunzio e Pascoli," in *Al limite. L'idea di margine nel Novecento italiano* (Firenze: Le Monnier, 2007), 71-85.

interested in politics per se (and the election in fact was temporarily invalidated due to an adultery charge). He was deeply involved with Eleonora Duse and the idea of a new modern Mediterranean tragic theater at the time, and he saw politics, like theater, as a way to create a mass following for himself and his art and especially as a means to forge a new and nobler national consciousness for Italians.[3] While this speech is usually interpreted as a defense of the "beauty" and legitimacy of private property, its rhetorical foundation is in fact race, but understood in a new way.

The political use of the notion of race as a unifying *national* force is the new or newly rediscovered element, race itself being an imaginary construct and a literary *topos* that d'Annunzio at this time helps finally to pull together from various literary and scientific sources, crystallizing it and making it a part of the Italian collective imagination. In the speech, which is in part a prelude to the ideas later elaborated in the novel *Il Fuoco* (1900), d'Annunzio affirmed that the best of any given ethnic group or *stirpe* is always necessarily achieved through a process of "natural selection," not by any given class or regional group, but by a select group of superior individuals – artists, poets, and intellectuals – through whom the *stirpe* perpetuates its highest and ancient heritage

---

[3] The project for a new "tragedia moderna e mediterranea" was outlined by d'Annunzio in the article "La Rinascenza della tragedia," *La Tribuna*, August 3, 1897, now in *Scritti giornalistici 1889-1938*, ed. Anna Maria Andreoli (Milano: Mondadori, 1996). See Valentina Valentini, *La tragedia moderna e mediterranea. Sul teatro di Gabriele d'Annunzio* (Milano: Franco Angeli, 1992). For a formal and thematic analysis of *Più che l'amore* in relation to the innovations and problems of modern tragedy, see Mary Ann Frese Witt, *The Search for Modern Tragedy* (Ithaca: Cornell University Press, 2001) pp. 78-88. Her reading emphasizes especially the theme of the individual hero as Nietzschean superman. For an insightful reading of the play within the ideological context of Italian and European colonialism in Africa, see Giovanna Tomasello, *La letteratura coloniale italiana dalle avanguardie al fascismo* (Palermo: Sellerio, 1984), chaper 2.

and "genius."[4] The beautiful, ennobling image of an Italic race that, through its superior poets and intellectuals, will go beyond even the achievements in the Mediterranean of the Greco-Roman and Latin world whose spirit it has inherited, is at the center of d'Annunzio's vision in the first decade of the twentieth century, and will reach its peak in the Dantesque "La canzone del sangue" from the *Canzoni della Gesta d'Oltremare* cited in the above epigraph, written to celebrate the Italian invasion and the colonial conquest of Libya in 1911.[5]

It is through an essentially esthetic and utopian vision that d'Annunzio hopes to overcome both the dehumanizing, exploitative, and debasing logic of capitalism and the "equalizing" materialism of socialism. In the notion of race and racial pride, d'Annunzio identifies not only a powerful antisocialist and anticapitalist rhetorical instrument, but also a powerful myth eventually capable of transcending and overcoming all social, economic, cultural, religious, and sexual differences and unifying the Italian imagination like never before. In the "Discorso della siepe," reversing entirely the individualistic perspectives of his own novelistic heroes Giorgio Aurispa (*Il trionfo della morte*) and Claudio Cantelmo (*Le vergini delle rocce*), d'Annunzio appeals to his prospective voters of Abruzzi (but implicitly to all Italians) as members of the same *stirpe*, inviting them to recognize in him the superior "interprete delle eterne aspirazioni che sollevano la

---

[4] *Prose di ricerca*, 1:475: "Avete dinnanzi a voi, rivelata, la vostra essenza. Voi credete che io trasformi tutto in mia poesia, mentre io non altro fo se non obbedire al genio cui voi medesimi siete soggetti. Voi mi giudicate dissimile, mentre io vi somiglio come un fratello purificato. [. . .] Accoglietemi come si accoglie un fratello più puro e più lucido."

[5] The ten *Canzoni della Gesta d'oltremare*, published by *Il Corriere della Sera* between October 1911 and January 1912, were published together by Treves in 1912 as the fourth volume of d'Annunzio's *Laudi del cielo del mare della terra e degli eroi*, under the title *Merope*. For the controversy surrounding this publication and the subsequent editions of the volume, see D'Annunzio, *Versi*, 1291-2.

stirpe verso il suo destino [. . .] le profonde cose che dice in voi l'antico sangue ereditario" (*Prose* 467). D'Annunzio in his speech refers specifically to an autochthonous, *mixed* Italic race and even to the primitive, colonized tribes of Abruzzi that through the fierce struggle against Rome helped forge the dominant Italic race, which inherited the "Latin spirit": "Nella storia delle stirpi umane come in quella delle specie animali è manifesto che la condizione prima di ogni ascesa verso le superiori forme di vita è la lotta" (*Prose* 472). Struggle and war, in other words, are crucial to the refinement of the race. D'Annunzio's is in fact an estheticized version of the social, political, and ethnic Darwinism shared by many other Italian and European intellectuals of the era – for example, in Italy, anthropologists such as Giuseppe Sergi and social historians such as Guglielmo Ferrero. But while for Giovanni Verga's *vinti*, for example, being poor and working class meant, tragically, being racially inferior and doomed (the protagonist of the ground-breaking story "Nedda" is a case in point), social and racial inferiority no longer coincide in and for d'Annunzio.

What is new and astute in d'Annunzio is the use of race as both a regional *and* national ethnic category, deployed as a unifying, beautiful and holy image to displace divisive class, region, and gender conflicts (and potential solidarity) along those lines. The lower peasant and working classes, and the colonized southerners, are no longer seen or represented as biologically and intellectually inferior (as they were in Verga) and, thus, doomed to extinction or dangerous degeneration, but rather as an integral part of a powerful and ascending Italian mixed race, whose consciousness must be awakened, forged and elevated by the militant poet-intellectual. D'Annunzio was hardly invested in the politics of the right, and in fact in 1900, with a widely publicized, defiant gesture, he seized the opportunity to gain some notoriety by passing "from the right to the left," joining the socialists. He shared none of their political ideas, but wanted to be associated in the public imagination with revolutionary fervor and change. What he wanted more than anything else was to talk the masses into seeing the need to go beyond class consciousness and class struggle and accept instead the higher principle of racial and national consciousness, embracing the beautiful challenge to fight for Italy in the grandiose international "war between the races." By 1900, he had effectively become himself a prophet and a floating signifier of the Italian race.[6]

The "tragedia moderna" *Più che l'amore*, written in the summer of 1905 after the formal end of the long *sodalizio artistico* and liaison with Eleonora Duse, and following the immensely creative period of the *Laudi* with the publication of the epic poem *Maia* in 1903 and the success of the tragedy *La figlia di Iorio*, represents a key step in the evolution of d'Annunzio's literary writings and thinking about race. It opened at the Costanzi in Rome in October with Ermete Zacconi in the role of the hero, Corrado Brando. To the bourgeois audience in Rome, its plot seemed openly to justify and even exalt murder and the defilement of innocent young women, and the defiance of all law, morality and common sense of decency.[7]

The action is as follows. Corrado Brando, a desperate and

---

[6] See the speech "Della coscienza nazionale" published in *Il Giorno*, May 21, 1900; and see also the "Ode Leonis" in *Le Figaro*, December 18, 1898, now in d'Annunzio, *Scritti giornalistici*, vol. 2, ed. Annamaria Andreoli and Giorgio Zanetti (Milano: Mondadori: 2003), pp. 410-17; 498-505. For a more comprehensive reading of d'Annunzio's role in the formation of an Italian discourse on race, see my "Italians and the Invention of Race: The Poetics and Politics of Difference in the Struggle over Libya, 1890-1913." *California Italian Studies Journal* 1.1 (2010): 1-58.

[7] The play was subsequently picked up in January 1907 by Ruggero Ruggeri and Emma Gramatica's company in Turin, and performed again by Zacconi's company in Milan the same month; the reception of the play in the northern cities was on the whole rather positive compared to Rome. For an account of the play's production and reception, see Gabriele d'Annunzio, *Tragedie, Sogni e Misteri* vol 2, ed. Annamaria Andreoli and Giorgio Zanetti (Milano: Mondadori, 2013), pp. 1539-42.

destitute architect and engineer is a veteran explorer of East Africa languishing in Giolittian Rome and longing to return to the Dark Continent where he lived many adventures with his faithful servant and fierce ally, the Sardinian Rudu. Corrado and Rudu now live together, sharing memories of their glorious past. Corrado's long-time fraternal friend in Rome is the hydraulic engineer Virginio Vesta, a man of impeccable virtue and admirable industriousness. Corrado loves Virginio's beautiful and virginal young sister, Maria, and is loved in return. She has given herself to him and expects his child. Corrado rejoices in his future paternity, but his departure for Africa is imminent. Maria selflessly refrains from trying to hold him back, accepting his desire to resume his mission as an explorer. The lovers sadly embrace the need to separate, as there is a destiny more important than love or "beyond love" awaiting the hero. The title phrase "Più che l'amore" refers to this destiny, but is also a distinct homage to Eleonora Duse as d'Annunzio's enduring tragic muse. The phrase is in fact one of Foscarina's distinct leitmotifs in *Il Fuoco*. In *Più che l'amore* Corrado hides his truly tragic situation from both Maria and Virginio. He sought to finance the new expedition across the Mediterranean by gambling, but lost all his money to a usurer, a despicable man who kept his own family members in abject poverty. Overwhelmed by uncontrollable violence and mad passion, Corrado (as he finally reveals to his friend Virginio), killed the usurer. He knows that the law will soon hunt him down. Virginio, faithful and forgiving as ever, sees Corrado's mission in Africa as an opportunity for redemption. But the play closes as Rudu announces the arrival of three policemen and the two old comrades, defiant and refusing to give themselves up, pick up their guns and get ready for the deadly shootout that will bring their end.

On opening night *Più che l'amore* caused a riot and a huge scandal as the outraged audience rose up in indignation, calling for the police to arrest the author. A similar reaction oc-

"*Più che l'amore*"

curred in Padua and other Italian cities. In defense of his text, d'Annunzio wrote a long prologue to the tragedy in the form of a letter addressed to his only defender, the critic Vincenzo Morello. This letter is both an amazingly learned and rhetorically complex explication of his own classical and philosophical subtexts to his work, full as well of self-quotations, whose significance apparently the audience failed to grasp, and a passionate, bitter and linguistically very rich neo-classical invective against his enemies, written in a high style meant to emphasize the immense distance between the poet and his vulgar and ignorant critics. The bitter author of the invective in fact mirrors the bitter and superhuman protagonist of *Più che l'amore*, Corrado Brando, whose criminal yet heroic and even Promethean and untimely passion is, in the degraded and distinctly un-heroic era of the "Third Rome" profoundly misunderstood.

As d'Annunzio points out in the prologue to the play, Corrado Brando's self-immolation is meant to echo that of Ajax in the tragedy by Sophocles, the "o tenebra mia luce" explored by Paolo Valesio in *The Dark Flame*, yet it is also clearly a figure for d'Annunzio's own self-conscious and highly successful provocation of the bourgeois audience. Nonetheless, the prologue also emphasizes a dimension of the play that would soon become quite timely, thanks largely to d'Annunzio himself, namely the images of blood and race as foundations for Italian colonialism in Africa. "Voglio essere e sono il maestro che per gli Italiani riassume nella sua dottrina le tradizioni del gran sangue ond'è nato: non un seduttore né un corruttore, sì bene un infaticabile animatore che eccita gli spiriti [e insegna] la necessità dell'eroismo."[8] The lyric exode, meant to conclude the performance and clarify its significance for the audience, highlights the image of the son who will come, celebrating the hero's sacrificial death

---

[8] Gabriele d'Annunzio, "Più che l'amore. Tragedia moderna" in *Tragedie, sogni e misteri*, p. 128.

as the seed for rebirth and regeneration: "La mia cenere è semenza" (*Tragedie* 1231).

Blood and Seed, *sangue* and *seme* or *germe* are the symbolic signifiers around which the entire play in fact revolves. In 1905, despite the widespread belief among the ruling elites since the unification that Italy, like the other more powerful European nations, deserved its own overseas colonial empire, and that the Mediterranean was to become once again the *Mare Nostrum*, the discourse of blood and seed in connection with Italian colonialism in Africa was still largely unpopular. It was limited to rather small nationalist circles, and had little or no support from the left, from Catholics, and from women. It even lacked support from the right. There was lack of information and indifference towards the colonies that Italy had started acquiring as early as 1885 in Eritrea and then Somalia on the south side of the Horn of Africa. The first Italian colonial war in Africa against the Ethiopian empire in 1895-96 was generally unpopular, and the tragic defeat at Adwa became a national trauma that made Italian colonialism more controversial and unappealing than ever. Adwa was the first defeat by an indigenous people of a colonial power and a major blow to the Italian empire in East Africa, as well as to the Italian self-image and prestige.[9] The loss of Italian *blood* was widely seen as tragic, but not as justification for further colonial penetration, quite the contrary in fact. Not until the Libyan war of 1911 would a substantial consensus and even enthusiasm develop regarding the legitimacy of Italian colonial aspirations in Africa, much of it attributable to the dissemination of new racialist notions of blood and seed that d'Annunzio was among the first to bring to public attention in *Più che l'amore*. By 1911, d'Annunzio's influence had grown exponentially

---

[9] On the so-called "complesso di Adua," see Nicola Labanca, "Memorie e complessi di Adua," in Angelo del Boca, ed., *Adua, le ragioni di una sconfitta* (Bari: Laterza, 1997), pp. 397-416.

"Piú che l'amore"

along with those of the new nationalist movement, and his Libyan *Canzoni della Gesta d'oltremare*, written during his "exile" in France, met with unprecedented success, paving the way for d'Annunzio's triumphal return home.

The tragedy's simple plot is based in part on Dostoevsky's *Crime and Punishment*, and in part on Nietzsche's ideas. D'Annunzio and Nietzsche explain, confuse and struggle with one another, as Valesio has shown. *Più che l'amore* in fact clearly stands in opposition to Nietsche's racialist ideas of "purification" even as it embraces the Nietzschean ideal of the redemptive hero.[10] The text is constructed on the basis of images of blood and seed, which function as signs and emblems on several levels. At the most literal level, the plot is about "un fatto di sangue." Corrado Brando in fact murders, strangling him with his bare hands, the vile moneylender and gambler who has ruined him, and takes from him a large sum that he hopes will enable him to go back to east Africa and continue his adventurous life of exploration and colonization. The grotesque moneylender is a symbol of the cowardice and corruption of the *terza Roma* under Giolitti. Although the character of Corrado Brando is not based on any specific historical figure, he is surely inspired by the likes of Vittorio Bottego, Ugo Ferrandi and other figures of Italian adventurers who, in the name of exploration and often through official military missions, in the 1880s and 1890s (before the Adwa tragedy, the fall of Crispi and the consequent lull in colonial activities), made their way often violently through Somalia and Ethiopia, sacking burning and pillaging with the help of native mercenaries and *ascari*, under the flag of Italy.[11] The bloody violence of Cor-

---

[10] See Nietzsche's well know aphorism 272 about the "Purification of Race" in *Daybreak* (1881), in which the ancient Greeks are invoked as a model for Europeans because as a people they have succeeded in achieving higher beauty and vigor through racial purification.

[11] See *Più che l'amore, Tragedie*, pp. 47-55. In the play, D'Anuunzio refers in fact to the actual explorer Ugo Ferrandi. In the conversation between the

rado Brando's endeavors in Africa is made vividly clear through the text, and it is to that bloody violence that the hero wishes to return in order to live again. Life in Rome under Giolitti is on the other hand equivalent to a kind of slow and deadly *dissanguamento*, or bleeding to death for the hero and for the nation.

The image of blood becomes important in turn as a metaphor for race. And indeed the word *razza*, along with the words *sangue* and *stirpe*, begin to circulate more and more in Italy in this period, and in d'Annunzio's own work. But for d'Annunzio, unlike other European intellectuals of this era, there is no innate purity or nobility of blood, nor is there genetic racial superiority. It is through violent sacrifice, courage and the spilling of blood, that blood itself is ennobled. The hybrid and mixed blood of the composite Italic race, described by the Italian school of anthropology as encompassing extensive zones of chronic and irremediable degeneration and criminality in the south and the islands, can, the d'Annunzian text implies, be rendered noble, and the nation sacred, through violent sacrifice. The function of sacrifice (from the Latin *sacer* and *facere*) is indeed to perform or make sacred. This violent economy of blood is in fact not far from that of Georges Bataille, for blood is in itself the sign of the necessary symbolic performance of sacrificial violence in d'Annunzio's tragedy.[12] The moneylender thus becomes a sacrificial scapegoat figure whose death signifies the nation's

---

two friends Virginio and Corrado, Corrado announces his intention to return to Africa, where Ugo Ferrandi is currently waiting for him at Brava. Virginio observes that "i grandi esemplari stanno per riapparire dalla profondità della stirpe" and Corrado relates his new mission explicitly to the idea of an Italic race of daring explorers: "Io sono un italiano della razza dei Caboto." Using a Latin phrase often cited by d'Annunzio, he describes his dream as follows: "Ho il mio pensiero, una parola romana da rendere italica: *Teneo te, Africa*. The expression "Teneo te, Africa" was attributed to Julius Caesar by Svetonius.

[12] See the essays on sacrifice in Georges Bataille in *Visions of Excess. Selected Writings 1927-1939*, ed. with an introduction by Allan Stoekl.

potential liberation from the dominant regime of capitalist corruption and *Giolittismo*.

Corrado's Sardinian attendant, Rudu, "non servo ma compagno," whose presence in the text is most often ignored or a source of critical puzzlement or even condescension, symbolizes through his fierceness, endurance and courage the nobility of the Sardinian race, otherwise vilified by Cesare Lombroso and then by Alfredo Niceforo in *L'Italia barbara contemporanea* (1898) and *Italiani del Nord e Italiani del Sud* (1901) as corrupted by the influx over the centuries of degenerate, primitive and inferior African blood in the south.[13] D'annunzio like Grazia Deledda reiterates at various points that Sardinian blood, *sangue sardo*, is indeed black, *nero*, infused with African influences; but rather than a racial slur, this is a point of pride.[14] D'annunzio is among the first artists in Italy to cultivate, even before the futurists, and before Picasso (whose *Les Demoiselles d'Avignon* dates from 1907), the surrealists and Georges Bataille, the cult of the African primitive, the savage and the barbaric, and to be fascinated by the violent performance of the sacred through sacrifice. The hero himself, Corrado Brando, repeatedly asserts to have Africa in him. The African paraphernalia, including masks, skulls, weapons and lion skins that decorate Corrado's rooms described in the elaborate stage directions at the opening of the second act have an unmistakable orientalist flavor that may recall the lore of Emilio Salgari's adventure novels, but

---

[13] About the racialization of Sardinia and the south in the anthropological and political literature as well as in the press at the turn of the century, see Michele Nani, *Ai confini della nazione. Stampa e razzismo nell'Italia di fine Ottocento* (Roma: Carocci, 2006).

[14] See the sculptural portrait of Rudu in *Più che l'amore*, p. 128: "Egli è di membra snelle, asciutto e muscoloso come quei veltri sardeschi addestrati alla 'piga' contro la bestia e l'uomo, fosco in viso come un indigeno dell'alto Egitto, raso i neri capelli, nerissimo gli occhi sagaci tra cigli lunghi e folti, con tutti i piani facciali della fronte e del mento ridotti su l'osso alla più semplice singolarità quali nel masso calcàrio li scolpiva l'arte egizia dell'Antico Impero."

there is a sense of savage cruelty in this claustrophobic space which renders it uncanny, like a chamber of ritual horrors.[15]

Shortly before the play's conclusion, which will bring their ultimate "sacrifice," Corrado recalls a scene of torture endured together with Rudu at the hands of a black African tribe after a bloody massacre. In this scene, the two men, whose names (Corrado and Rudu) echo one another, became one single terrifying demon in the eyes of the natives, who acknowledged their superhuman and god-like power and finally submitted to it:

> A Olda, sopraffatto dal numero, atterrato, disarmato, stretto in un cerchio ostile, mi sollevai di sul cumulo nero degli uccisi (sotto i mille sguardi di terrore e di furore sentivo il bianco del mio vólto divenire soprannaturale e quasi dalla potenza dell'anima assumere la luce dell'immortalità), mi sollevai e dissi pacato per la bocca dell'interprete: 'Io sono un dèmone, e voi non potete farmi né soffrire né morire'. Dissi e mantenni. Il mio buon Sardo era al mio fianco; e per obbedirmi seppe esssere il mio pari. 'Né soffrire né morire.' Cantammo e ridemmo, nella tortura. Vedemmo colare il nostro sangue, udimmo scricchiolare le giunture delle nostre ossa; e cantammo e ridemmo, sempre fissando i carnefici che non sostenevano lo sguardo sgomenti. 'Né soffrire né morire'. Il Fato mi contraccambiò d'amore! Il pànico a un tratto spense la ferocia; il supplizio fu tralasciato; la tribù si sottomise al dèmone; inalzato dal coraggio sopra il dolore e sopra la morte. Il vólto bianco parve immortale.[16]

The political and racial message could not be clearer. Italy, which Lombroso, quoted by Niceforo in *L'Italia barbara contemporanea*, defined as "united, but certainly not uni-

---

[15] *Più che l'amore*, pp. 105-6.
[16] *Più che l'amore*, p. 161. A similar scene is recalled earlier, p. 51.

fied,"[17] can be made truly and once again one victorious race, as it was when Rome ruled over the *Mare Nostrum*, only through ennobling, unifying and ultimately sacred violence. The whole body of the land, including its islands and the peninsula jutting into the Mediterranean towards Africa, must be revered and celebrated as sacred space through violent sacrifice, rather than exploited and profaned. Corrado, who is by training an architect and an engineer, rebelled long ago against the system of internal colonialism and land exploitation which enslaved the Sardinian working class to northern entrepreneurs, and refused to keep working on the island's mines or build factories. He dreamed instead of "divenire un costruttore su terre di conquista, ritrovare quell' architettura coloniale che i Romani piantarono nell'Africa degli Scipioni."[18] Ultimately, however, his is not a constructive but a sacrificial instinct. His atavistic *istinto ferino*, which makes him yearn to return to fight in Africa, is effectively a death wish, a yearning for sacrificial self-immolation, and for a primitive destiny that he and the faithful Rudu finally embrace together. Fused together they thus become icons of the higher sacredness of the nation cleansed of the corrupting influence of *Giolittismo*.

Corrado's double, *deuteragonista* and alter-ego in the tragedy is his friend Virginio, once his roommate at school in Rome, and an engineer himself, but, unlike Corrado, a humane, rational and thoughtful human being whose job is to build bridges and dams and control the flow of the Tiber through Rome. The two men complement each other in an allegorical symmetry: Corrado is as primitive, vehement, cruel and passionate as Virginio is civilized, controlled, gentle, and rational. Their union is symbolically necessary to the greatness of the nation. Their brotherly and nearly inces-

---

[17] Alfredo Niceforo, *L'Italia barbara contemporanea* (Milano-Palermo: Sandron, 1898) p. 296.
[18] *Più che l'amore*, p. 54.

tuous and homoerotic bond is meant to highlight another meaning of *blood* in the play. What matters in the economy of the text is not *consanguineità*, not the biological bond of blood or family, which, we are given to understand, may be tainted, weak or compromising, but rather the kinship one chooses to embrace. Corrado and Virginio have chosen to be brothers and to love one another. The only female character in the play, Maria, is but a shadowy figure for this male love, and a vessel for its final incarnation, "il germe che tu nutri" (p. 122) – the transformation of blood into seed. Maria's incestuous attachment to her brother only highlights her role as the link between the two men, the means through which they can become one. Seduced and made pregnant by Corrado, this typically D'annunzian figure of pure female self-devotion and self-denial is there only to bring the blood of her brother Virginio to this ideal union and fusion of the two opposite types of man – the primitive and the civilized, the passionate and the rational, the dreamer and the builder. Through this future human being, Corrado hopes, "la mia ragione eroica di vita sia perpetuata." In his eyes, Maria's child promises in fact to redeem "tutta la mia *razza* imperitura." Corrado's seed mixed with Maria's and Virginio's blood will rekindle the fire of the heroic spirit, and spark a general rebirth: "M'è parso che nel *germe* ancor cieco del nuovo essere sia entrata la più fulgida favilla del mio spirito."[19]

The essentially religious logic of this "Mediterranean tragedy" that, in its attempt to imagine a possibility of redemption for the Italian "race" at the beginning of the 20th century, manages syncretically to incorporate so many disparate textual elements from classical Greece, the ancient Mediterranean and the imagined, exotic and otherworldly African continent, could and did indeed seem delirious and far-fetched on the Roman stage at its 1906 opening. Yet, this

---

[19] *Più che l'amore*, pp. 122; 141 (emphasis mine).

redemptive logic soon began to appear less abstract. D'Annunzio returned to many of the same *topoi* in his later works (most notably the "Canzone del sangue"). By 1911, his audience was enthralled and ready to embrace the nation's destiny across the Mediterranean, in Libya.

Works Cited

Bataille, Georges. *Visions of Eccess. Selected Writings 1927-1939*. Ed. Alan Stockl. University of Minnesota Press, 1985.

Becker, Jared M. *Nationalism and Culture. Gabriele d'Annunzio and Italy after the Risorgimento*. New York: Peter Lang, 1994.

D'Annunzio, Gabriele. "Più che l'amore. Tragedia moderna." *Tragedie, sogni e misteri*. Ed. Annamaria Andreoli and Giorgio Zanetti. Milano: Mondadori, 2013. Vol 2.

_____. *Prose di Ricerca*. Milano: Mondadori, 1947. Vol I.

_____. *Scritti giornalistici* 1889-1938. Ed. Anna Maria Andreoli. Milano: Mondadori, 1996.

_____. *Scritti giornalistici*. Ed. Annamaria Andreoli and Giorgio Zanetti. Milano: Mondadori: 2003. Vol. 2.

_____. *Tragedie, sogni e misteri*. Ed. Annamaria Andreoli and Giorgio Zanetti. Milano: Mondadori, 2013. Vol. 2.

_____. *Versi d'Amore e di Gloria* Annamaria Andreoli and Niva Lorenzini. Milano: Mondadori, 1984. Vol. 2.

Frese Witt, Mary Ann. *The Search for Modern Tragedy*. Ithaca: Cornell University Press, 2001.

Labanca, Nicola. "Memorie e complessi di Adua." *Adua, le ragioni di una sconfitta*. Ed. Angelo del Boca. Bari: Laterza, 1997. 397-416.

Moroni, Mario. "1897, scrivere i confini: la retorica della siepe in D'Annunzio e Pascoli." *Al limite. L'idea di margine nel Novecento italiano*. Firenze: Le Monnier, 2007. 71-85.

Nani, Michele. *Ai confini della nazione. Stampa e razzismo nell'Italia di fine Ottocento*. Roma: Carocci, 2006.

Niceforo, Alfredo. *Italiani del Nord e Italiani del Sud*. Torino: Bocca, 1901.

———. *L'Italia barbara contemporanea.* Milano-Palermo: Sandron, 1898.
Nietzsche, Friedrich. *Daybreak. Thoughts on the Prejudices of Morality.* Transl. R.J. Hollingdale. Ed. Maudemarie Clarck and Brian Leiter. Cambridge: Cambridge University Press, 1997.
Re, Lucia. "Italians and the Invention of Race: The Poetics and Politics of Difference in the Struggle over Libya, 1890-1913." *California Italian Studies Journal* 1.1 (2010): 1-58.
Tomasello, Giovanna. *La letteratura coloniale italiana dalle avanguardie al fascismo.* Palermo: Sellerio, 1984.
Valentini, Valentina. *La tragedia moderna e mediterranea. Sul teatro di Gabriele d'Annunzio.* Milano: Franco Angeli, 1992.
Valesio, Paolo. *Gabriele d'Annunzio: The Dark Flame.* Trans. Marilyn Migiel. New Haven and London: Yale University Press, 1992.

UNDEFENDED COMMUNICATION

Laura Wittman
Stanford University

> If I could come back from the dead, I would –
> I'd come back for an apple,
> and just for one bite, one break,
> and the cold sweet grain on the tongue.
> There is so little difference between
>
> an apple and a kiss, between desire
> and the taste of desire.
> Anyone who tells you other-
> wise is a liar, as bad
> as a snake in the quiet grass.
>
> You can watch out for the snake and the lie.
> But the grass, the green green wave
> of it, there below the shadows of the black
> and twisted boughs, will not be
> what you thought it would be.
>
> S. Stewart, *Columbarium* (2003, pp. 23, 26)

L'organismo retorico che abbiamo parzialmente (*non* sinteticamente e *non* frammentariamente) analizzato è quello di un pensiero *violentemente esploso* in frammenti. Ciò a cui assistiamo infatti è insieme una parodia *e* una celebrazione del pensare filosofico come sforzo onnicomprensivo. Parodia [...] perché un pensiero presentato come frammento è [...] un pensiero indifeso. È una sentinella perduta, [...] La sua è una retorica del vagabondaggio. [...] Che lezione scaturisce da tutto ciò? Che quasi nessuna questione filosofica [...] è risolubile sul piano filosofico. Resta soltanto la via della contemplazione retorica [...] Per recuperare, appunto, [...]

From: *Discourse Boundary Creation*. Bordighera Press, 2013

un'*insinuazione* della morte dentro la vita; [...] [...] un silenzio interruttivo, che come tale volge in crisi ogni progetto di continuità. Questo silenzio si insinua come un cuneo tra (se vogliamo usare la terminologia fenomenologica) l'atto noetico e il suo contenuto noematico – è un silenzio bruno, non solare.

P. Valesio, Ascoltare il silenzio (1986, pp. 237, 248, 249, 381)

ha sognato l'incontro vita/morte:
guardava una chiazza
di terreno dall'alto
(violetto era il colore)
dove un bimbo incontrava,
gli pare, un altro bimbo.
Ha sentito
come una crepa al cuore –
prima di ricadere nel risveglio.

P. Valesio, "La soglia" (2009, p. 84)

My reflections will cover three things that I hope emerge from these opening quotations. First, I want to discuss coming back from the dead, and ask what might seem like the redundant question: why return to life? Second, following the inspiration of *Ascoltare il Silenzio*, I will propose that the answer to this question is by its very nature not "sul piano filosofico," but located rather in that experience Valesio describes as "insinuazione," "interru[zione]," "silenzio bruno," and especially, "pensiero indifeso." Finally, third, I will draw on Valesio's recent collection of poems, *Il volto quasi umano*, to consider how this sort of experience might be related to poetry.

1. COMING BACK TO LIFE:
   TRANSCENDENCE VERSUS TRANSFORMATION

First, then, why return to life? In the Gospel of John (11:41-44), Lazarus is remarkably silent about his experience,

"Undefended Communication"

but I think it is fair to say that more or less up to the nineteenth century this silence is one of ineffable plenitude, such that even for the Romantic poets it still contains clear "intimations of immortality." After that, in contrast, his silence becomes more and more "interruttivo," in the era when, indeed, all "progetti di continuità" are in crisis. It becomes fragmentary, and its intentions are uncertain.

Maurice Barrès is a typical example, as he imagines a dialogue between Lazarus and Seneca in which the latter ironically harangues the former:

> quoique vous ayez observé la plus grande discrétion sur cette anecdote désormais historique, il est évident que vous êtes renseigné sur le problème de l'au-delà. Si vous balancez comme je vois, c'est que la vérité ne s'en impose pas [...][1]

Barrès then uses his dialogue to pose the question that in modernity is typical of the Lazarus story: what sort of reasons to live – what sort of vitality, enthusiasm, or inspiration – remain to Lazarus, now dispossessed of the afterlife? Having come back, really, through no choice of his own, Barres asks, is his only option to continue believing in Jesus or rather, in life after death, for lack of a better illusion? More broadly, after the 1850s or so, focus is on how Lazarus has been transformed by an experience that, in and of itself, remains impenetrably obscure. So it is now his transformation, his return, that we must read in order to divine why or whether life is worth living. A crucial related question is, of course, what does the very obscurity of Lazarus' experience mean? Is it merely a blank space upon which we can only project, or does it have a more palpable, experiential realness to it?

I am going to draw on D. H. Lawrence and Luigi Pirandello to give an idea of some recurrent features in modern versions of Lazarus' resurrection. Lawrence's short novel,

---

[1] Maurice Barrès, *Le Culte du moi, III: Le Jardin de Bérénice*, pp. 149-150.

The Man Who Died, is also the last one he published, in 1929. It conflates Jesus and Lazarus to tell the story of who Jesus became, after he returned not to the father and the transcendent, but to the very same world and times he had preached in. As Lawrence himself commented, "Jesus gets up and feels very sick about everything, and can't stand the old crowd any more – so cuts out – and as he heals up, he begins to find what an astonishing place the phenomenal world is, far more marvelous than any salvation or heaven – and thanks his stars he needn't have a 'mission' any more."[2] The theme is familiar and Nietzschean: the morality that proffers an elsewhere cuts us off from the sacredness of reality here and now. But there are two remarkable things about Lawrence's novel that are typically "Lazarean."

First, the emphasis on the body's vitality as the very essence of the phenomenal world:

> Strange is the phenomenal world, dirty and clean together! And I am the same. Yet I am apart! And life bubbles variously. Why should I have wanted it to bubble all alike? What a pity I preached to them! A sermon is so much more likely to cake into mud, and to close the fountains, than is a psalm or a song. I made a mistake. I understand that they executed me for preaching to them. Yet they could not finally execute me, for now I am risen in my own aloneness, and inherit the earth, since I lay no claim to it. And I will be alone in the seethe of all things; first and foremost, forever, I shall be alone. But I must toss this bird [the cock he freed from the peasant's house] into the seethe of phenomena, for he must ride his wave. How hot he is with life! [...] the body of my desire has died, and I am not in touch anywhere. Yet how do I know! All at least is life.[3]

The celebration of vitality, in a tone that often turns to the elegiac, is per se not unusual in this period. What is notable

---

[2] Cf. letter to Earl Brewster, 3 May 1927, in D.H. Lawrence, *The Letters of D.H. Lawrence* (Cambridge: Cambridge University Press, 1991), p. 50.
[3] D.H. Lawrence, *The Man Who Died* (New York: The Ecco Press, 1994), p. 35.

is that embodied life suffers from its aloneness: this is no lofty solitude, but a symptom of incipient depression, a sense that for all that "all is life," something is missing or hollowed out. For me, this is a symptom of what feminist critics such as Françoise Meltzer and Elizabeth Grosz describe as the modern (and postmodern) nostalgia for an identity associated with an imaginary, pre-Cartesian, holistic body. For them, this is a failure to address the body in its situatedness and historicity. I would add that it is an attempt to reenchant the phenomenal world, which founders against the problem of the relationship of the one to the many, or also of individual mortality, which the "seethe of all things" cannot undo. Another way of putting this is that Lazarus has seen that he cannot transcend mortality but he still has to learn the inner transformation this implies (Grosz, 1994; Meltzer, 2001).

This brings me to the second Lazarean element of Lawrence's novel: though purportedly a novel about life, we find in it a fascination with death, whose dual nature cannot be evaded. On the one hand death is the very opposite of the phenomenal Lawrence wishes to celebrate, for it suddenly dawned on him:

> "I asked them all to serve me with the corpse of their love. And in the end I offered them only the corpse of my love. This is my body – take and eat – my corpse." A vivid shame went through him. "After all," he thought, "I wanted them to love with dead bodies. If I had kissed Judas with love, perhaps he would never have kissed me with death. Perhaps he loved me in the flesh, and I willed that he should love me bodilessly, with the corpse of love – "[4]

As we will see more clearly in Pirandello, this corpse as total end of the self, total disenchantment of the phenomenal, is depicted as the result of rationalism, scientism, and positivism, as well as Christianity as distinct from Jesus himself. In

---

[4] Ibid., p. 75.

this view, death becomes pure negative, the opposite of life, that which can only be pushed away. On the other hand, at the end of Lawrence's novel, Jesus encounters a young woman who is a priestess of Isis, and in their sexual encounter they reenact the story of Osiris and Isis. Their sexuality is more than the wish for a holistic body I mentioned above, however. Osiris is the god of the dead, or indeed of death itself; he has been associated with Lazarus and is also known as the lord of silence. Since Isis is associated with motherhood, fertility, and magic, as a couple they represent the interpenetration of death and life. Their presence in Lawrence's novel is not mere nostalgia for religion, displaced onto a non-Western tradition (though it is that, too): it is also a strong if oblique claim that we cannot properly see the phenomenal as "astonishing" and "marvelous" if we do not learn that death too is a god, death too is "astonishing" and "marvelous."

For reasons of space I cannot dwell much on Pirandello's 1930 play, *Lazzaro*, which is the second of his three myth plays (with *La nuova colonia* and *I giganti della montagna*). The play is set in the present, and is about Diego Spina, a man of rigid and uncompromising Catholic faith, who is pronounced dead after a car accident, but is brought back to life by his doctor. As he remembers nothing, his entire family tries to keep this passage through death a secret for fear that losing his faith will truly kill him. The one exception is his son, Lucio, who depicts this as a chance for his father to find a truer faith:

> Vedi com'è? Per non finire noi, annulliamo in nome di Dio la vita, e facciamo regnare Dio anche di là (non si sa dove) in un presunto regno della morte, perché ci dia là, un premio o un castigo. Quasi che il bene e il male potessero esser quelli di uno che è di parte, mentre Egli solo, che è Tutto, sa ciò che fa e perché lo fa. Ecco, vede, dottore? questo dovrebbe esser per lui, com'è stato per me, il vero risorgere dalla morte: negarla in Dio, e credere in questa sola Immortalità, non nostra, non per noi, speranza di un

> premio o timore di castigo: credere in questo eterno presente della vita ch'è Dio, e basta. E Dio allora veramente, dopo quest'esperienza che gli ha concesso di poter fare, compirà – e soltanto Lui – il miracolo della sua risurrezione.[5]

There are some remarkable convergences with Lawrence's novel. In Pirandello, the idealization of embodied life is found in Spina's estranged wife Sara, who could not agree with how he cut off his children from nature, pushing Lucio into the seminary and causing Lia to become paralytic. Sara has made a new life for herself with the peasant Arcadipane, and they with their two other children are fully embedded in that marvelous phenomenal we saw in Lawrence. But the drama revolves around Lucio, for at the play's opening he intends to leave the seminary to embrace his mother's vitality. Here we have an echo of Lawrence's aloneness, since for Lucio there is something sadly mute about the life his mother embodies, and he cannot quite join her in it.

In the end, faced with his father's near-death experience, and most of all with his father's despair at losing his Catholic image of the afterlife (the father tries to kill Arcadipane and himself after he finds out what happened), Lucio reverses course again and decides he must become a priest. This is very clearly for Pirandello a rejection of the scientific view of death embodied by the doctor, Gionni, who does not find anything mysterious in the father's reanimation. This echoes Lawrence's aversion for a purely material understanding of death. But where Lawrence draws on ancient Egypt to make a philosophical point, Pirandello is concerned with the connection between myths and institutions. Lucio thus explains at the end:

> Ora intendo e sento veramente la parola di Cristo: CARITÀ! Perché gli uomini non possono star tutti e sempre in piedi, Dio stesso vuole in terra la sua Casa, che

---

[5] Luigi Pirandello, *Lazzaro: mito in tre atti* (Milano: Mondadori, 1930), p. 94.

prometta la vera vita di là; la sua Santa Casa, dove gli stanchi e i miseri e i deboli si possano inginocchiare [...].⁶

There may be something quite opportunistic about returning to the institutional Church right after the Lateran Pacts of 1929, but this does not invalidate the still unresolved question Pirandello is raising. Even those who have direct experience – like the modern Lazarus, direct experience of the re-enchantment of both life and death – even they need myths, and thus languages, cultures, and institutions to uphold and transmit their experiences.

To sum up: many different Lazarus stories say that, yes, we come back to life, perhaps nostalgically, in search of a fresh look on reality, and also in search of a more direct and honest engagement with mortality but, more fundamentally, the return requires an inner transformation in which communication with self and others plays an essential role. As we are about to see, and as Pirandello already suggested, this desire to communicate is fraught with dangers, and they are all about reification. Or, as Stewart writes, to come back for an apple, the first bite, means also to meet the snake and the lie.

2. TELLING THE STORY: TRANSFORMATION VERSUS REIFICATION

Second, then, what do I mean by reification? Basically, the desire to fix, to freeze, to pin down the mysterious astonishment of the return to life. (In this respect, it is notable that for Stewart the snake and the lie come after the first bite, not before: evil is not in the appetite for knowledge but in a second degree reflection on it or desire to grasp it.) In the case of Lazarus stories, a common expression of reification is the feelings of fear, contempt, or anger he causes, at times even in those closest to him. They find his silence about his experience – his inability or unwillingness to reify it – unbearable.

---

⁶ Ibid., p. 143.

"Undefended Communication"

I will mention briefly a salient case, which is Leonid Andreyev's 1906 short story, "Lazarus," in which Lazarus' gaze is described as "the unfathomable *There* gaz[ing] upon humanity." All who meet this gaze fall into a terrible depression, and even a great positive solar classical artist who attempts to conquer it ends up producing nothing but sculptures that are "crooked, strange, [..] shapeless, [...] inside out, [...] wild fragments." For Andreyev, as moderns, we can only be obsessed with a death that is unfathomably empty: condemned to fix our gaze on Lazarus in the vain attempt to pin down what he knows, all we do is fragment our own experience, cut ourselves from life.

When we look at the literature on near-death experiences, we find a different, yet symmetrical struggle with reification. The term itself dates from the 1970s, and is meant as an equally scientific alternative to terms like reanimation. Its apparent neutrality is however undercut by the title of the book that launched it, Raymond Moody's *Life After Life* (Moody, 1976). Moody's book is in fact mild compared to the innumerable, often cultish books that followed, claiming that all near death experiences are essentially the same, across cultures and times – containing, at the very least, a dark tunnel, a light, and spiritual entities – and that this proves there is life after death. Such books – even when they are sincere stories by experiencers themselves – reveal most of all the power of our desire to make death understandable, to give Lazarus' silence a coherent and predictable shape (Holden et al., 2009).

Serious study of near-death experiences, from a scientific and a cultural perspective, is relatively new, but it already shows a lot more diversity and a lot less certainty about life after death. To the humanist, one particularly provocative if very preliminary finding is that modern Westerners have experiences that are a lot more abstract – reduced, indeed, quite often to the tunnel and the light – whereas in other cultures and in earlier eras people's experiences are far more dramatic, populated by mythological figures and extraordinary otherworldly domains. The point has been made that our era has a rather poor imagination when it comes to death and dying, and what we see here is how this poverty actually changes what we are able to experience when we die (d'Aquili and Newberg, 1999; Zaleski, 1987). A similar claim has been made about hypnosis, which has been experienced differently in various historical periods depending on cultural expectations (Harrington, 2008). Reification is a sort of willful denial of this complex role of the imagination in shaping what we call reality, and also a willful attempt to understand something we have not given ourselves time to meditate upon – whether we insist on Andreyev's dark nihilism or on a more postmodern neon-bright salvation.

There are, of course, a number of writers, thinkers, and poets who seek to explore Lazarus' silence without reifying it, proposing ways to dwell with and in his astonishment. One fascinating example is Miguel de Unamuno's 1930 short story, *San Manuel Bueno, Mártir*. I lack space to discuss it in detail, but must mention that in this story, Lazarus is a political activist who is converted to a very unique version of Christianity: he dies to socialism in order to believe in a here and now governed by charity; but most important, he says he does not believe in God or the afterlife, only in this life. There is great deal of irony in Unamuno's story, especially because there are three levels of imbricated narration, but the overall point is that both Lazarus and Don Manuel, the title character and priest, experience and act out a certain faith while using their conscious unbelief to undo the reification that both Christianity and socialism are subject to. As Angela puts it in her version of the story, "without believing in their belief, they actually believed."

The very fact that there are other, more skeptical perspectives in Unamuno's story brings us to the key question: short of coming back to life, literally, again in each moment, how do we explore the nexus of life and death without reifying it? Or also: in our era of self-conscious abstraction, how do we populate death with believable myths? Valesio offers us a possible direction in his meditation on a kind of silence that cannot be reified:

"Undefended Communication"

> Ciò che, in questo silenzio, esaspera ogni ideologia è che esso non è sinonimo di segreto, è un silenzio trasparente. Non è un segreto soggettivo, poiché non si propone di celare nulla; né è un segreto oggettivo, poiché non si aggira attorno a uno specifico contenuto, impermeabile alla parola. Per questo silenzio, che è (ripeto) non una modalità silenziaria tra le altre, ma la piena realizzazione del silenzio, per questo silenzio l'ineffabile non è la caratteristica di certe privilegiate strutture dell'Essere, ma è uno stato pervasivo di tutto l'essere (nella sua generalità, dal sublime al quotidiano, con la « e » iniziale, appunto, minuscola).
>
> E' questo, insomma, un silenzio non edificante [...] un silenzio testardo [...] *pig-headed* – come dice l'inglese [...] E' stato attaccato come ateistico e sovversivo dalle varie chiese, e d'altro canto è stato deriso come un'effusione misticheggiante, irrazionalistica.[7]

Interestingly, like this silence, near-death experiences exasperate both religious and scientific ideologies. However, what I want to stress at this turn in my argument is the range of Valesio's "pig-headed" "non-edifying" silence – "dal sublime al quotidiano." One answer – a major answer I think – to how we combat reification and recover enchantment, especially as regards supposedly lofty ultimate questions, is a turn to the everyday.

Before I turn to Valesio's poetic practice, I want to mention two recent examples of a completely fresh look on near-death experience thanks to the everyday. The first is Jill Bolte Taylor's *My Stroke of Insight*, in which the author, a brain scientist, details her experience of slowly losing her critical, rational, linguistic – more or less her left-brain – faculties due a hemorrhage.

> I remember that first day of the stroke with terrific bitter-sweetness. In the absence of the normal functioning of my left orientation association area, my perception of my physical boundaries was no longer limited to where my

---

[7] Paolo Valesio, *Ascoltare il silenzio*, pp. 361-62.

skin met air. I felt like a genie liberated from its bottle. The energy of my spirit seemed to flow like a great whale gliding though a sea of silent euphoria. [...] it was obvious to me that I would never be able to squeeze the enormousness of my spirit back inside this tiny cellular matrix. [...]

Without a language center telling me: "I am Dr. Jill Bolte Taylor. I am a neuroanatomist. I live at this address and at this phone number," I felt no obligation to being her anymore. [...] Although I felt enormous grief for the death of my left hemisphere consciousness – and the woman I had been, I concurrently felt tremendous relief. [...] I shifted from the doing-consciousness of my left brain to the being-consciousness of my right brain. I morphed from feeling small and isolated to feeling enormous and expansive. [...] My entire self-concept shifted as I no longer perceived myself as a single, a solid, an entity with boundaries that separated me from the entities around me. I understood that at the most elementary level, I am a fluid. Of course I am a fluid! [...]

And I must say, there was both freedom and challenge for me in recognizing that our perception of the external world, and our relationship to it, is a product of our neurological circuitry. For all those years of my life, I really had been a figment of my own imagination![8]

In many ways, Taylor's adherence to a language of scientific observation and to naturalistic metaphors allows her to sidestep the sort of ironic and unhappy consciousness of Unamuno, or before him Andreyev.[9] This leads her to a poetic paradox: on the one hand, the self is a product of neurological circuitry; on the other, there is now a vaster voice, a speaker who can perceive this self as "a figment of my own imagination." Ultimately Taylor's account is part of a new mythology of death and dying that I will provisionally call

---

[8] Jill Bolte Taylor, *My Stroke of Insight*, pp. 67-70.
[9] As an aside, recent neuroanatomy shows that we have language areas in both our left and right brain: losing the left one means losing our normal ability to speak and understand, but the right one, Taylor's experience suggests, is related to a more silentiary language, or also a more holistic one.

"Undefended Communication"

"The Marvelous Brain." This mythology refuses to separate the mind, or the soul, from matter and its processes, but at the same it acknowledges and even celebrates their nexus as unfathomably mysterious – a modern "mysterium tremendum."

My second example is Kathryn Davis' novel, *The Thin Place*. It belongs to the same mythology as Taylor's account, but gives it a more poetic expression. In it, Mees is a girl who has an uncanny capacity to draw the nearly-dead or the recently dead back into their bodies. She is a rather unremarkable girl otherwise, who likes pink clothing and occasionally has slight temper tantrums, and the reader gets the impression all the people in the small town where the novel is set fail to notice what she is doing because she is too commonplace to be seen. In fact, they go about their lives, even after some strange returns from death take place, as though nothing had happened. They don't want to see Mees and what she does, and so they don't. Here is one instance, in which Mees brings a dog back to life – notably the style and metaphors used are exactly the same as for people:

> What was inside Buddy was like stars connected by strings of light, a chain of stars, strings linking star to star, and not just in *there* but the strings were everywhere, in her arms, for example, and whole of them strung to the star at the back of Buddy's nose. The closer she got, the more densely knitted it all was and also clumped with debris, dark clots of stinking matter, buzzing like bees and restless, fidgeting around, bumping themselves into place and taking up all the room. [...] Buddy, Mees wanted to say. But you couldn't talk. You couldn't be in the world and in there at the same time. You couldn't scratch the backfly bites behind your ears no matter how much they itched, no matter how crazy they were driving you. Otherwise, you might never get back. [...]
> But if blood and pieces of bone were where they weren't supposed to be, it made the clumping worse. Mixed with those buzzing stinking clots, and the stars going out like matches. There were only so many of them – if you didn't

get in soon enough they'd all have gone out and then there wouldn't be a thing you could do. Nothing.[10]

You can see "The Marvelous Brain" in the association of neurons firing with the life and death of stars – the implication being that we live in a sentient universe, where matter and the incorporeal meet just as do the micro and the macro. But the magic of Davis' novel lies in the narrating voice – via free indirect speech, closest to Mees' voice: it has the kind of bumpy materiality of pre-adolescence, and a lack of self-consciousness that is, crucially, associated with animal life. In the end, Davis makes us picture God like an eleven-year-old girl playing house in the mud. Thus she slips in under the unhappy consciousness of our modernity to associate death with childhood enchantment.

3. THE POETICS OF UNDEFENDED COMMUNICATION

So let me address more directly, in this third and last part, the question implicit in what I just wrote: how do you capture poetically the fluidity of the everyday? what sort of poetics helps us to counter the skeptical eye we have developed for the nexus of life and death, and for spiritual transformation? how does "pensiero indifeso" become poetic practice without losing its freshness or falling into solipsism?

This is of course an old problem, and I will simply mention that Baudelaire, Valéry, and d'Annunzio all compare the poet to Lazarus, invoking the "risveglio ingenuo e terribile," of an "oeil frontière entre l'être et le non-être [...] regard d'agonisant, d'homme qui perd la reconnaissance" (d'Annunzio, 1990, 121; Valéry, 1992, 74; Baudelaire, 1968). Valéry's play on "perdre connaissance" – to lose consciousness or to faint – implies that the poet acquires a new consciousness by losing his ability to recognize, thus acquiring an ability to see as though for the first time. However "re-

---

[10] Kathryn Davis. *The Thin Place: A Novel* (New York: Little, Brown and Co., 2006), pp. 61-62.

"Undefended Communication"

connaissance" also means gratitude, and so Valéry implies the poet must be wary of losing that as well.

But it has become harder, I believe, since the last turn of the century, to "perd[re] la reconnaissance," as we have seen the darker side of myths of rebirth. I have already suggested that the everyday – a light touch rather than a grand gesture, a "Lazzaro-piccino" rather than a grand miracle – can help us here. In Valesio's *Il volto quasi umano* this rendering modest of lofty questions is an active pursuit, and thus I will conclude with a few salient examples.[11]

First, we find in these poems an attention to the silence of animals that recalls the observation made in *Dialogo coi volanti*: "[gli animali] ci stimolano, poi ci offendono e disturbano e tormentano, poi tornano a stimolarci, e così via, in vertiginose alternanze; insomma, gli animali non ci trasmettono idee" (Valesio, 1997, 30; see e.g., "Il Crinale," Valesio, 2009, 85). This attention is very much the sort of meditative state or even enlightenment that numerous religious traditions pursue but, in rather Zen fashion, taken down a notch. Related is the focus on "quelle piccole lacune / [...] quelle feritine e fenditure / attraverso cui passa la salvezza," which echo the "crepa al cuore" of the "incontro vita/morte" I cited in the beginning, again chipping away at the lofty ("A-morte, e vita," and "La soglia," Valesio, 2009, 90, 84).

In "Albare," we find a second element of this poetics, which consists in evoking high poetic models only to shroud them with uncertainty:

> Nel lucernaio dell'alba
> gli è sembrato
> vedere una macchia rossa
> sopra il guanciale dove poco prima
> era giaciuta la bocca
> e poi si è reso conto
> che era il piccolo stemma dell'albergo
> ma qualcosa è restato

---

[11] See Valesio's take on Catherine of Siena as "caterina-piccina," Valesio, 2009, p. 235.

> di sanguìneo e affocato:
> il marchio era il ricordo
> di un passaggio infernale
> in troppe ore prima della luce
> che non eran nemmeno
> riuscite a salire
> alla dignità degli incubi.[12]

The journey to the underworld – of Orpheus, Aeneas, or Dante – ultimately inheres in a sign chosen through an initial mistake, a misrecognition. There is a palpable sense of human frailty in this error – and I would say also of that gratitude Valéry speaks of, in the willingness to accept this sign after all, to welcome the error. But this is also a meta-moment, a comment on how experience is translated into poetics: rather than using the everyday as a springboard for a departure into the world of the imagination, and of myths of the afterlife, the poem reverses course, indicating that we must gently dig beneath the clarity of myth until we find what Davis calls those "dark clots of stinking matter, buzzing like bees and restless."

Hence a third, crucial, element of poetics is a relationship to prayer epitomized by words like "perdonanza," "corazone strappazzato," and most of all "avvilitudine" (Valesio, 2009, 33, 67, 46). Prayer, of course, implies a certain immediacy, a lack of self-consciousness, that Valesio refers to in his title *Dardi* (2000). In *Il volto quasi umano* Valesio returns to the elusiveness of such immediacy, to the paradox of pursuing it and even more of setting it down into poetry. His "personaggio" is a recognition of this problem, at once not him (a mere persona) and yet terribly also him (who else may speak here?). But his neologisms and borrowings from Spanish are where we find at the very core of the poetic word a kind of breaking – "feritine e fenditure" – of poetry into prayer. "Perdonanza" and "corazone" are, to the Italian ear, a little clumsy, reminding us that prayer is neither adroit nor masterful.

---

[12] Paolo Valesio, "Albare," 2009, p. 107

"Avvilitudine" is more complex and takes me to my fourth and last point: this is a poetics of learning to see not what is hidden but what is too obvious to be noticed. "Avvililtudine" modifies "avvilimento," of course, but also echoes words like "beatitudine," "gratitudine," or "finitudine," as well as the French "négritude." It thus takes that state of slight depression and turns it into a moral choice; like "finitude" with respect to "finiteness," it says that human recognition of our condition is difficult – we so often fail to see what is right in front of us – but also that there is an ethical striving in word choices. This I believe is the essence of "undefended communication." The novelist Jeanne Hyvrard has done something similar in coining the term "meurtritude," which modifies "meurtri" ("wounded") but also "mort" ("death") (Hyvrard, 1977). What such modifications do, in the end, is allow us to encounter the unexpected, "l'ovvietà incomprensibile / d'essere un essere umano" that lies before us when "è tutto così nitido e chiaro / che lui non sa che cosa significhi" ("Affrontamento," and "I vuoti," Valesio, 2009, 154, 181).

As Stewart warned us in the beginning:

> But the grass, the green green wave
> of it, there below the shadows of the black
> and twisted boughs, will not be
> what you thought it would be.

To which Valesio would respond:

> Siamo quello che non pensavamo
> siamo la nostra
> gloriosa limitatezza.[13]

---

[13] Paolo Valesio, "L'unico," 2009, p. 143.

Works Cited

Barrès, Maurice. *Le Culte du moi, III: Le Jardin de Bérénice*. Paris: Perrin et Cie, 1891.
Baudelaire, Charles. "Le peintre de la vie moderne." *Oeuvres complètes*. vols. Paris: Editions du Seuil, 1968.
d'Annunzio, Gabriele. *Di me a me stesso*. Milano: Mondadori, 1990.
d'Aquili, Eugene G., and Andrew B. Newberg. *The Mystical Mind: Probing the Biology of Religious Experience*. Minneapolis: Fortress Press, 1999.
Davis, Kathryn. *The Thin Place: A Novel*. 1st ed. New York: Little, Brown and Co., 2006.
Grosz, E. A. *Volatile Bodies: Toward a Corporeal Feminism. Theories of representation and difference*. Bloomington: Indiana University Press, 1994.
Harrington, Anne. *The Cure Within: A History of Mind-Body Medicine*. 1st ed. New York: W.W. Norton & Co., 2008.
Holden, Janice Miner, et al. *The Handbook of Near-Death Experiences: Thirty Years of Investigation*. Santa Barbara, Calif.: Praeger Publishers, 2009.
Hyvrard, Jeanne. *La meurtritude*. Paris: Minuit, 1977.
Lawrence, D. H. *The Letters of D.H. Lawrence*. Ed. James T. Boulton. Cambridge: Cambridge University Press, 1991.
_____. *The Man Who Died [The Escaped Cock]*. 1929. New York: The Ecco Press, 1994.
Meltzer, Françoise. *For Fear of the Fire: Joan of Arc and the Limits of Subjectivity*. Chicago: The University of Chicago Press, 2001.
Moody, Raymond A. *Life After Life*. 1975. Harrisburg, Stackpole Books, 1976.
Pirandello, Luigi. *Lazzaro: mito in tre atti*. Milano: Mondadori, 1930.
Stewart, Susan. *Columbarium*. Chicago: University of Chicago Press, 2003.
Taylor, Jill Bolte. *My Stroke of Insight: A Brain Scientist's Personal Journey*. New York: Plume, 2009.
Valéry, Paul. "La soirée avec M. Teste." *Oeuvres*. Ed. Jean Hytier. Vol. 1. 2 vols. Paris: Gallimard, 1992.
Valesio, Paolo. *Ascoltare il silenzio. La retorica come teoria*. Bologna: Il Mulino, 1986.
_____. *Dialogo coi volanti*. Napoli: Cronopio, 1997.

"Undefended Communication"

———. *Il volto quasi umano: Poesie-dardi, 2003-2005*. Bologna: Lombar Key, 2009.

Zaleski, Carol Goldsmith. *Otherworld Journeys: Accounts of Near-Death Experience in Medieval and Modern Times*. New York: Oxford University Press, 1987.

Gratulatoria / Testimonials

Gian Maria Annovi
University of Southern California

Su *Il volto quasi umano* di Paolo Valesio

L'ultimo libro di versi di Paolo Valesio, *Il volto quasi umano* (Bologna, Lombar Key 2009), che raccoglie oltre duecento poesie scritte, con poche eccezioni, tra il 2003 e il 2005, si presenta come un oggetto particolarmente complesso, a partire dal suo titolo. Il "quasi" posto in maniera provocatoria prima dell'aggettivo "umano," infatti, crea uno spazio di sospensione, una soglia d'arresto per il lettore, che si ritrova di fronte a un nome reso *indecidibile*. L'avverbio colloca il "volto" che Valesio ci invita a guardare a un passo prima e a un passo dopo dall'umano, tra quello che ancora non ha saputo (o potuto) diventare umano e la dimensione del divino. Tra il sub e l'ultra. Tra il troppo e il non ancora abbastanza. Tra la bassezza della terra e l'irraggiungibilità del cielo. Che questo spazio di sospensione—spazio, dunque, d'interrogazione sulla natura dell'uomo e sulla propria umanità—sia lo spazio del tipo di parola poetica che Valesio ha deciso di abitare lo mostra anche uno dei testi più belli della raccolta:

Per El Greco
Qualcheduno mi ha chiesto nella notte:
"Qual è quadro più bello
che tu abbia mai veduto?"
E senza esitazione io ho risposto:
"El entierro del conde de Orgaz",
perché non ho mai visto più vicini
quelli del cielo e quelli della terra.
   [*La sepoltura del Conte di Orgaz*]

"Su *Il volto quasi umano* di Paolo Valesio"

Questa poesia dedicata al famoso capolavoro toledano di El Greco, *La sepoltura del Conte di Orgaz,* non solo rende visibile lo spazio di sospensione cui accennavo, l'accostarsi—senza toccarsi—di cielo e terra, ma lo fa attraverso un'esperienza di natura estetica, in cui il *vedere* è però assai prossimo alla *visione* e alla fede nella realtà di quella visione. Scrivo fede perché *Il volto quasi umano* è anche—e dichiaratamente—la tormentata testimonianza di un credente che si interroga sul come si diventi umani, sul come l'uomo possa raggiungere il pieno della propria umanità, ma anche sul come Dio abbia saputo farsi uomo. Anche la fede, infatti, almeno secondo uno dei filosofi con cui Valesio intrattiene da anni i suoi dialoghi silenziari, Søren Kierkegaard, è una condizione di sospensione: "la corda alla quale si rimane appesi, senza impiccarsi."[1] Il volto quasi umano è la parola di questo soggetto fisicamente ed esistenzialmente sospeso, in lotta contro l'apnea dell'essere.

Nella storia della letteratura italiana meno frequentata, e per questo sicuramente battuta da Valesio, che ha peregrinato tra gli infiniti fogli-foglie della foresta filosofico-letteraria occidentale, c'è un'opera teatrale che inizia proprio con un personaggio che parla da impiccato, o meglio, da sospeso. Si tratta di *Orgia* di Pier Paolo Pasolini, un autore cui Valesio ha dedicato pagine pregnanti e che ancora costituisce il centro delle sue riflessioni sulla letteratura dell'estremo, insieme a Marinetti e d'Annunzio. Il nome di Pasolini non viene qui evocato per caso, infatti, lo si ritrova nel testo intitolato *Alba pratalia,* che rimanda a *Poesia in forma di Rosa:* "...alba pratalia, alba pratalia, alba pratalia...i prati bianchi!" Quest' immagine è la metafora—ancora una volta—di una scrittura sospesa: la scrittura dell'indovinello veronese, tra italiano e latino, lingua in transito, in cammino, *quasi*-lingua. Quella degli alba pratalia è allora anche la scrittura del "pellegrino della mente," per applicare a Valesio l'espressione da lui

---

[1] Søren Kierkegaard. *Aforismi e pensieri.* Ed. M. Baldini. (Roma: Newton & Compton, 1995).

riservata a Guido Guglielmi,[2] scrittura mentale, bianco su bianco, come sembra suggerirci in *Ecco un vivente arazzo d'improvviso, 1*, memore forse della "cette blanche agonie / par l'espace infligée" del *Cygne* di Mallarmé:

> Come si distinguono i due cigni
> dentro il banco di nebbia in fondo al lago?
> Perché risalta il loro candore
> dentro il più sfilacciato biancore.

Quella degli alba pratalia è dunque anche l'immagine di una scrittura come delirio bianco, soprattutto nel senso etimologico di delirare, "uscire dal solco"—quello bianco della pagina—per ritrovarsi fuori, nella vita:

> quando scrive lui strascina una pietra
> da un angolo del campo verso l'altro
> lasciando un solco sull'erba.
>
> [*Alba pratalia, 1-3*]

È, quella di questi versi di Valesio, un'immagine affaticata e sisifea del *Solo et pensoso* petrarchesco, dove il moto fisico nel campo è al tempo stesso mozione poetica. Proprio Petrarca è forse il più gigantesco tra i volti-fantasma dell'opera valesiana. Si legga, a conferma, quanto egli scrive nella *Nota* al volume: "la prima parte [...] descrive quei materiali sparsi che un soggetto raccoglie preparandosi a scrivere un resoconto di se stesso" (p.19). L'eco degli sparsi frammenti petrarcheschi, tra "fragmenta" e "rime sparse," è evidente.

Ciò che mi pare sia andato rincorrendo Valesio in quindici libri di poesia, compreso quest'ultimo, è proprio la *forma* di un canzoniere assoluto: canzoniere non come *raccolta di forme* ma come *forma che raccoglie* il resoconto di sé attraverso scaglie d'esistenza, tanto più piccole e insignificanti tanto più fortemente *significate,* fatte segni, indicazioni

---

[2] Paolo Valesio. "Guido Guglielmi, pellegrino della mente," in *Moderna* V/2, 2003.

per quel pellegrinaggio mentale cui si accennava pocanzi. Quella del frammento d'esistenza è, di fatto, l'unica forma metrica che conosca la poesia di Valesio in questa sua fase, anche a dispetto di quanto abbia scritto il diretto interessato nella sua *Nota*, in merito alla struttura dei testi:

> Ho voluto finora, nelle mie poesie-dardi, raccogliere in una entità unitaria il testo della poesia in senso stretto insieme con gli elementi che di solito si definiscono para-(o peri-)testuali, e che qui invece sono pienamente testuali. Insomma, *tutti* gli elementi di ciascuna delle poesie che costituiscono la maggioranza in questo libro—il titolo, l'epigrafe o motto, la dedica, la indicazione cronotopica finale [...] perfino le poche note esplicative a piè di pagina— concorrono a costituire il testo della poesia, senza fondamentale distinzione tra un centro e un contorno. (p. 17)

Data questa precisazione dettagliata, il lettore si aspetterebbe di trovare nella raccolta copiosi elementi para- o peri-testuali, invece, su oltre duecento testi, s'incontrano solamente dieci note, altrettante epigrafi e una ventina di dediche. Non molto, pare, per giustificare quella che parrebbe una vera e propria dichiarazione di poetica. Non siamo però di fronte ad una svista: anche questo elemento auto-esegetico va inteso come *delirio del soggetto*, qualcosa che, nell'intento di segnare un percorso definito, devia, prende altra via. Quello che emerge in questa nota è così il tentativo inconscio del soggetto scrivente di giustificare retoricamente ciò che appare, piuttosto, come la tendenza generale delle propria poesia: il superamento della distinzione "tra un centro e un contorno."

Per capire meglio cosa intendo, occorre considerare il contorno testuale in maniera radicale—ossia letterale—come *altro* del testo. Come ciò da cui lo scritto-centro è circondato e assediato: la vita. È questa l'immensa aspirazione del canzoniere valesiano, infinito dunque quanto può esserlo una stele di Brancusi, la non separazione tra testo ed esistenza. Lo spaesamento che coglie il prefatore del volume, Davide Rondoni, di fronte a uno spazio "dove la poesia non è più poesia, o meglio diventa la propria continua e per così dire salutare oltranza," (p. 11) è l'effetto radicalmente straniante di un'opera che non vuole distinguersi dalla vita, ossia che non si vuole perfetta, ma in cerca della propria realizzazione. Date, note, luoghi, epigrafi, dediche, non sono che il dito retorico dietro il quale il soggetto nasconde la propria necessità di radicare il testo nel vissuto, di incarnarlo. L'anima, insomma, come la pagina, deve essere sfondata:

> Ciò ch'è dentro è inferiore a ciò che è fuori:
> bisogna sfondare
> la tenda dell'anima
> perché il livello interiore
> salga all'altezza
> della esterna bellezza,
> della bontà circostante.
>
> Laghetto, 18 Giugno 2003
> [*Anti-introspezione*]

Questa necessità di non separare estetico ed esistenziale (che si ritrova forse in un'idea di Scrittura come Verbo, Parola concepita per ricadere nell'esistere) produce stranamente effetti molto prossimi a quelli riscontrabili nell'ultima stagione poetica pasoliniana, quella scandalosa di *Trasumanar e organizzar*. Il nome di Pasolini non lo s'è dunque fatto precedentemente invano. Anche in *Trasumanar*, innanzitutto, date ed elementi paratestuali sono inglobati in componimenti che sembrano costantemente e sfrontatamente violare formalmente il limite del poetico convenzionale. Anche quella di Valesio è una poesia che oscilla (come il volto sottoposto al "quasi" del titolo), che si muove *anche* al di sopra e al di sotto del poetico: tra saggio e appunto, folgorazione e annotazione, riflessione filosofica e pensiero nella doccia. Trasumanare sembra allora proprio il verbo più adatto a descrivere parte dell'operazione compiuta ne *Il volto quasi umano*. Che cos'è, infatti, la trasumanazione pasoliniana se non il superarsi del soggetto nell'offerta cruda, disperata e non mediata di un personaggio messo a nudo nella sua debolezza, nei suoi dubbi di essere umano? Facendosi personaggio,

"Su *Il volto quasi umano* di Paolo Valesio"

anche Valesio rende il lettore partecipe delle peripezie di un soggetto oggettivato ("O diverso individuo, / raccontami le tue peripezie," *Semivigilie*), che passa però alla terza persona, al "lui," distaccandosi in questo modo dall'operazione pasoliniana, dove il personaggio non smette mai d'identificarsi con l'autore. Ecco allora parzialmente spiegata la ragione per cui il titolo della sezione più imponente del *Volto* è proprio *Il personaggio della vita*, un titolo non privo d'implicazioni. Infatti, se la vita si rivela abitata di personaggi, ci ha insegnato Pirandello a suo tempo, essa non può che essere testo: opera. Scrittura ed esistenza si confondono, si assestano in uno spazio sospeso, in un quasi.

Per tornare a quanto si diceva all'inizio, anche la definizione che l'autore fornisce dei propri componimenti, quella di "dardi," da intendersi come "*giaculatoria*, vale a dire: preghiera breve lanciata verso/contro il cielo come un dardo," (p. 15) è immagine di questa sospensione che sembra costituire uno dei fili conduttori di tutta la raccolta. E lo è in quanto lanciare qualcosa contro il cielo significa—di fatto—collocarla nell'infinito. Il personaggio della poesia di Valesio è questo dardo sospeso nell'infinito. Tra il troppo del cielo e il troppo poco della vita. È l'aspirazione a farsi confine, quel confine invisibile della tela di El Greco, dove cielo e terra s'avvicinano senza mai davvero toccarsi.

Patrizio Ceccagnoli
University of Massachusetts - Amherst

Il lombrico e la nuvola. Una testimonianza

Paolo Valesio è un uomo straordinariamente umano, e un colto letterato con una lunga bibliografia e una grande biblioteca. Un prolifico protagonista delle umane lettere nel Nord America e un degno rappresentante della cultura italiana degli ultimi decenni. Che fosse essenzialmente, puramente, un letterato o meglio quello che noi chiamiamo un uomo di lettere, glielo disse anche Harold Bloom ai tempi di Yale, dove era arrivato con le referenze di Roman Jakobson e di Italo Calvino, lo studioso e lo scrittore.

Ho imparato molto standogli vicino. Per una questione di *kairos*, direbbe lui, ho avuto la fortuna di collaborarci durante, e dopo, il mio dottorato alla Columbia University. Ha guidato la scrittura della mia tesi sull'ultimo Marinetti, e a volte io mi domandavo se quello che vedevo fosse anche lui stesso un tipico esempio di stile tardo, un ultimo Valesio. Alla fine della sua illustre carriera, non rifugge dal pericolo dell'impressionismo. Se lo concede, forse coraggiosamente. Dice "poroso" e probabilmente non pensa a se stesso. Eppure porosa è la mente di Valesio. Ancora, sempre.

Sia come sia, ho imparato molto da lui e lo capisco quando, lontano dai libri e dai saggi, dico una cosa che ho appreso dalle nostre conversazioni. Perché qualcosa la impari veramente quando poi diventa tua, la prendi e la tieni con te, e poi la riusi come vuoi. Parlargli è stato, ed è, sempre un piacere: discute solo di lavoro eppure mai di lavoro. Parla sempre di libri, di parole, di pensieri. Se eccezionalmente parla di sé è come se le cose che gli accadono abbiano una connessione con la vita del mondo intero, con qualcosa di più grande. Il narcisismo non ha mai prevalso sulla sua

From: *Discourse Boundary Creation*. Bordighera Press, 2013

"Il lombrico e la nuvola: Una testimonianza"

saggia, cristiana modestia. Secondo me Paolo Valesio è timido eppure sa essere molto affabile, generoso, sempre signorile. Valesio è signorile come chi non è nato signore e non si dimentica la fatica di diventarlo, la volgarità di non esserlo, l'obbligo della nobiltà che nobilita.

Dalle nostre conversazioni ho appreso molto, soprattutto perché Valesio è incredibilmente colto principalmente perché curioso. Gli interessa ancora scoprire un bel libro. Tra gli ultimi che mi ha consigliato ci sono quelli di Clarice Lispector. Il primo romanzo della scrittrice brasiliana si chiama *Vicino al cuore selvaggio* (*Perto do Coração Selvagem*), una citazione da un passo di James Joyce. Nel primo capitolo la protagonista bambina, Joana, recita un paio di poesie al padre. Una è questa, teneramente bambinesca, ma sottilmente meditativa:

> Ho visto una nuvola piccola
> povero lombrico
> credo che lui non l'abbia vista[1].

Contraddistinto da originale semplicità, questo testo è inserito all'inizio del romanzo, dove si osserva nel giardino del vicino «il grande mondo delle galline-che-non-sapevano-che-sarebbero-morte». A terra, «qualche lombrico oziava prima di essere mangiato dalla gallina che la gente avrebbe mangiato»[2]. È una variazione dell'antico *topos* del *tempus edax*, lo stesso che si ritrova nella crudele rivelazione della morte di Polonio, nella terza scena del quarto atto dell'*Amleto*: «Il Verme è il solo Imperatore, per quanto riguarda la dieta! Noi ingrassiamo tutti gli altri animali per ingrassar noi, e quindi ci ingrassiamo a nostra volta per ingrassare i vermi»[3]. Nella confusione di chi mangia e di chi viene man-

---

[1] Clarice Lispector. *Vicino al cuore selvaggio*. Trad. Rita Desti. (Adelphi, Milano 2003): 13.
[2] *Ibidem*.
[3] William Shakespeare. *Amleto*. Introduzione, traduzione e note di Gabriele Baldini. (BUR, Milano 1980): 203-05.

giato si svolge il ciclo eterno della natura, tra l'innocenza di Joana e la colpevolezza di Amleto.

Ma se penso per questo a Valesio è perché, come critico, mi ha insegnato che «*there are no small things*» e, come poeta, proprio perché poeta, pensa al lombrico mentre vede la nuvola e alla nuvola quando vede il lombrico.

Come il monito a non sottovalutare nulla, neppure le piccole cose, tanto etico quanto metodologico, così il richiamo all'importanza del piccolo (il lombrico) non è mai stato disgiunto dall'imperativo di puntare in alto (le nuvole). Spesso nei momenti di difficoltà, quando si potrebbe esser presi dallo scoraggiamento e dalla stanchezza, Paolo Valesio mi ha sempre indirizzato con le parole di Leonardo che figuravano anche sotto l'omonima rivista fondata da Papini e Prezzolini: "Non si volge chi a stella è fisso." Per questo, credo, quando mi è capitato di avere Valesio come mentore sono stato guidato dalla mia buona stella.

Luigi Fontanella
Stony Brook University

Per Paolo Valesio: Una Testimonianza

Mi sono imbattuto la prima volta in Paolo Valesio grazie a un suo romanzo che lessi 35 anni fa poco prima di trasferirmi a Cambridge, Massachusettes (estate 1978), per il mio Ph.D. in Lingue e Letterature Romanze alla Harvard University. Il "romanzo" in questione (da me virgolettato in quanto è un'opera narrativa singolare che si muove tra memoria e invenzione para-autobiografica) è *L'ospedale di Manhattan* (Roma, Editori Riuniti, 1978). Ad esso avrebbero fatto poi seguito altre opere narrative: *Il regno doloroso* (Milano, Spirali Edizioni, 1983), *S'incontrano gli amanti* (Roma, Ed. Empiria, 1993), e *Dialogo coi volanti* (Napoli, Edizioni Cronopio, 1997). Per una mia esegesi su questi libri mi permetto rimandare il lettore al mio denso saggio *Paolo Valesio prosatore*, nel volume a cura di Victoria Surliuga *Analogie del mondo. Scritti su Paolo Valesio* (Modena, Edizioni del Laboratorio, 2008).

Devo qui dire, per inciso, che Valesio è stato anche, insieme con Dante Della Terza, Luigi Ballerini, Joseph Tusiani, Giose Rimanelli, Franco Ferrucci e Alfredo de Palchi (quest'utimo però conosciuto più tardi), lo scrittore italiano espatriato in America con il quale mi sono maggiormente confrontato almeno nei primissimi anni del mio soggiorno statunitense.

Dell'*Ospedale di Manhattan*, suo romanzo d'esordio, mi aveva parlato Giuliano Manacorda, con il quale avevo avuto un intenso scambio epistolare durante l'anno accademico 1977-78, quando—Fulbright Fellow all'università di Princeton—stavo decidendo del mio destino esistenziale e professionale: da un lato rientrare in Italia a continuare a fare il precario presso La Sapienza, con nessuna garanzia per il futuro; dall'altro restare in America, accettare la prestigiosa *fellowship* che mi era stata appena offerta dalla Harvard University relativamente al conseguimento di un Ph.D. in Lingue e Letterature Romanze. Tutta acqua passata; se ne accenno è perché questi frangenti esistenziali sono a ridosso della mia prima conoscenza della scrittura di Paolo, voglio dire prima ancora che lo incontrassi di persona (il che sarebbe avvenuto solo l'anno seguente, nel 1979).

Il romanzo lo lessi durante la torrida estate del 1978 a casa di Dante Della Terza. Ne ricordo ancora adesso, mentre vado scrivendo questa testimonianza, la partecipazione emotiva, ancor prima che intellettiva, che mi procurò quella lettura. E devo qui ammettere che è un vero peccato che poi Paolo non abbia proseguito, intendo in modo prevalente e sistematico, la sua attività di narratore (benché so che da molti anni a questa parte è impegnato in una sorta di "pentalogia" paradiaristica, costituita da migliaia di fogli manoscritti di cui ho letto ogni tanto qualche spezzone nella rivista "Steve"), lasciandosi tentare proprio in quegli ultimi anni Settanta dal *daimon* della Poesia, alla quale ha poi dedicato la maggior parte del suo tempo nei decenni successivi pubblicando un enorme numero di raccolte poetiche (ormai sono quasi venti!) che, lo ammetto in tutta franchezza, non hanno mai trovato il mio pieno consenso critico, pur essendo stato io stesso promotore di almeno due di esse, uscite rispettivamente presso l'editrice Caramanica e presso l'editrice Gradiva Publications.

Perché quel romanzo mi piacque così tanto? Perché di esso mi attraeva soprattutto la scrittura "nervosa," zigzagante, a tratti febbrile, iper-analitica, tramite la quale Paolo raccontava la propria esperienza di intellettuale italiano nel "nuovo mondo"; un intellettuale italiano che, quasi scaraventato nella quotidinanità di una città magmatica come New York, sapeva coglierne umori e risvolti, stimoli e sorprese, gioie e patimenti. Leggendo quelle pagine ritrovavo una parte di me stesso, con il sentimento acuto di una problematica linguistico-antropologica, talora psicologicamente traumatica, all'interno della quale continuavano a misurarsi la mia precedente educazione e le esperienze culturali della mia vecchia Italia della/nella quale mi ero pur sempre nutrito.

Nel romanzo di Valesio ritrovavo anche la ricerca di una purezza incontaminata, l'esaltazione del corpo percepito come "santo" (se ben ricordo il titolo originario di questo romanzo doveva essere proprio *Corpo santo*, poi scartato per ragioni editoriali), il concetto di "umana fratellanza" contro l'individualismo sentito come "una menzogna apportatrice di morte," e poi ancora una stendhaliana tenerezza e un'acutissima introspezione; infine, ma non alla fine, un linguaggio originale, eletto e al contempo umile (aggettivo da considerare nel pieno significato del suo etimo), senz'altro atipico rispetto a quello fin troppo ideologizzato e sprezzante che imperversava nella narrativa e nella pamphlettisca di quegli anni.

Ma la Poesia era in agguato e l'anno seguente (siamo al 1979) lessi il suo primo libro di poesia (*Prose in poesia*, Guanda, 1979). Da quell'anno in poi la mia frequentazione con Paolo fu abbastanza assidua almeno fino alla soglia degli anni Novanta, e nell'ottobre 1980 avremmo trascorso vari giorni insieme in occasione di un indimenticabile congresso internazionale su Pier Paolo Pasolini a Yale, da lui organizzato, cui parteciparono scrittori e critici americani ed europei tra i più significativi (*Pier Paolo Pasolini. A Meeting. Five Years Later*, si veda ora *Italian Quarterly*, nn. 82-83, Fall 1980—Winter 1981, che raccoglie gli atti di quel memorabile convegno).

Tornando alla problematica linguistico-antropologica cui accennavo poc'anzi, in *L'ospedale di Manhattan* essa diventa spesso il perno su cui ruota l'infinito auto-affabulio dello scrivente, le cui elucubrazioni partono spesso proprio da situazioni in cui la lingua *nova* si pone come momento di disquisizione mentale che va ben oltre la pura e immediata accezione semantica. Conoscere la lingua d'adozione—in questo caso l'inglese—diventa il momento d'agnizione di

"Per Paolo Valesio: Una testimonianza"

una cultura *autre*. Ecco allora che anche una semplice parola udita per caso, ma assunta per errata omofonia in un significato diverso, può scatenare un rovello inquietante, tanto più quando esso, una volta chiarito, porta alla scoperta di esiti tragici e strazianti

Pagine, quelle dell'*Ospedale di Manhattan* abbastanza emblematiche del modo di procedere autonarrante di Valesio: il suo ripassare accanito drammatici ricordi degli anni Sessanta equivale, a mio avviso, anche a una sorta di *decantazione della propria storia*. In altre parole, ripassare e filtrare dettagliatamente quei ricordi significa—così come si fa col vino (chiedo scusa del brutale ma credo efficace paragone) - rendere più tersa e trasparente la propria vita vissuta; significa in ultima analisi dare un senso che sia unico, personale e *irripetibile* alla propria esistenza, sia fisica sia spirituale, conferendole una sacralità che le è propria.

Credo che quest'ultimo termine, *sacralità*, possa suggellare il fine ambizioso—neppure troppo *abscondito* - di questa singolare opera narrativa, a metà strada tra la cronaca, i ricordi, e l'ossessiva autointerrogazione: e cioè—come avverrà più tardi e ancor più in maniera estremamente composita nel *Regno doloroso* - far rivivere, liricamente, attraverso la forma descrittiva del mondo moderno, in tutta la sua natura disperata e degradata, la categoria del *sacro*.

Se poi penso—a una rilettura odierna—che questo romanzo fu scritto in anni in cui c'era una concentrazione quasi assoluta sul "materialistico," esso non può che apparire come una sfida, un atto di coraggio, perfino commovente, teso a riscattare lo "spiritualistico" (versus l'immanentistico laicizzante): una categoria che la stragrande maggioranza degli intellettuali di quegli anni rifiutava quasi provandone vergogna.

Da quell'ultimo scorcio degli anni Settanta irruppe poi, travolgente, intenso, fluviale, il lavoro in poesia: dapprima in una particolare forma di "prosa lirica" che permeerà anche la narrativa (si veda, in particolare, il secondo romanzo di Paolo (*Il regno doloroso*, uscito nel 1983), poi nelle tante raccolte che egli pubblicò a getto continuo dagli anni Ottanta in poi. Un lavoro enorme sia come scritture poetiche in proprio sia come "promozione" della poesia di poeti italiani-in-America. Vanno menzionate almeno le co-curatele di due importanti antologie, che dimostrano, per l'appunto, l'attenzione di Valesio alla poesia italiana in America: *Italian Poets in America*, curata insieme con il sottoscritto (*Gradiva*, nn. 10-11, 1992, fascicolo monografico) e *Poesaggio. Poeti italiani d'America*, antologia curata insieme con Peter Carravetta (Treviso, Ed. Pagus, 1993). Un lavoro affiancato dalla rivista "Yale Italian Poetry" prima, e da *Italian Poetry Review* poi, tuttora attiva, e condiretta da Alessandro Polcri, allievo di Paolo e ora italianista alla Fordham University.

Credo che il venticinquennio 1978-2003 sia stato tra i più fecondi nell'attività di Valesio come narratore, poeta e studioso (fra i suoi volumi critici spicca quello su D'Annunzio *The Dark Flame*, senz'altro a mio avviso il più appassionato e appassionante); attività che ancora oggi continua, si capisce, sebbene in questi ultimi quindici anni non ci sia più stata tra di noi quella feconda frequentazione e quello scambio di idee—a volte animoso ma sempre animato dalla nostra comune Passione Poetica, pur da prospettive e visioni divaricate (Sartre direbbe da "posizioni" ideologiche distanti tra di loro)—che c'erano state nei primi anni Ottanta, quando forse c'era un maggiore entusiasmo e una maggiore volontà di cooperazione reciproca.

Vorrei infine sottolineare di Paolo Valesio, il suo straordinario impegno didattico, eticamente responsabile nei riguardi dei suoi innumerevoli allievi che nel corso di tutta la sua carriera di docente non è mai venuto meno, consigliandoli, assistendoli, indirizzandoli e concretamente aiutandoli nella ricerca di un incarico accademico in tante università americane.

Erin Larkin
Southern Connecticut State University

Studium and *Caritas*

When I have thought of Paolo lately, a conversation we had some years ago comes to mind. We were talking about Futurism and the idea of the sacred, and he confessed to not knowing what Marinetti meant when he once wrote that he prayed each night before his electric light bulb. Paolo said, "I don't know what he means, but *he is saying something*." I have come back to this memory again and again; first, because—even with the recent flurry of attention to Futurism—Paolo's insistence on its spiritual dimension is one of the most compelling yet under-explored contributions to this conversation. But I know that others will comment on his scholarship, they will pay tribute to how he has changed the way we look at the authors we touch each day, their works, their times. What struck me about this admission is the humility with which he could say, "I do not know." Yet of course this humility belies a great erudition, greater than any I have known. In fact, his "petites questions stupides" tease out the complexities of works that are unfamiliar, as well as those we think we know. Sometimes these questions make matters clearer; sometimes, truthfully, they lead to a place where ideas we would take for granted—or want to be so—seem to lose their footing. Talking to Paolo, at times, one loses one's footing.

As an American student of *italianistica*, I remember poring over all that I thought I should put to memory; there was simply so much to know. In those years, Paolo was an enigmatic figure, whose flamboyant choice of socks and well-worn oxblood pocket watch case were objects of fascination for his undergraduates, as much as his scholarship. After

From: *Discourse Boundary Creation*. Bordighera Press, 2013

more than two decades, I am finally comfortable admitting that I do not always understand what Paolo is talking about; in fact, I'm quite sure this will always be the case. Fortunately, I have learned to pay more attention to the questions he asks than my ability to come up with any one answer. That is his lasting lesson.

It was an honor to take part in the spring 2010 celebration dedicated to Paolo, which he himself called a gift of *studium* and *caritas*. That was fitting, since in his person, they are really one and the same; for Paolo has always taken the time to listen to his students, to comment, to engage, to foster dialogue. It has been his life's work to convey to his students not only the substance of volumes representing a time, a place, and the ideas they have borne, but also that of the human condition; attesting to this is not only his scholarly work, but a formidable body of creative activity spanning decades. What unites the two is a constant search for dialogue, between authors and aesthetic texts of all kinds, but more importantly—and, I think, with increasing urgency in recent years—with others: his students, colleagues, fellow writers, and friends. I count myself fortunate to be among the latter, and I am humbled to call Paolo not only a mentor and interlocutor, but also a true friend.

I have a picture in my mind from a recent dinner we shared. Paolo had spoken of his students, a seminar he was preparing, a book presentation, his own writing; and when he broke off and left the table, he stooped down and did a surprisingly nimble two-step with my family dog, his face awash with levity. I wish that the next chapter of his career be flavored by such humble, little joys as this one.

Michael Palma
Poet, Translator, Independent Scholar

As has been the case with a number of poets, including some others that I have translated, I came to know Paolo Valesio as a person, and a colleague and a friend, before I knew him as a writer. We met in 1996 at the first meeting of IPSA, the Italian Poetry Society of America, which had just been founded by Luigi Fontanella. From the very beginning, I was impressed by his energy and enthusiasm. He seemed to be overflowing with ideas, and with the readiness to see them carried out. As I grew to know him better, I was impressed as well with the depth and range of his scholarship, with the passionate intensity that he brought to everything he cared about, and, of course, with the excellence of his poetry.

In that same year of 1996, Paolo published one of his finest collections, *Avventure dell'uomo e del figlio*. I especially liked the eighteen "Sonetti profani e sacri" that concluded the volume. They were poems of a kind that I am particularly responsive to: formally structured, and thus paying proper homage to the rich heritage that has shaped our culture, and yet at the same time original and even daring in their use of that heritage; all this while displaying everywhere an eager and alert intelligence in their content. In these sonnets I immediately recognized a kindred spirit (aesthetically, if not spiritually: my sensibility is tilted much more than Paolo's is to the profane), and I translated two of them for a packet of contemporary Italian poets that I was preparing for an issue of *Chelsea*.

My pleasure in translating them, and Paolo's apparent pleasure with the outcome, led to our discussing the possibility of my translating the entire sequence. This possibility stimulated Paolo—that enviable energy and fecundity of his

From: *Discourse Boundary Creation*. Bordighera Press, 2013

once again—to write another twelve sonnets to complete the sequence, and to revise its overall structure. Working on the book with him proved to be a pleasant experience. He was always helpful and encouraging, and his suggestions made the translation stronger than it would otherwise have been. The final result, *Every Afternoon Can Make the World Stand Still*, remains one of my favorites among the books that I have published.

Now that project has led to another, larger one, a volume of Paolo's selected poems on which I have collaborated with Graziella Sidoli, who has exemplified her given name so well that the enterprise hardly deserves the name of work. Thus Paolo contains to challenge me, to enlarge my knowledge and my sensibility, and to reward me with the pleasure of the experience. And in all my dealings with him, Paolo himself has exemplified that now too little heard phrase, "a gentleman and scholar," and he has become, and will always be, a vital inspiration and a valued friend.

Graziella Sidoli
Convent of the Sacred Heart, Greenwich (CT)

Concerto a quattro voci
A Reading in Tongues of Paolo Valesio's Poetry

In tongues? Yes, the reading "a quattro voci" by Michael Palma, Erin Larkin, Gian Maria Annovi and myself, was in more than one language. Echoes of Peter Carravetta's *Poessays*, begun in the mid-eighties and spanning almost two decades of variations, were a source of inspiration. I selected the poems for this celebratory occasion from the entire Valesian poetic opus, which included the original Italian, as well as English and Spanish translations. Thus in various tongues.

The resulting polyphony did produce, in those whose listening was acutely attuned to the sensorial experience that poetry expects, a concert of sounds that could be not so dissimilar from that of the evangelicals' choirs that are known to elevate perceptive and receptive souls to a place unknown where languages blend into a babelic pastiche that leaves the unbeliever completely mesmerized.

And is not poetry reaching often if not always that same whirlpool of swirling sound that leaves one wondering what just happened, what was said, and where it came from? If poetry inhabits such mysterious sphere, then ironically it should leave us, the reader or the audience, both spell bound and speech less.

Something like that did indeed occur at the concerted reading on April 23, 2010. Someone, and only one, came to me later and said: "That was the most beautiful moment of the celebration." He added words to the effect that listening to poetry instead of conferences or testimonials as the others had done for Paolo Valesio, in his praise, was so much more

From: *Discourse Boundary Creation*. Bordighera Press, 2013

striking, penetrating and truthful. I think he was trying to say that the poet had then appeared, invisibly, in all his being. His soul had been bared, his word had been heard, his authorship revealed.

Once again, I am offering here the poet's words, not words about words, but the words written by Valesio, and this time not those collected for that special afternoon but from a different collection, and from his most recent publication, *La mezzanotte di Spoleto* (Rimini, Raffaelli Editore, 2013). As his principal translator I know that to widen his readership, via versions in other tongues, remains a heroic and precious yet ultimately doomed attempt at rendering the original voice of the poet. Thus, I give you some of Valesio's verses in his own tongue, the one that rises before, after and above the babelic lure of tongues, i.e., translations.

The poems featured here represent a wide spectrum of themes dear to Valesio, cutting across a narrative that bridges eros and agape, a fabular bestiary and a theological existentialism.

ECATE

Ogni suo apparire lo stupisce.
L'ha veduta, in questi giorni, crescere
con un'ammirazione
che preparava l'amore
ma che era nutrita di timore.
Ogni sera lasciava che l'umido biancore
invadesse la stanza un poco più.
Ma al momento del sonno
chiudeva gli scuretti.
Ieri notte: nel caldo che scendeva
dal soffitto basso di legno
ricurvo come un ventre di balena,
ha spalancato
la finestrella più vicina al letto.
Si è poi riscosso fra lo scuro e l'alba

prima che si sentissero gli uccelli,
con il petto schiacciato e gli occhi torbi.
Gli era balzata addosso
e il suo bianco malato
aveva offuscato –
gran cappuccio di cobra dispiegato –
il cielo del soffitto.

GOODBYE, MONTELUCO...

Il corno di corriera è ancora allegro
quando passa la curva non visibile
di là dal viale e il prato e la striscia di bosco;
il fischiare del treno
è ancora melancolico.
Tutto in ordine, dunque—il paesaggio
si adatta alla sua propria descrizione,
si traveste da *locus amoenus*.
Ma il sibilo del vento è già cambiato:
è divenuto oscuro.
Adesso solamente,
sotto il segno di questo avvertimento,
egli quando distende
sopra gli occhi il ricamo delle palpebre
la vede:
abietto obietto della sua peggiore
esausta nostalgia,
la morbida la dolce
più di ogni segno, la rada
l'insenatura oltre il fiume
l'accennante, insensibil
mente declinante—la riva buia.
Mezzo luglio: e l'estate è già finita.

La tentazione della danza

Se la pensa la teme; se la sente
con gli scalpiti e i colpi del cuore minacciato
da lei—è come un vento
di desiderio forte e profumato.
Se la teme è vile, e se la brama
è un codardo, affermano i campioni
della vita; i sempre-pronti all'amo
aureo di pervicaci illusioni.
Il terrore ci fa correre innanzi
(dicono) incontro al nemico e al fatale.
È per ciò che lui balza e pare che danzi
un barcollante ballo rozzo e crudo
con la scura fanciulla in-ospitale,
per questo che offre il petto senza scudo?

Paradiso

> "L'acteur est las, et vous triste; c'est qu'il s'est
> démené sans rien sentir, et que vous avez senti
> sans vous démener"
> D. Diderot, *Paradoxe sur le comédien*

Il paradiso piccolo con l'arco
del soffitto affrescato
che quasi tocca la testa:
il loggione del Caio Melisso.
Ecco: il gran lampadario
al centro del soffitto—di poche braccia
distante—si spegne
ma le piccole luci dei palchi
restano accese qualche istante ancora.
Poi, il buio; ma presto si rivela
la luce, doppiamente artificiale,
della scena denudata, al segnale
degli orchestrali in basso.

L'opera che si srotola in questa matinée
è un inferno dolce e bonario;
inferno di salotto e *boudoir* –
color di pesca
lievemente inturgidita
pieno di specchi e gabbie e pappagalli
e divani turcheschi.
E non importa quale poi sia il dramma
in questa mattinata;
chi s'agita su quelle assi è Dives,
e chi osserva dalla piccionaia
è un Lazzaro: egli spera
che un volo di colombe lo porti in paradiso,
al benvenuto di Abramo.

GLI ANIMANTI
(Glossa a San Francesco)

Regno animale e regno vegetale
e regno umano e regno angelicale:
i confini sembrano
indebolirsi come in una nebbia –
paiono graffi, superficialmente
graffiti e graffiati
sopra la pelle del mondo.
Cerchio degli animali,
degli animati animanti –
metamorfico cerchio.
Uno stormo di uccelli sopra un albero:
chiacchiericciano come
(pare che Béla Bartók abbia detto
in una sua lettera)
scimmie.
Gli uccelli come scimmie
le scimmie come uomini
gli uccelli fluttuanti

"*Concerto a quattro voci*"

nell'aria come pesci
gli uccelli sono spiriti
dispersi poi subito ripresi
al volo, spiriti contesi
tra gli angeli e gli umani
gli uccelli sono angeli
rimpiccioliti
ma restano aggraziati
gli uccelli sono angeli terricoli.
Gli animali, tutti, sono
agli uomini quasi eguali.
Ma i confini non sono cancellati:
attraverso questi, gli sguardi
si reciprocamente interrogano
con separato rispetto
(non vedono più l'altro come oggetto).
Come gli angeli, gli animali
richiamano in questione
l'affaticata congiunzione
di corpo e d'anima.
È forse per questo che sono
più belli degli uomini –
appesantiti dall'anima
che si portano in petto.

DESIDERANDO PAROLA

Ogni giorno che vola, egli sente
dentro di sé un rombo premente:
son le parole che vorrebbe dire
prima che scocchi l'ora del finire,
le parole accorrenti a tutti quelli
che ha scoperto essere fratelli
e sorelle (se alcune furono amate
più d'altre, invidie e insidie son passate).
S'egli rappresentasse ad ogni uno

Graziella Sidoli

l'onda della vita come un dono,
riscatterebbe la sua tramontante
esistenza oscura e pesante
che non trova in se stessa più valore
se non nel tuttassurdo dell'amore.

MEDITAZIONE DELLA ROSA

Preferisci le rose oppure le spine?
Si chiede quando guarda le rovine
della sua a volte vita sorridendo,
come dentro se stesso discendendo.
Preferisci le spine ovvero le rose?
Forza di seduzione delle cose,
con la voce bambina del piacere…
Ma affiorano severe rose nere
subito nella mente a ricordare:
il soffio del rovaio invernale,
il tortuoso cammino nel roveto,
la traccia (sangue-cervo) sulla neve
che racconta un dolore non breve
e prepara al riposo del roseto.

PROSSIMANDOSI ALLA FIAMMA

Il desiderio è punta dell'osceno
e coltello appuntito d'assassino;
il desiderio è fiotto di veleno
e laccio di velluto nel giardino.
Il desiderio è scala alla purezza
ed è lacrima della trasparenza;
il desiderio vive in tenerezza,
contento della propria presenza.
Il desiderio giudica il soggetto

e viene valutato dal suo oggetto.
Desiderio non cura diletto.
Il desiderio ascolta e poco dice.
Il desiderio è come la Fenice:
la cenere d'ascesi è sua matrice.

LA SFIDA

Ha seguito le orme di Francesco
lungo un erto sentiero secco bresco:
su dai gradini della cattedrale,
nella polvere dello stradale.
Sono saliti in volta a Monteluco,
verso il romano antico bosco cupo.
Ma a un certo punto, in margine ad un fosso,
gli si rivolta come un gatto rosso:
"E tu che cosa vuoi da me, o tristo?
Le orme da seguire, son di Cristo!
Accódati al maestro e non al servo –
fatti disindividuo, fatti cervo
che non ha occhi per il santo idolo
ma segue solo il richiamo e lo stimolo".

CONTRIBUTORS

GIAN MARIA ANNOVI is Assistant Professor of French and Italian at the University of Southern California. He is the author of *Altri corpi: poesia e corporalità negli anni Sessanta* (Bologna: Gedit, 2008), and of a collection of essays on Pasolini and youth: *Fratello selvaggio: P. P. Pasolini fra gioventù e nuova gioventù* (Massa: Transeuropa, 2013). He also edited a selection of Antonio Porta's poems, *Piercing the Page: 1958-1989* (Los Angeles: Seismicity, 2012)

TEODOLINDA BAROLINI, Da Ponte Professor of Italian, Columbia University, is author of *Dante's Poets: Textuality and Truth in the "Comedy"* (1984; Italian 1993), *The Undivine Comedy: Detheologizing Dante* (1992; Italian 2003), *Dante and the Origins of Italian Literary Culture* (2006; Italian 2012), and the editor and commentator of Dante, *Rime giovanili e della "Vita Nuova"* (2009), revised and translated *Dante's Lyric Poetry: Poems of Youth and of the "Vita Nuova"* (2014). She has coedited *Dante for the New Millennium* (2003) and *Petrarch and the Textual Origins of Interpretation* (2007). She is working on the second volume of her commentary to Dante's lyric poetry.

PETER CARRAVETTA is Alfonse D'Amato Professor of Italian Studies at Stony Brook University and author of several works in philosophy and criticism, including *Prefaces to the Diaphora. Rhetorics, Allegory and the Interpretation of Postmodernity* (1991); *Del postmoderno* (2009); *Sulle tracce di Hermes. Migrare vivere riorientarsi* (2011), and *The Elusive Hermes. Method, Discourse, Interpreting* (2012). Founding editor of *Differentia, review of italian thought* (1986-1999), he has translated Vattimo & Rovatti's *Weak thought* (2012) and written seven books of poetry, including *The Sun and Other Things* (1998) and *L'infinito. Poesie scelte 1972-2012* (2012, winner of the Lorenzo Montano Prize).

ALESSANDRO CARRERA is Professor of Italian Studies and World Cultures at the University of Houston. His fields of interest include Italian and Comparative Literature, Continental Philosophy, and Music Criticism. In recent years he has published *La consistenza della luce. Il pensiero della natura da Goethe a Calvino* (2010) and *La distanza del cielo. Leopardi e lo spazio dell'ispirazione* (2011). He has edited two books by Massimo Cacciari, *The Unpolitical* (2009), and *Europe and Empire* (forthcoming), and guest-edited *Italian Critical Theory* ("Annali d'Italianistica" 29, 2011). He has translated into Italian three novels of Graham Greene and all the lyrics and prose of Bob Dylan.

PATRIZIO CECCAGNOLI received his Ph.D. from Columbia University and is currently teaching Italian at the University of Massachusetts/Amherst. Along with Paolo Valesio he just published the first edition of Marinetti's posthumous novel *Venezianella e Studentaccio* (Mondadori 2012). In collaboration with Susan Stewart, he translated the last two books of poetry written by Milo De Angelis (U Chicago P, 2013).

ANDREA CICCARELLI is Professor of Italian Studies and Chair of the Department of French and Italian at Indiana University. He is the author of *Manzoni: la coscienza della letteratura* (1996) and he is editor or co-editor of several collections, including, *L'esilio come certezza* (1998), *The People's Voice: Essays on Romanticism* (1999), and *The Cambridge Companion to the Italian Novel* (2003). He has served as Editor of *Italica*, the oldest journal of Italian studies in North America, since 2003.

LUIGI FONTANELLA (Ph.D., Harvard) is Professor of Italian and co-director of the Italian program at Stony Brook University. Poet, critic, translator and novelist, he has published fifteen books of poetry, nine books of criticism and three books of narrative. His most recent works include *Pasolini legge Pasolini* (2005, translated into several languages), *Controfigura* (2009), *Migrating Words* (2012), and *Bertgang* (2012, winner of the Prata Prize, and the Murazzi Prize). He is the editor of *Gradiva* and Gradiva Publications (Prize for Translation by the 'Ministero dei Beni Culturali'). In 2005 the President of Italy, Carlo Azegli Ciampi, recognized Fontanella as "Cavaliere della Repubblica Italiana."

ERIN LARKIN is Assistant Professor of Italian at Southern Connecticut State University. She received a Ph.D. in Italian literature from Yale University in 2008, and has recently published on Futurist theatre as well as on the works of Benedetta Cappa Marinetti. She is working on a manuscript on the women of Italian Futurism.

ERNESTO LIVORNI is Professor of Italian Language and Literature, and Affiliate of Comparative Literature, at the University of Wisconsin-Madison. His scholarly publications include *Avanguardia e tradizione: Ezra Pound e Giuseppe Ungaretti* (1998) and *T. S. Eliot, Montale e la modernità dantesca* (forthcoming). He has published articles on medieval, modern and contemporary Italian, English, American, and Italian-American literature. Livorni is the founding editor of *L'ANELLO che non tiene: Journal of Modern Italian Literature*, and author of three collections of poems: *Prospettiche illusioni (1977-1983)* (1987), *Nel libro che ti diedi. Sonetti (1985-1986)* (1998), and *L'America dei Padri* (2005).

MARIO MORONI is Professor of Italian at Binghamton University. As a critic, he has written *Essere e fare* (1991), *La presenza complessa* (1998), and *Al limite* (2007), and co-edited *Italian Modernism* (2004), *From Eugenio Montale to Amelia Rosselli*, (2004), and *Neoavanguardia* (2010). He has published seven volumes of poetry and one of poetic prose. In 1989 he was awarded the Lorenzo Montano prize for poetry. In 2006 he released *Reflections on Icaru's Lands*, a DVD of poetry, music, and images in collaboration with composer Jon Hallstrom. In 2013 he released a CD of poetry and music for piano and soprano entitled *Reciting the Ashes*.

MICHAEL PALMA has published two poetry chapbooks, *The Egg Shape* and *Antibodies*; two full-length collections, *A Fortune in Gold* and *Begin in Gladness*; and an online chapbook, *The Ghost of Congress Street*. His translations of modern Italian poets include recent editions of Maurizio Cucchi and Giovanni Raboni with Chelsea Editions and prize-winning volumes of Guido Gozzano and Diego Valeri with Princeton University Press. His fully rhymed translation of Dante's *Inferno* was published by Norton in 2002 and reprinted as a Norton Critical Edition in 2007.

ALESSANDRO POLCRI is Associate Professor of Italian at Fordham University. He has published essays on Teofilo Folengo, Matteo Maria Boiardo, Luigi Pulci, Marsilio Ficino, Cosimo de' Medici, Martino Filetico, and on the debate about "Magnificentia" in Quattrocento Florence. He has also written on contemporary Italian Poetry. His publications also include the volume *Luigi Pulci e la chimera. Studi sull'allegoria nel "Morgante"* (2010) and a poetry collection, *Bruciare l'acqua* (2008). He serves on the editorial board of *Interpres. Rivista di studi quattrocenteschi*, and is Associate Editor of *Italian Poetry Review*.

LUCIA RE received her Ph.D. in Comparative Literature from Yale University. She is Professor of Italian and Gender Studies at the University of California in Los Angeles. Author of *Calvino and the Age of Neorealism* (1990; winner of the MLA Marraro Prize), she has published on modern and contemporary literature and culture, has translated works by Rosa Rosà and Amelia Rosselli and is one of the founders of the electronic interdisciplinary scholarly journal *California Italian Studies*, for which she co-edited the volume *Italy in the Mediterranean* (2010). She is working on a book on Italian Modernism and Africa.

GRAZIELLA SIDOLI holds an M. Phil. in Comparative Literature from New York University. Professor of Spanish language and literature at Sacred Heart Preparatory School in Greenwich, Connecticut, she is a scholar in translation studies and Italian Futurism. Her literary translations include texts by Marinetti, Antonio Porta, and Maria Luisa Spaziani. She has provided the English translation and the Spanish-language supervision for Paolo Valesio's trilingual collection of poetry, *Volano in cento* (2002), and co-translated his selected poems, *The Red Servant*, forthcoming with Chelsea Editions. Sidoli is on the Advisory Board of *Italian Poetry Review*.

LAURA WITTMAN is Associate Professor of French and Italian at Stanford University. She is the author of *The Tomb of the Unknown Soldier, Modern Mourning, and the Reinvention of the Mystical Body* (University of Toronto Press, 2011; winner of the Marraro Award of the Society for Italian Historical Studies for 2012), the editor of *Futurism: An Anthology* (Yale University Press, 2009), and has written articles on d'Annunzio, Marinetti, the fin-de-siècle, and Italian cinema. Her current project is a cultural history of near-death experiences and rewritings of the Lazarus story in the twentieth-century West, entitled *Lazarus' Silence*.

CENTER FOR ITALIAN STUDIES

THE ALFONSE M. D'AMATO CHAIR
IN ITALIAN AND ITALIAN AMERICAN STUDIES

PROGRAM

Logos, Nomos, Poiesis
A *Festschrift* in honor of Paolo Valesio on his 70th birthday

Friday, April 23, 2010
9:00 am to 7:00 pm

STONY BROOK MANHATTAN
110 EAST 28TH STREET

FREE AND OPEN TO THE PUBLIC

STONY BROOK
STATE UNIVERSITY OF NEW YORK

PROGRAM OF THE DAY

Logos, Nomos, Poiesis

Friday, April 23, 2010

9:00 am • Welcome

Nicholas Rhzevsky, Chair, European Languages, Literatures,
and Cultures, Stony Brook University
Introductory Remarks: Peter Carravetta, Alfonse M. D'Amato Professor of Italian
and Italian American Studies, Stony Brook University

9:30 am to 12:00 pm • Papers (Morning Session)

Alessandro Carrera, University of Houston
"The Logic of Poetic Genealogy"

Davide Rondoni, Università di Bologna
"Bianco su bianco: la visionarietà di Valesio"

10:40 am to 10:50 am • Coffee Break

Barbara Spackman, University of California/Berkeley
"Photography and Fantasy at the *Fin-de-Siècle*: Rodenbach's *Bruges-la-Morte*"

Lucia Re, University of California/Los Angeles
"'*Più che l'amore*': D'Annunzio's Bitter Passion"

12:00 pm to 1:10 pm • Lunch Break

1:15 pm to 4:00 pm • Papers (Afternoon Session)

Laura Wittman, Stanford University
"Undefended Communication"

Mario Moroni, SUNY/Binghamton
"La meditazione continua: A partire da 'Dialogo coi volanti' di Paolo Valesio"

Ernesto Livorni, University of Wisconsin/Madison
"Poetry, Dialogue, Silence"

2:40 pm to 2:50 pm • Coffee Break

Teodolinda Barolini, Columbia University
"The Poetry of Theology and the Theology of Poetry: From Dante's Lyrics to the *Paradiso*"

Andrea Ciccarelli, Indiana University
"Abroad and Beyond: Paolo Valesio and the Empty Nest"

PROGRAM OF THE DAY

4:00 pm to 4:30 pm • Testimonials
Brief interventions by Peter Carravetta, Alessandro Polcri,
Luigi Fontanella, and others from the audience on their personal/professional
relationship with the honored guest.

4:30 pm to 5:30 pm • Poetry Reading
A selection from the poetry written by Paolo Valesio read by Graziella Sidoli,
Michael Palma, Patrizio Ceccagnoli, Gian Maria Annovi, and Erin Larkin

5:45 pm to 6:15 pm • Lecture
Paolo Valesio, Columbia University
"Expression versus Communication"
Followed by a Q&A from 6:15 pm to 6:30 pm

6:30 pm to 7:00 pm • General Discussion and Concluding Remarks

8:30 pm • Dinner
At own expense; restaurant to be announced

This conference has been organized and sponsored by the Alfonse M. D'Amato Chair in Italian and Italian American Studies at Stony Brook University, with partial support from *Italian Poetry Review* (Columbia University, Italian Academy for Advanced Studies in America, and Fordham University) and *Gradiva Publications* (Stony Brook University). The organizer would like to thank Alessandro Polcri and Graziella Sidoli for their help and support.

Paolo Valesio

Linguist, philosopher, essayist, novelist, poet, humanist, and maestro to scores of students for two generations, Paolo Valesio was born in Bologna in 1939. He obtained his *Laurea in Lettere* in 1961 and the *Libera Docenza* in 1969 from the Università di Bologna, where he was *assistente* at the Istituto di Glottologia from 1961 to 1962 and 1966 to 1968. He was a researcher and visiting professor in the Department of Romance Languages at Harvard University from 1963 to 1966 and 1968 to 1973. Subsequently, he was an associate professor of Italian studies at New York University from 1973 to 1975, and a professor of Italian language and literature at Yale University from 1975 to 2004. He is currently Giuseppe Ungaretti Professor of Italian Literature at Columbia University.

Valesio has held seminars and been a visiting professor at numerous universities on both sides of the Atlantic, and has been a fellow at the Center for the Humanities at Wesleyan University, the Guggenheim Foundation, and the Whitney Humanities Center at Yale University. In 1997 he founded *Yale Italian Poetry*, which became *Italian Poetry Review* in 2006.

Author of more than 200 articles, reviews, prefaces, and short stories in periodicals throughout the world, Valesio has written four books of criticism: *Strutture dell'allitterazione* (1968), *Novantiqua: Rhetorics as a Contemporary Theory* (1980), *Ascoltare il silenzio* (1986), and *Gabriele d'Annunzio: The Dark Flame* (1992); and a critical-narrative essay, "Dialogo coi volanti" (1997).

Valesio is also the author of two novels, *L'ospedale di Manhattan* (1978) and *Il regno doloroso* (1983); a collection of short stories, *S'incontrano gli amanti* (1993); a novella, *Tradimenti* (1994); and a dramatic poem in nine scenes, *Figlio dell'Uomo a Corcovado*, staged in Italy in 1993 and 1997.

But Valesio's greatest output has been in the field of poetry, in which he has published 16 books to date: *Prose in poesia* (1979), *La rosa verde* (1987), *Dialogo del falco e dell'avvoltoio* (1987), *Le isole del lago* (1990), *La campagna dell'Ottantasette* (1990), *Analogia del mondo* (1992, winner of the "Città di San Vito al Tagliamento"), *Nightchant* (1995), *Sonetos profanos y sacros* (Italian original with facing Spanish translations, 1996), *Avventure dell'Uomo e del Figlio* (1996), *Anniversari* (1999), *Piazza delle preghiere massacrate* (1999, winner of the "Delta Poesia"), *Dardi* (2000), *Every Afternoon Can Make the World Stand Still/Ogni meriggio può arrestare il mondo* (Italian original with facing English translation, 2002), *Volano in cento* (Italian original with Spanish and English translations, 2002), *Il cuore del girasole* (2006, winner of the "Colli del Tronto," 2007), and *Il volto quasi umano* (2009). He received a lifetime achievement award in 2007, the international poetry prize "Senigallia."

For years Valesio has been engaged in the simultaneous writing of five "quotidian fictions," which make up a narrative *Pentalogia* and of which only a slight portion of the more than 20,000 manuscript pages has appeared in print.

Index of Names

Agamben, Giorgio, 66, 70, 73, 74, 108
Ahmed, Ali J., 25
Alexander, King, 26, 29,
Alexander VI, Pope, 32
Amabile, Luigi, 21, 38
Anceschi, Luciano, 64,
Anderson, Benedict, 25,
Andreoli, Anna M., 133, 136, 146
Andreyev, Leonid, 156, 157, 159
Annovi, Gian M., 169-74, 187
Antonioni, Michelangelo, 64
Ariosto, Ludovico, 119
Aristotle, 10, 96, 112
Asher, Linda, 81, 89
Augustine, 3

Baldini, Enzo, 47, 52
Baldini, Gabriele, 176
Baldini, M., 170
Ballerini, Luigi, 178
Barenghi, Mario, 73, 74
Barolini, Teodolinda, 1-18
Barrès, Maurice, 150, 165
Bataille, Georges, 141, 142, 146
Baudelaire, Charles, 65, 161, 165
Becker, Jared M., 132, 156
Belpoliti, Marco, 73, 74
Benjamin, Walter, 63, 65, 75,
Bertoni, Alberto, 113, 120
Bettiza, Enzo, 80, 81, 89
Blumenberg, Hans, 70, 73
Boccaccio, Giovanni, 16, 119
Bodei, Remo, 70, 73
Bodin, Jean, 23, 47
Bodini, Vittorio, 108
Boiardo, Mattea M., 116
Bolinger, Dwight, 95
Bottego, Ugo, 140
Brewster, Earl, 151
Boyde, Patrick, 7, 17
Bruno, Giordano, 48
Burros, Virginia, 2

Burton, Robert, 63, 67,
Butor, Michel, 64
Bynum, Caroline, 4,17

Campanella, Tommaso, xii, 19-54
Cachey, Theodore, 122
Caesar, Julius, 29, 141
Caligula, Emperor, 30
Calvino, Italo, 62-66, 68, 70-73, 173
Carravetta, Peter, 19-54, 80, 89, 93, 182, 187
Carrera, Alessandro, 55-75
Cavalcanti, Guido, 14, 16
Ceccagnoli, Patrizio, 175-77
Celati, Gianni, 62-65, 68, 72, 74
Cesaro, Tommaso, 35, 52
Chabod, Federico, 43, 53
Charlemagne, Emperor, ("Charles the Great," "Carolus Magnus"), 33, 40
Charles V, Emperor, 30, 34, 40, 42
Ciccarelli, Andrea, 76-90
Cicero, 72,
Clement VIII, Pope, 38
Clemente, Francesco, 34, 53
Colilli, Paul, 102, 104, 107, 108, 112
Columbus, Christopher, 29
Conde, Aurora, 93, 113
Conrad, Joseph, 132
Coward, Noel, 109
Crahay, Roland, 48, 53
Creagh, Patrick, 73
Crispi, Francesco, 140

da Lentini, Giacomo, 3, 8, 12, 13
d'Anjou, Charles, 30
D'Annunzio, Gabriele, x, 55-58, 60, 61, 72, 74, 91, 119, 131-147, 161, 165, 170, 182, 199

Dante, 1-18, 32, 44, 45, 50, 60, 95, 119, 134, 163
d'Aquili, Eugene G., 157, 165
d'Arezzo, Guittone, 3, 6
Davis, Kathryn, 160, 161, 163, 165
de Castrillo, Alonso, 47
Del Boca, Angelo, 139, 146
Deledda, Grazia, 142
Deleuze, Gilles, 64, 69, 70, 74
Della Terza, Dante, 178, 179
de Marselha, Folquet, 3
De Mattei, Rodolfo, 22, 53
De Mauro, Tullio, 106, 114
de Médicis, Marie, 38
de Palchi, Alfredo, 178
De Robertis, Domenico, 5, 17
Derrida, Jacques, 61, 64, 65
Diderot, Dennis, 190
Dieckhoff, Alain, 25
Dostoevsky, Fyodor, 131, 140
Duse, Eleonora, 133, 136, 137
El Greco, 170, 174
Eliot, Thomas S., 117
Emerson, Jan S., 4, 18
Ernst, Germana, 20, 21, 22, 38, 47, 52, 53
Ezzelino, da Romano ("il tiranno"), 30

Fabry, Nathalie, 20, 52
Falcetto, Bruno, 73
Feiss, Hugh, 4, 18
Fernández-Santamaria, J. A., 47, 53
Ferrero, Gugliemo, 135
Ferrucci, Franco, 178
Ficino, Marsilio, 127, 129
Firpo, Luigi, 21, 26, 38, 47, 53
Folengo, Teofilo, 119
Fontanella, Luigi, 80, 89, 100, 112, 178-182
Foster, Kenelm, 7, 17
Foucault, Michel, 63, 65, 66, 67, 72, 74
Fournel, Jean-Louis, 48, 53
Frajese, Vittorio, 25, 53

Franklin, Julian H., 23, 48, 53
Fredric, Emperor, 33
Freese, John H., 96, 112
Frese Witt, Mary A., 133, 146

Galilei, Galileo, 48
Garzoni, Tommaso, 67
Gide, André, 131
Gilbert, Neil, 23, 53
Ginzburg, Carlo, 62, 63, 64, 66, 74
Giolitti, Giovanni (& "giolittismo"), 137, 140, 141, 142, 144
Gosselin, Edward, 31, 53
Gragnolati, Manuele, 1, 17
Gramatica, Emma, 136
Gregory XV, Pope, 38
Grosz, Elizabeth, 152, 165
Guglielmi, Guido, 113, 171
Guinizzelli, Guido, 3, 8 ("Guido" 10, 11)

Harrington, Anne, 157, 165
Hay, Denys, 43, 53
Headley, John M., 30, 31, 45, 46, 53
Heidegger, Martin, 101, 104, 112
Henry, King ("Arrigo"), 33
Herodotus, 43
Hesiod, 59
Hobbes, Thomas, 45, 46, 47, 49, 54
Hobsbawn, Eric, 25
Hofmannsthal, Hugo von, 121, 129
Holden, Janice M., 156, 165
Hyvrard, Jeanne, 164, 165

Jabès, Eduard, 119
Jakobson, Roman, 55, 95, 112, 120, 175
John, Apostle (St. John), 17, 149
Joyce, James, 176
Julius II, Pope, 32
Jung, Carl G., 99, 108

Kant, Immanuel, 64,
Keller, Catherine, 2, 17
Kierkegaard, Søren, 123, 170
Krase, Jerome, ix
Kundera, Milan, 81, 89

Labanca, Nicola, 139, 146
La Boëtie, Etienne, 47
Lansing, Richard, 5, 18
Lapo, Gianni, 10, 11
Larkin, Erin, 183-84
Lawrence, D.H., 150-54, 165
Leclercq, Jean, 128, 129
Leo XI, Pope, 38
Leopardi, Giacomo, 55, 72, 109, 110, 116, 117, 118
Leoussi, Athena, 46, 54
Lerner, M. Pierre, 22, 40, 54
Lévi-Strauss, Claude, 64
Leyra, Ana M., 93, 113
Lispector, Clarice, 176,
Livorni, Ernesto, 91-115
Lombroso, Cesare, 142, 143
Luisetti, Federico, 97, 114
Lunetta, Mario, 97, 114

Machiavelli, Niccoló, 23, 25, 28, 29, 30, 31, 34, 42, 44, 45, 46, 50
Mallarmé, Stephane, 67, 68, 74, 171
Manacorda, Giuliano, 178
Mandelbaum, David G., 95, 113
Manetti, Giovanni, 77, 107, 114
Manzoni, Alessandro, 77, 78, 79, 119
Marinetti, Filippo T., 57, 72, 97, 119, 170, 175, 183
Marsilius of Padua, 32, 50
Martucci, Roberto, 25
Masciandaro, Franco, 107, 112
Matilda, Countess, 32
Melandri, Enzo, 62-64, 66-68, 74
Meltzer, Françoise, 152, 165
Mendras, Henri, 43, 54
Migiel, Marylin, 75, 91, 114, 131, 147

Moevs, Christian, 4, 18
Moody, Raymond, 156, 165
Moroni, Mario, 116-18, 132, 146
Mudimbe, 25

Nani, Michele, 142, 146
Neri, Guido, 62, 64
Nero, Emperor, 30
Neppi, Enzo, 93, 113
Newberg, Andrew W., 157, 165
Niceforo, Alfredo, 142, 143, 144, 146
Nietzsche, Friedrich, 59, 133, 140, 147, 151
Nygren, Anders, 2, 3, 4, 18

Ong, Walter J., 23, 54

Palma, Michael, 110, 113, 185-86
Papini, Giovanni, 177
Parmenides, x
Pasolini, Pier P., 55, 119, 170, 173, 174, 180
Pascoli, Giovanni, 72, 132
Paul V, Pope, 38
Pedace, Pietro, 106, 114
Peirce, Charles S., 58
Pepin (Pippin the Short), 33
Petrarch, Francis ("Petrarca"), 3, 171
Philip II, King, 23, 37
Picasso, Pablo, 142
Picchione, John, 92, 114
Pico della Mirandola, Giovanni, 24, 27, 50
Pietropaolo, Laura, 92, 114
Pirandello, Luigi, 150, 152-55, 165
Plouchart-Cohn, Florence, 39, 40, 41, 52
Polcri, Alessandro, 119-130, 182
Ponzio, Paolo, 38, 52
Prete, Antonio, 68, 74
Prezzolini, Giuseppe, 177
Psaki, F. Regina, 4, 18
Pseudo-Dionysius, 3

Pythagoras, 27
Rabelais, François, 119
Ranger, Terence, 25
Re, Lucia, 131-47
Rendall, Steven, 73
Richeleau, Cardinal, 22, 39, 41, 45
Rimanelli, Joseph, 178
Rimbaud, Arthur, 132
Robbe-Grillet, Alain, 64
Rondoni, Davide, 122, 124, 129, 130, 172
Rossetti, Dante G., 58
Rotenberg, Joel, 129
Ruggeri, Ruggero, 136

Sapir, Edward, 63, 74, 94, 95, 99, 113
Sartre, Jean P., 182
Savage, Robert, 73
Schelling, Friedrich W. J., 68
Schmidt, Carl, 28
Schmidt, Dennis J., 112
Scrimieri, Rosario, 113
Sepúlveda, Juan Gines de, 47
Sereni, Vittorio, 64
Sergi, Giuseppe, 135
Shakespeare, William, 58, 123, 176
Sidoli, Graziella, 186, 187, 188
Sinopoli, Franca, 43, 53
Smith, Anthony, 46, 54
Solmi, Renato, 65, 75
Somigli, Luca, 97, 114
Sophocles, 69, 138
Stambaugh, Joan, 104, 112
Stasi, Annio G., 106, 114
Stewart, Susan, 148, 155, 164, 165
Suárez, Francisco, 47
Surliuga, Victoria, xii, 97, 112, 114, 129, 178
Svetonius, 141
Svevo, Corradino, 30

Tamburri, Anthony J., xiii
Taylor, Jill B., 158, 159, 160, 165

Telesio, Bernardino, 28, 48
Tedeschi, Anne C., 74
Tedeschi, John, 74
Tomasello, Giovanna, 133, 147
Truffaut, Françoit, 64
Tusiani, Joseph, 178

Unamuno, Miguel de, 157, 159
Uranio, Martino, 127
Urban VIII, Pope, 38
Vacchina, Maria G., 92, 114
Valentini, Valentina, 133, 147
Valéry, Paul, 161, 162, 163, 165

Valesio, Paolo, x, xi, xii, 1, 15, 20, 55-75, 76-90, 91-115, 116, 117, 119-130, 131, 138, 140, 147, 149, 157, 158, 162-166, 169, 170-174, 175-177, 178-182, 183-184, 185-186, 187-188
Valla, Lorenzo, 24, 32
Verdicchio, Stefano, 74
Verga, Giovanni, 135
Vico, Giambattista, 19, 27, 45, 72

Waldbaum, Serge, 20, 52
Wallerstein, Immanuel, 41, 49, 54
Watson, Philip S., 2, 18
Weaver, William, 74
Weinfield, Henry, 74

Wittman, Laura, 109, 115, 148-66
Zacconi, Ermete, 136
Zaleski, Carol G., 157, 166
Zanetti, Giorgio, 136, 146
Zizzi, Michelangelo, 93, 108, 115

www.ingramcontent.com/pod-product-compliance
Lightning Source LLC
Chambersburg PA
CBHW031142160426
43193CB00008B/220